END OF THE ROAD

End of the Road

Inside the War on Truckers

Gord Magill

CREED & CULTURE

NASHVILLE, TN

First published 2026 by Creed & Culture Books

Printed in Canada

Hardback ISBN: 9781967613021
E-book ISBN: 9781967613076

Library of Congress Control Number: 2026930154

To the memory of Marty Paddock

Contents

Introduction

Friday, January 28, 2022:
Thousand Islands border crossing between the United States and Canada.

"If you can't produce a vaccination card I can't let you in."

"I'm Canadian. You have to let me in."

"You are supposed to provide us with a quarantine address."

"I'm not quarantining anywhere for the two-week period. I'm only here for a couple of days."

"But you still have to provide us with an address."

"I don't have to provide *you* with *shit*."

And so it was that I was welcomed back to Canada.

Having crossed the U.S.–Canadian border hundreds if not thousands of times in my life as a professional trucker, I had become inured to the various delays and subtle insults of the petty tyrants who typically wear the uniforms of customs officials. This time it felt different, as if the "guards" of the Canada Border Services Agency (CBSA), buttressed by plain-clothes bureaucrats from the Public Health Agency of Canada (PHAC), had been issued letters of marque granting them permission to maximally harass any traveler that crossed their bow. In January 2022, getting myself over the border in my pickup truck proved more difficult than crossing with any load I had ever hauled in an eighteen-wheeler, but cross it I did, somehow avoiding fine or penalty in my newfound position as a second-class citizen, an *Auslander* in the eyes of my home and native land.

As I made my way east along the 401, Canada's busiest road and the most heavily trafficked highway in North America, I kept looking in my rearview mirror, expecting police to give me a hard time in the same manner I had just given customs. They never appeared, though looking backwards made me think about how I was driving ahead of a past that may never return.

Over beers later that evening a friend and I recounted tales of the depravities and impositions forced upon us as *purebloods*—the vernacular term for the unvaccinated. My buddy, a sales rep for one of Canada's biggest supplement and health-food distribution companies, regularly traveled across the country to meet retailers and suppliers, often by airplane (Canada is the second-largest country on Earth, geographically, spanning six time zones west to east, and ranging from the U.S. border nearly to the North Pole). He was no longer able to make in-person sales calls; for his refusal to be vaccinated against COVID-19 he had been *unpersoned* by Prime Minister Justin Trudeau, whose mandates had put my friend on the wrong side of Trudeau's medical-apartheid regime. My friend was no longer allowed to board airplanes or trains or engage in any other federally regulated area of life.[1] His kids were prevented from taking part in various activities, and he and his wife endured severe social censure. I could certainly relate, given that I now live in a very blue college town, home to an Ivy League university, whose citizens proclaim open-mindedness yet can sometimes be the most narrow-minded and provincial people I've ever met— second only to a certain type of "CBC Canadian."

The next morning was the big day: Saturday, January 29, 2022, when the Freedom Convoy rolled into Ottawa, the capital city of my country of birth and home to a decrepit political class that had exploited concerns over a virus whose serious effects were largely limited to clearly identified groups—the elderly and those with certain comorbidities—to completely turn society upside down. Spontaneously organized via Zoom calls in kitchens across the country and using social media to garner support, the Convoy snowballed into an international sensation before it ever hit Ottawa. The Freedom Convoy represented a form of salvation to the long-suffering people of Canada, who had endured some of the harshest lockdown and mandate measures in the world. Its truckers in big rigs were folk heroes to many, recalling a time not so long ago when North American truckers were celebrated as archetypal rugged individualists, doing right by themselves and their families in spite of overbearing feds and spiteful law enforcement. I had driven home from the United States to welcome the Western Canada convoy to Ottawa in a show of solidarity with my fellow citizens and the truckers who had been my colleagues and comrades since I was a kid.

The treatment I experienced at the hands of CBSA and PHAC officials at the Thousand Islands border crossing was not unique. It had become a daily fixture in the lives of a group of people who really were essential to the functioning of the economy, both in normal times and in the Days of COVID. Many of the truckers who helped organize the Freedom Convoy had suffered the same indignities. They worked sixty to seventy hours a week (or more) yet were treated like mere vectors of disease everywhere they went.

My friends had decided to display their support on an overpass crossing Highway 417. As we approached the side-road overpass in our own miniconvoy of four vehicles, it became clear that the buzz around the Freedom Convoy was absolutely real. We arrived about ninety minutes before the Convoy was to drive past en route to Ottawa, and already dozens of cars were lining the sides of the road; in time, it would be hundreds. Hockey sticks holding Maple Leaf flags were popular with this patriotic crowd, and despite bone-penetrating temperature of −25 Celsius, the warmth and smiles all around were infectious. It was an incredible moment, the euphoria of sweet relief from a pain long endured and shared by an entire country. For the first time in my life I was drunk with patriotism, in love with every person I met, and they were in love with me.

As the Convoy made its approach to the overpass, the cheering reached a symphonic volume that nearly drowned out the airhorns of the trucks as they slowly rolled below us on their way east, letting loose the honks that would become their signature battle cry as they settled into downtown Ottawa for the largest peaceful protest in Canadian history.

After my friends and I joined the party at Parliament Hill, it didn't take long for me to sense that this protest, this collective scream of relief, was about much more than the vaccine mandates that threatened not only truckers' bodily sovereignty, and potentially their health, but also their livelihoods. No, the protest was anchored in something much, much deeper, and the government knew it, which is why it had already plotted a media campaign against the Convoy before it had even gotten to Ottawa, likening it to "January 6th North."[2] In a move meant to solidify this narrative, Justin Trudeau, like a king fleeing his castle, skipped town immediately, showing cowardice rather than the diplomacy required of a nation's leader.

By the time I returned to Upstate New York after that weekend, the media smear machine had revved into overdrive, accusing the Freedom Convoy of various heinous crimes and statements, all of which were eventually disproven. As the old saying goes, a lie has traveled halfway around the world before the truth has its shoelaces tied, and with the Freedom Convoy that lie was like a sports car getting the jump on a Kenworth pulling a Super B-train load of Canadian softwood lumber.

As thoughtful observers wondered just what the Freedom Convoy was all about, I found myself the guest on many podcasts, trying to disentangle the truth from the web of lies spun by the government and its press agents. After writing about the Convoy for *Newsweek* and other outlets, I tried to formulate an answer to a question I was regularly asked: *Why truckers? Why not some other group of workers? If the COVID regime was harming everyone in society, where was everyone else?*

I have wrestled with this question for four years now. My answer was the genesis of this book.

Why truckers? Well, truckers—in Canada, the United States, and elsewhere— have been the target of a long-running and mostly silent war, unremarked upon by nearly everyone except those of us who have felt and suffered the wounds. Many who have studied labor and the economics of the trucking industry point to the deregulation of the business by Jimmy Carter with the enactment of the Motor Carrier Act of 1980, and similar legislation brought to Canada several years later, as the source of truckers' problems. But the Motor Carrier Act was simply the first volley in a war on a very particular subset of the working class. Many others volleys have followed, each extracting its own toll and making the job more difficult while also decreasing its pay and prestige.[3]

Justin Trudeau's vaccine mandates were the proverbial straw that broke the eighteen-wheeled camel's back, and this book is going to take a good hard look at the straws that were piled on earlier. From passage of the Motor Carrier Act, which opened the industry up but sent truckers' wages spiraling downward, to the industry-wide employment of surveillance technology right out of George Orwell's *Nineteen Eighty-Four*, to the flooding of our highways with ill-trained immigrant drivers, many of whom are brought to North America under arrangements of indentured servitude, to the Tech Bros and their dreams of replacing us with robot trucks, we're going to visit the frontlines of this silent war, searching for the answers to two questions:

Why truckers? And: *Is this the end of the road?*

1

A Family Tradition

I was totin' my pack along the dusty Winnemucca Road
When along came a semi with a high an' canvas-covered load
"If you're goin' to Winnemucca, Mac, with me you can ride"
And so I climbed into the cab and then I settled down inside
He asked me if I'd seen a road with so much dust and sand
And I said, "Listen, I've traveled every road in this here land"

—Geoff Mack, "I've Been Everywhere"[1]

The North American trucking industry stands on the precipice in 2026. For nearly half a century, its biggest players and biggest customers have failed to properly contend with the monumental changes brought about by the deregulatory measures of the Motor Carrier Act of 1980. As this book was being written, a confluence of policy corrections, tariff uncertainty, a flat market flooded with excess capacity, a steady increase in truck collisions, public exasperation with the behavior of certain truck drivers, and the looming imposition of robot-driven trucks have combined to force a reckoning.

The question: What the hell has happened to the truck driver during the past five decades?

Despite the best efforts of niche players in specialized parts of the business doing their part to pay drivers well, truckers' wages stubbornly refuse to account for inflation, cost-of-living increases, or the devaluation of the dollar by decades of terrible fiscal mismanagement on the part of central bankers. And the Biden Administration, though told directly by an MIT researcher that the inefficiencies created by truckers' detention time at loading docks were a critical weakness in our supply chains under the COVID regime, and likewise told by many experts that there was no shortage of truckers, only a shortage of pay, expanded the pool of "truckers" through a suspicious program of giving out commercial driver's licenses (CDLs) to migrants and refugees of dubious training and vetting. As a result, a cavalcade of dangerous truck drivers have been loosed upon our roads—and there has been carnage.

Yet nothing has been done to beef up lax training systems, and efforts to remove the incompetents from the road have only just begun. Instead, veteran seasoned truckers like myself, people with a lifetime of safe operation and clean driving records, are forced to work under ever more punishing scrutiny and surveillance technologies that insult our professionalism. Trucks themselves are now built to accommodate lower-skilled drivers, perpetuating a cycle that further degrades the respect and honor once afforded us. Life on the road continues to deteriorate in numerous ways: there's not enough parking, truck stops are closing or converting to fast food only, and surveillance technology and the flooding of the industry with recent arrivals have completely upended our culture. How we relate to each other, how we are treated at customer facilities— it's all part of a pattern of dehumanization. And despite warnings from many corners about the dangers of artificial "intelligence" and historical examples of what becomes of a society when major technological innovation is imposed at warp speed and without consideration for the displacement of labor, it appears that Trump 2.0 and the federal government are allowing autonomous-truck developers to proceed—while removing obstacles and oversight. Are we being set up for a repeat of what happened in early nineteenth-century England, when weavers and garment workers, their very livelihoods taken away by steam-driven looms, engaged in an industrial rebellion that gave us the term "Luddite"? Will truckers lie down and take what's happening to them quietly?[2]

It seems that we have been trained over these past five decades to do exactly that—take it quietly, say nothing, just work harder and harder in the belief that things will get better.

It reminds me of *Animal Farm* (1945), the classic anticommunist satire from George Orwell.

In Orwell's parable of communism under Stalin, the character Boxer, a horse, represents the working class, whose members dutifully go about their work, no matter how mistreated they are by the pigs in charge, such as Napoleon and Snowball, Orwell's stand-ins for Stalin and Trotsky. Eventually Boxer works himself to exhaustion and death, and his body is sent to "the knackers." Are America's truckers bound for the glue factory of history, after so many years of government and industry leadership viewing us as easily replaceable?

Like Boxer, some of us have worked our butts off for our entire lives, seventy-hours-plus week in, seventy-hours-plus week out. We're guys (and women) living fairly austere lives who don't spend much time at home with our families, all while serving an economy whose beneficiaries don't work nearly as hard. Yet unlike Boxer, we can see what is happening here—and how the story we are being told about truckers doesn't line up. We see how a nearly forty-year-old driver-shortage narrative was a lie, and how instead of promoting and honoring safe and professional drivers, many within the industry have convinced the government to flood the market with new entrants in order to keep our wages down. Some of us are the sons of an intergenerational commitment to the industry. We understand how it used to function, and we have seen enough creeping impositions and poor policy over the years to know the score. And there are more than a few academic works out there nibbling around the edges of these questions, some of them by truckers who transitioned to the life of the mind.

The conditions are there for some serious blowback—maybe.

You may ask: Who am I to say anything about this?

In the lead-up to the Allied effort to liberate Europe during World War II, planning for the D-Day invasion took on great significance across the Allied nations, and Canada was no exception. In Burlington Bay, at the western end of Lake Ontario, a young sergeant by the name of James Magill was tasked with testing the latest version of something called the Davis Escape, short for Davis Submerged Escape Apparatus, or DSEA. The sergeant, being fit and a good swimmer, was sent to the bottom of the harbor, simulating a scenario where an amphibious tank might no longer float, should the inflatable skirting around it succumb to enemy fire and the crew need a quick escape to safety. Burlington Bay, later renamed Hamilton Harbour, turned out to be a somewhat ironic place to test what happens when a tank sinks in the drink, given the presence on that harbour of Canada's two biggest steel mills. Sergeant Magill proved up to the task, and also up to the task of amphibious landings; he later landed on Juno Beach at Normandy, D-Day plus three, and took part in the liberation of Europe from the forces of Hitler's Germany. One might say he fought real Nazis, not those imaginary Nazis who possess the minds of so many deranged leftists eighty years after his sacrifices.

Driving a Sherman tank across Europe turned Sergeant Magill into a pretty good mechanic, so after he returned home from the war, his services were in high demand in the postwar economic expansion that accelerated the United States, and to a lesser extent Canada, into industrial powerhouses. Moving from Sudbury, Ontario, down to Hamilton, Canada's Steel City, Sergeant Magill eventually came to be in the employ of Fred Norton, the proprietor of Norton Motor Lines, a major trucking concern in the 1950s and '60s.

In addition to maintaining and fixing Fred Norton's fleet of B-Model Mack trucks and various trailers, Grandpa drove them as well, mostly back and forth to Winnipeg, which at the time meant cutting through the United States or tackling

Now that was a truck: a B-model Mack of Norton Motor Lines, Stoney Creek, Ontario, early 1960s.

the nascent Trans-Canada Highway along the north shore of Lake Superior, that section not being completed until 1960.[3]

Trucking then was a different game. Sergeant Magill's rig had no sleeper, no air conditioning; back then, it was either sleep with your feet kicked up on the passenger seat or get a bunk in Fort William, later merged with Port Arthur to become the city of Thunder Bay, nine hundred miles into the route from Hamilton to Winnipeg. For someone who had been subject to death at any minute from an 88-mm German gun or Panzer tank, the lack of modern conveniences didn't even register, nor did the possibility of freezing to death should one of those old B-Models gel up in the winter.

It was into this history that my father, one of seven children ultimately sired by Sergeant Magill, was born. Along with his older brothers, my Uncles Chris and Bruce, Dad came into trucking the old-fashioned way. He learned from the ground up at Norton's trucking yard in Stoney Creek, Ontario, just east of Hamilton. Dad washed trucks on weekends, helped my grandfather and other mechanics, and learned from the cast of characters who made up the truck-driving scene around Hamilton: Earl Paddock and his sons, Joe Mordeca, Orly Robertson, Lacey Dalton, the brothers Lawrence and Gerald Marshall. . . . They were hard men, in a way, but excellent operators and mechanics who all had successful businesses. The boots presented for me to fill were very large indeed.

My uncles both lived as archetypes worthy of any young man's admiration. Bruce, an owner-operator for most of his career, left Hamilton to seek his fortune in the north. He hauled out of a mine in the Yukon for a while, but ultimately spent most of his life in Armstrong, Ontario, working in forestry and trucking an awful lot of logs down to Thunder Bay. Though Uncle Bruce is no longer with us, his shadow is long, and my many trips to Armstrong to visit him were marked with wisdom downloads, "talking-to's" over my many mistakes, and a lot of enjoyable fishing trips. Canadian readers might imagine Bruce as Red Green from *The Red Green Show*, but with a much harder edge, and supremely competent with heavy equipment over and above any mastery of duct tape.

Uncle Chris has also led a very successful life in trucking. Working his way up from being an over-the-road driver for Earl Paddock, he became a dispatcher and terminal manager for a couple of different companies before striking out on his own, opening a load brokerage in 1985 when such a third-party service

A chip off the old block? My Father and me in front of a Hayes Clipper at the Paddock 60th anniversary party, 2017.

provider became possible after deregulation came to Canada. Uncle Chris and his partners, my aunty Gina and his colleague Jeff Moore, built up a tiny freight brokerage into one of the biggest 3PLs (third-party logistics providers) in Canada. After Uncle Chris retired, Jeff ultimately sold the company, and eventually the house Uncle Chris built became Uber Freight Canada.

My Old Man, God bless him, is still on the road at the age of seventy, driving a Kenworth for the Paddock family back home. The Paddocks are one of the best trucking companies in the business. Their equipment is sharp and top-notch, maintaining the same arrangement of black with red-and-gold striping that has been turning heads since the 1970s. Dad, like my Uncle Bruce, had a thing for the north. He spent time in the Yukon and had two spells of living in Armstrong, hauling logs and generally enjoying life in the bush. Armstrong is where I was conceived, perhaps as a testimony to the long winters there. My mother, unfortunately, was easily convinced by her parents to move back to Hamilton, and poor old Dad hadn't much of a choice in the matter, so it was in Hamilton I was born. It seemed destined that I would one day leave.

A heritage is no guarantee that the next generations will follow, especially in this modern era of atomization and illusory notions of infinite choice and emancipation from social bonds. Perhaps it was during all the times I rode with my Dad as a small child and later during summer break between grades eight, nine, and ten that the seeds of my obsession with the road were planted. I also rode with one of Dad's friends, a fellow by the name of Mark "Mouse" Williams, who was one of those characters whose personality was so large that it made his truck work a whole lot harder just carrying it around. I spent most of a summer with Mouse as he hauled containers for a company contracted to Kodak in Rochester, New York. One could say I was part of Kodak's last gasp as I rode with Mouse down to the pier in New Jersey to export the last rolls of film to be used before digital technology took over the camera and image industry. I learned about patience while sitting in massive backups at the terminals of steamship lines, and I learned a lot about incentives and the small doses of corruption one had to employ in order to get the job done. These lessons were usually delivered to me peppered with Mouse's signature humor and what you might call coarse language. "Gordon, if you ever decide to go trucking—and I suggest that you don't, as you are far too smart for this shit—you have got to be careful around all of these fuckers here in New Jersey. They are just a different species than those back home."

The last time I rode with Mouse he had a secondhand cabover Freightliner that used to belong to one of America's biggest companies, Werner Enterprises. He had custom lettering on that cabover: "Owned, Steered, and Geared by Mark Williams." Mark's previous Freightliner was emblazoned with the Woody Woodpecker symbol of the Thrush Muffler Company. Mark hauled Thrush's mufflers all over North America, at least until its Toronto plant closed. We neighborhood kids knew Mouse by the Woody Woodpecker truck, and it was deeply ironic that a guy with such character hauled something meant to quiet down a motor. These proud symbols of personal ownership are becoming a rare sight on today's trucks, for reasons that will be revealed along the way.

I too went to work for the Paddocks, starting from the ground up in their shop facilities, learning how to drive and secure loads from their local drivers, and eventually getting my Class AZ license (Ontario's highest commercial-driving level) at age eighteen. The first few years I drove locally around Hamilton and other parts of Southern Ontario, especially the Greater Toronto Area, delivering loads of all descriptions that had arrived in our yard as backhauls from the United States. I also did a lot of preloading of trailers for the over-the-road (OTR) drivers—or "highway guys," as we called them—before I graduated to that position. This informal quasi-apprenticeship system gave me and a lot of other young guys a great foundation, and I worked for the Paddocks for many years; they were amazingly tolerant of my proclivity for traveling to work in other places and always gave me my job back when I returned home. After many years of trucking in Western Canada, New Zealand, Australia, and the United States for a number of different companies servicing various industries, I can say with some certainty that the Paddocks set the gold standard for trucking. It is a great pity the rest of the industry doesn't operate like them.

Throughout my adventures in trucking I have witnessed the slow and steady degradation of what it means to be a trucker, and how policies and complexes have manifested themselves in our day-to-day lives and employment relations. I have also witnessed what it looks like to operate correctly and with honor in spite of it all, thanks to my relationships with many friends and colleagues, true professionals who have shouldered their burden and continue to get it done.

In 2026, my upbringing might seem rare or even anachronistic, and my advocacy for an industry that is erroneously believed to be facing imminent automation might seem to be something of a lost cause, doomed to the same historical black hole occupied by the Luddites. Defending what we inherit from our forefathers was once standard operating procedure for most of humanity, but with many smaller and medium-sized trucking companies having been absorbed into much larger companies in a decades-long process of consolidation, the number of defenders is shrinking. The Paddocks have resisted this trend. How long they and companies like them will survive and carry the torch for their fathers remains to be seen. That is one of the urgent questions animating this book.

2

The Journeymen

Bobby and I thumbed that diesel down.

—Kris Kristofferson, "Me and Bobby McGee"

The professional trucker, once rolling from the start of his day, or after having completed loading, especially when hauling flatbeds or pulling a heavy equipment trailer, will stop within half an hour or so of departure to check his load. Chains can come loose, settling or slightly swaying; bungee cords and ropes holding down tarps may require minor adjustment; and tires always require a look. Then there is the matter of eliminating the copious amounts of coffee with which you may have started your day.

While I was working in Australia, pulling road trains up and down the West Coast of the "Lucky Country" (or Cursed Island, depending on one's perspective) between Perth and Karratha/Dampier, nearly one thousand miles north of the most isolated city on Earth, I often stopped at a little roadhouse gas-station joint, or "servo" in Ozzy parlance, called Ginger's Roadhouse, in a tiny place called Upper Swan, about twenty minutes north of Perth. Ginger's

*The Wanderjahre Three
(Ze Germanz).*

had enough parking to fit about four road trains. It also had an espresso machine where one could get a "flat white," which is an upgraded version of a cappuccino and seems to be the coffee of choice for that part of the Australian population that is descended from prison officers. Many truckies stopped at Ginger's to check the chains and tarping on their loads before "heading up the track," and so did I. When in Perth, do as the Sand Gropers.

On one typically warm afternoon, as I was loaded and rolling northbound, I pulled into Ginger's, hopped out, and had a look around my two forty-five-foot flatbed trailers, checking the chains holding down the offshore oil-rig baskets bound for the port at Dampier, where they would be transloaded onto rig tenders and taken to one of the drilling rigs working the North West Shelf oil field in the Indian Ocean.

On my way in for a coffee, something like a scene out of one of my many trips to Burning Man was assembled in front of the servo in the form of three gentlemen wearing identical costumes. As one of them approached me, thoughts of Burning Man switched to thoughts of Oktoberfest, although this gentleman wasn't carrying a stein of lager.

"Hello sir, would you happen to be traveling north? Do you have room for me and my friends?" Spoken in pretty decent English but with a very heavy German accent.

I had a look over the threesome. One was ginormous, about 6'6", and could probably take me out with one punch. The other two were more my size and appeared a little younger than I. All of them looked like they had just left a Bavarian beer garden. Bummer they didn't bring any Biermädels with them.

"Sure," I said. "I'm heading up to Dampier. How far would you like to go?"

One of them whipped out a paper map that, just like their costumes, hearkened back to a different age. After consulting the map their leader, Christian, the kid who had first approached me, said they would like to go the whole way.

"Not sure where you're going to sleep, because there is only one bed in the truck and none of you have the right equipment for that. It's a little over a day's ride, and I'll be camping out somewhere along the way."

Christian laughed. "Okay, no problem, we will sleep outside."

After we had hopped into the Ozzy-built Kenworth T-904 I was driving, with Christian in the passenger seat and his boys seated in the bunk, I quickly relayed some rules to Ze Germanz.

"You guys need to be paying attention. If I tell you to duck, duck."

Turns out the two in the bunk didn't speak much English. The taller of the pair spoke zero.

"The problem," I said to Christian, "is that I'll get in shit from my employers if they see you in here. We are not supposed to pick up hitchhikers or have anyone in the truck."

"Ah, I see. We will duck, no problem."

When I had taken this job, I was still in Canada. I had made the connection through my friend Gavin and then traded a few emails and phone calls with the owner. I had to operate on Gavin's word, which is golden as far as I'm concerned, about what this company was like. He had heaped praise on the family who owned it, averring that its owner, Jim Currie, was a "top bloke." As regards hitchhikers, Gavin told me that he had flown his wife over from New Zealand to ride along with him.

No more.

Not long after I arrived in Perth, the company was broken up and the trucking half sold to an offshore energy outfit from Scotland. The transition to the new owners resulted in the incursion of spreadsheet-brained management types more concerned about compliance than maintaining a family-friendly and humane work environment. My wife Jenna was going to come trucking with me, as part of our plan for an extended work adventure in Australia. That plan was nixed by new policies.

I have spent most of my life picking up hitchhikers and have often been a hitchhiker myself. Nothing terrible has ever come of it—I have never picked up Rutger Hauer or the creepy guy in that *Twilight Zone* episode—and I wasn't about to let a bunch of management nerds tell me who I could or could not bring in the truck, which was effectively my home. Never mind the lonely existence of a "truckie" operating across the vast expanses of Western Australia. That

Ozzy state has some of the loosest hours-of-service rules in the world. You can run for some ridiculous amount of time—like three weeks straight—before your employer is under any obligation to give you a day off. If I wanted to have passengers, I was going to have passengers.

Across North America, there aren't many to pick up anymore. Those who still travel the world by thumb tell me that truckers are increasingly less likely to pick them up. I spoke with my friend Andy Hickman about this, and he had some keen insights into the hitching lifestyle, given that he was a self-described hobo and homeless drifter for five years of his life:

Eulogies for the fine art of hitchhiking were already circulating widely by the time I first raised my thumb for a cross-country trip in 2013. "You younger guys don't know how it was," one older drifter told me at an encampment of vagabonds in Southern California. "In the '70s, it was semi-truck after semi-truck—so many rides from them guys they'd be radioing each other ahead on the CB and passing you off truck to truck across the whole country."

No more, of course—by the time I began the five-year hitchhiking odyssey that would carry me over more than a hundred thousand miles of American highway, I already knew that the end was near. "I'd love to pick you up," the truckers would always say, "but insurance rules mean I'd get fired if I did." Where old-timer hitchhikers had wild stories of riding with hotshot truckers back in the glory days, I was lucky if one let me sit on the floor of the cab, hiding from the sensor in the passenger seat. In the thousands and thousands of hitchhiking rides I took in my travels, less than ten were in semi-trucks, and of these, all but two were with owner-operators. Not even one human lifetime ago, this would have been totally inconceivable.

By 2018, hitchhiking meant standing on the Interstate on-ramp in the broiling sun, hiding from the cops, and aiming for rides from the few souls marginal enough—or drunk enough—to actually pick you up. COVID ushered in the complete death-knell of even this paltry form of travel; and these days, hitchhiking in all but the most far-flung backwaters is nothing short of a masochistic act, for you are effectively living as a fugitive in a landscape of leery motorists, anti-vagrant policies at truck-stop chains, aggressive police, and a trucking system that cannot tolerate the legal risk you might pose to them.

It brings me no joy to admit it, and I resisted conceding the point for many years—but hitchhiking is dead. It is essentially over with. I caught the last whimper of its heyday, and I'm glad I did—but it's dead, long gone, and it is a death that did not come about by way of natural causes at all. Hitchhiking was killed, not only by a paranoiac media, not only by COVID, but by lawyers and corporate policy officers, by insurance agencies and trucking companies and truck-stop chains. The American hitchhiker was, perhaps, too romantic a species for the new, efficient, neat-and-tidy world order our leaders sought to make—and so it was that we and our kind would find ourselves throwing in the towel, one by one.

Back to our German hitchhikers. Once we got the ground rules out of the way, the boys had to duck within a few minutes as I chanced upon a southbound road train I recognized immediately. I reached for the VHF radio.

"G'day Spider, not much traffic back to the yard. How's it looking going north?"

"You're clear, mate. Not much goin' on, aye. How ya goin', Gordie?"

"Not bad. Coffee'd up and ready to roll. Might pop in to see your girlfriend there in Cataby. Catch ya later, sir."

A burst of laughter squeals across the radio.

"Rog-ee mate, see ya later."

Once safely past my mate Spider, real name Greg, I motioned to the journeymen that they could sit up straight, and this is when the talk began in earnest.

Like most other young guys in the internet age, we shared a number of cultural and political references, and the obvious wanderlust which landed us all in Australia. I had to find out about the outfits, though, and what it all meant. Christian was only too happy to oblige. His recited oral history of the journeymen flowed so smoothly it was almost like he'd had to tell this story thousands of times. His answers to all my questions were delivered in the manner and with the confidence of an expert.

The German tradition of the *Wanderjahre*, or *Wanderschaft*, dates back to medieval times and is where we get the English term journeymen as a title for those who have completed an apprenticeship in the trades. The Wanderjahre, or "wandering years," are what Christian and his associates were undertaking after the completion of their three-year carpentry apprenticeship.

"There are many rules to the *Wanderschaft* which we still follow to this day," explained Christian. These include "wearing these outfits which identify us as journeymen. In the tradition, we would travel to different towns, and exchange work for lodging, and learn the ways of carpenters in other areas. We even carry a journeyman passport, which the mayors of towns would stamp, so as to prove that we are not vagrants."

With this, all three of them pulled out their carpenter's passports, as if I were some customs official at an airport.

A key component of this ancient German apprenticeship program is the restriction on when the *Wanderjahre* may begin: not until three years of training have been completed. The *Wanderjahre* act as a type of finishing program, where a newly minted carpenter, technically proficient though lacking in experience, learns the finer points of the trade through interaction with carpenters in other locales and gains experience by employing his skills along the way with whatever hosts will have him.

You would think this must line up at least somewhat with how truckers are trained and turned loose upon the highway. But you would be completely, utterly, and decidedly wrong. Truck-driver training is exactly back-asswards in America. Most new truckers, once they have learned the bare minimum to pass a state CDL exam, are sent out on their own to crisscross America without any experience whatsoever. The results are about what you would expect.

One recent study examined the question of whether age or experience was a factor in the likelihood of a trucker being involved in a collision or other serious incidents. It reached the same conclusion as those who had molded the rules of the *Wanderschaft* many centuries ago: experience matters, and training and mentorship should therefore be more emphasized.[1] Unfortunately, nearly all the megacarriers who operate in the United States have ignored this ancient wisdom. In the name of profiting from taxpayer funds lavished upon their internal CDL mills, they have come to depend on the steady flow of "steering-wheel holders" that these mills produce.

In most cases, a budding truck driver will sign up for one of these schools after he or she has been conned by a recruiter at a jobs fair or some such event. The student will discover that there is plenty of money available, whether from the federal Workplace Innovation and Opportunity Act (WOIA) or Pell Grants or various state programs, to subsidize or even completely pay for that training. Failing that, trucking companies will offer to pay for training through their own in-house financing, which often comes with many strings attached. Typically, this involves a contract stipulating that the trainee may not quit and work for another company in a specified time period without forfeiture of the training loan, which comes with interest rates that would make the credit-card companies blush. Many dodgy credit scams involving truck-driving schools have been investigated by an organization called the Student Borrower Protection Center. These scams often involve needless upfront administrative fees meant to juice the high interest rates that are the profit centers for these schools.[2]

For the price that the taxpayer or student is paying, the product delivered is of decidedly low quality. Most trucking schools only train to the test, which is to say they convey the bare minimum of knowledge and skill you need to drive a few miles and maybe back a trailer up under the supervision of a state driving examiner. Do these schools show you how to install tire chains such that you can take a loaded semi over the Donner Pass in the wintertime? Do they teach you the basic skills involved to navigate nasty weather?

Not a chance.

The investigation into a tragic accident that took place on an interstate in Fort Worth, Texas, in February 2021 reveals the state of the average American truck-driving school.[3]

On an icy morning commute, two people were killed when a recent immigrant to America from Haiti named Jean Marie Saint-Lot, driving for one of the no-name subcontractors often used by Federal Express and other large corporations, failed to slow down for the icy conditions and plowed his rig into stopped traffic, in which four other people had already died in a 133-vehicle pileup. An investigation found that FedEx had farmed the load out through a load broker, which then double-brokered the load through a company owned by a dude from Uzbekistan that later passed the load to the company for which Mr. Saint-Lot drove. Double-brokering is an all too common, if illegal, practice in America. Basement-dwelling cheap carriers employ inexperienced and dangerous drivers like Mr. Saint-Lot, who obtained his Class A CDL in a three-week course offered by a truck-driving school in Florida that, not surprisingly, taught him nothing about driving in winter conditions.[4]

》→

One of the functions of guild systems such as the *Wanderschaft* is to ensure that all practitioners of the trade do their jobs correctly. When you hire a carpenter, you are getting an actual carpenter who possesses the skill and craftsmanship expected by and of his fellow carpenters and will build you a house that won't collapse.

The driver-licensing regimes of Australia and New Zealand have a quasi-apprenticeship system built into them. The aspiring driver must graduate through levels of accrued experience on progressively larger equipment. Once you turn eighteen and have at least one year of car-driving experience, you can then test for what they call Down Under a "rigid," which is a straight truck without a trailer that would fall under an American Class B CDL. After one year driving one of these small trucks, you can apply for a trailer license, or Heavy Combination (HC) license in Ozzy-talk. Later you can apply for an MC, which is the Ozzy license for road trains and B-doubles. In Canada we call a B-double a Super B-train; it's two trailers connected by a fifth wheel on the lead trailer (not a dolly converter), with a total of eight axles on the ground holding up a weight of 140,000 pounds, which is 60,000 pounds more than the standard American tractor-trailer combo.[5]

One would think that those who cry the most about making our roads safe in North America would want to import this system from Australia rather than hand the keys to the likes of Mr. Saint-Lot, who after three weeks of tax-payer-subsidized training was competing against people, like me, who have been trucking since they were teenagers. We also might wonder why the trucking industry in Canada and the United States doesn't actively recruit highly skilled operators from, say, Norway, where truckers know how to drive in snow and navigate mountainous terrain, which implies high levels of operational skill.

I have been unable to locate any study comparing the safety or performance outcomes of the truck-licensing regimes of Australia or New Zealand to those of Canada or America, so we have to rely on bare statistics.

In 2021, 163 people were killed in crashes involving trucks in Australia, and 5,991 were killed in the United States.[6] Controlling only for population, you are three times more likely to be killed in a truck crash in the United States than you are in Australia. You might think Australia's much lower population density contributes to that outcome, but one must consider that Australia, contrary to the images put in our minds by films like *Crocodile Dundee* and *The Road Warrior*, is a highly urbanized society where 86.6 percent of the population lives in five coastal cities.[7] The U.S. population is a bit more spread out, though similarly urbanized at about 82 percent. (This total includes the suburban population.)

There has not been any well-publicized attempt to bring an obviously sane licensing system to North America, although my home province of Ontario imposed graduated licensing on car drivers. (I was in the first cohort of teenagers subjected to this regime.) Alabama, Alaska, Arizona, Arkansas, Missouri, and New Jersey have similar rules for car drivers, especially for those applying between the ages of sixteen and eighteen. There is no such system for truck licenses.

What we have consistently seen, instead, are calls to debase minimum requirements for truckers and those who train them, especially from large megacarriers, which have major driver retention and turnover problems.

The goal of the megacarriers, as reported by *FreightWaves*, seems to be to ensure that the blind lead the blind. For instance, they want the minimum years of experience necessary for a registered trainer halved from two to one.[8] I remember feeling uncomfortable when asked to train someone back in 2004 when I'd already had seven years under my belt; how could anyone feel comfortable training someone when he himself is still wet behind the ears? And how could anyone in good conscience advocate for such a policy?

Truckers are not at risk of building a house that is going to fall on you, but they are part of your daily life if you spend any time on the roads. The motoring public ought to have some assurance that those behind the wheels of trucks have the proper amount of training. If Americans are three times more likely than Australians to be killed in a truck collision, perhaps we ought to consider adapting our trucker-training system to more resemble theirs. Who would be hurt by this?

As the German carpenters and I kept rolling north, I rattled on about the system I was trained in, which looked and functioned an awful lot like an apprenticeship. At the risk of being the proverbial old man yelling at a cloud, I told them how it was Back in the Day.

My teenagehood was not normal. My parents divorced when I was eleven years

*From high school to the trucking life:
graduation day with my girlfriend Sarah Bailey
and a Paddock KW Cabover, June 1997.*

old, and the Old Man married a lady he met at Country Bob's, a legendary honky-tonk located next to the old Travel Port truck stop in Binghamton, New York. He later moved to that area. The summers when I was fourteen and fifteen were spent mostly going trucking with the Old Man and hanging out with his friend Mark "Mouse" Williams, who had also found female companionship at Bob's and moved south. Dad and Mouse had both worked for the Paddocks at different times, where I also got my start. My first job was working in the Paddocks' body shop, sandblasting trailers and preparing them for paint under the watchful eye of painter and body man Lynn Radford.

I eventually moved from Lynn's body shop to the main mechanics shop and spent most of one summer replacing wooden deck boards in many a flatbed and van trailer. This led to helping the mechanics at night and assisting the evening-shift local drivers in preloading steel at the steel mills, warehouses, and processing plants in and around Hamilton. I loved every minute of it, even the nights when I worked until midnight or later and then had to drag my tired ass into school the next day, usually tardily. The secretaries and vice principal of my high school often expressed concern about my late arrivals, Tim Horton's coffee in hand. In a moment of frustration I once asked them, "My mom doesn't work and we have no money, so what else do you want me to do?" This was to be the first of many instances where the tension between certain classes would be revealed to me, in spite of the pretense that we live in a classless society.

By the time I turned eighteen and was legally allowed to apply for my Class AZ (the Ontario CDL), I had already accrued two years of experience around trucks: greasing and adjusting brakes, chaining and tarping heavy loads of steel, operating a forklift, and backing trailers into a steel warehouse. I'd also come to understand the psychosocial and human aspects of the job that you can only learn from doing it: dealing with delays in loading, the self-organizing of truckers when in line at the mill, knowing who to help and who to avoid, and the pecking orders of the workplace, from the white hard-hats to shipping-office staff to crane operators and everyone else involved in the daily dances and exchange of making things move. It is impossible to learn any of this in a three-week CDL course.

When I told Christian that after receiving my license I stayed close to home, seldom going beyond Toronto in the first two years of my career, he mentioned the three years of training required before an apprentice undertakes the *Wanderjahre* and asked me if this was typical for all truckers. When I told him the truth about how most truckers get into the business in North America, he shook his head in disbelief.

There are exceptions to this messed-up paradigm, and a few bright sparks out there understand what they are getting into before going out on the road. One of these bright sparks is a young lady named Lora Andela, who until very recently hauled livestock for the Caruso Cattle Company out of Frankfort, New York.

Lora showed a lot of the initiative that is lacking in every new generation of young people, according to the laments of the Old Men Who Yell at Clouds, though perhaps in this age of screens and distractions the Old Men are more correct than they ever have been.

Lora describes her training:

I got one of those big study books for about a year before I got [my CDL] because I was super excited. I knew it was what I wanted to do. I was researching different companies and I didn't really want to go over the road right away if I didn't have to.

So I set up to go to a school that's in the area and then got an interview for a local milk company to work in their shop. And I told them, you know, if you're hiring drivers, I'm about to go to school, get my license.

And they said, don't waste your money on the school, we'll train you and we'll pay you while we're training you, just work in the shop for six months. And so I got really well acquainted with their equipment, moving it around the yard, backing into garages and whatnot.

I got the job in August of 2020 and then come February of 2021, I started going with the trainer and I drove with him for about three weeks and he told them, you know, she's pretty much good to go.

Lora is still out there, hauling livestock and getting it done, and with any luck she will find a husband who is likewise eminently competent and can keep up with her. Will that guy be a fellow truck driver, someone who completed the truckers' *Wanderjahre* and can build her a house that won't fall down?

I sure hope so.

Not all women entering the industry have been as successful as Lora. Many women who get into trucking have found themselves victims of one of the most ridiculous training phenomena in the country: the "team-training" model, where a rookie driver runs OTR team loads with a trainer. Over and above the facts that this training model is wildly unsafe, as the trainer is often in the bunk sleeping when the rookie is driving, and that the trainer himself often has very little in the way of experience, a new female driver is frequently assigned to run team with a male driver, and you can imagine that this arrangement produces some criminal situations.

Tammie Stuttle and Desiree Wood are board members of a group called REAL Women in Trucking, and they have reported on and advocated for the end of this ridiculous practice. Tammie and Desiree tell me:

The trucking industry's narrative of a "driver shortage" is a myth that masks a deliberate strategy to recruit vulnerable demographics—low-wage, inexperienced drivers such as women, immigrants, minorities, formerly incarcerated individuals, and even teenagers—who are easy to exploit. These new entrants are thrust into a system that prioritizes profit over safety and dignity. A cornerstone of this exploitation is the team-training model, where student drivers are forced to cohabitate with a trainer—often a near-stranger—in a confined truck cab for weeks to months. This setup, falsely marketed as a necessary training phase, is designed to maximize carrier profits by running team freight that delivers goods twice as fast, but at a steep human cost.

The American Trucking Associations' recent campaigns touting the recruitment of formerly incarcerated individuals as a way to "change lives" often gloss over how these programs force vulnerable drivers into team driving situations with minimal supervision, inadequate conflict resolution training, and insufficient tracking. This approach exacerbates workplace violence, as these high-pressure, isolated environments breed tension and abuse. Moreover, there is no mandatory sex offender registry tracking for truck drivers, unlike requirements for other professions interacting with communities, leaving both trainees and the public at risk.

For women specifically, the risks are amplified. Hundreds, if not thousands, of female drivers have reported sexual harassment, assault, and even same-gender violence during team training. Tragically, cases of murder have also been documented (REAL Women in Trucking, 2022, FMCSA Public Comment). In these arrangements, trainers, who often have minimal experience themselves (sometimes as little as six months), are tasked with mentoring novices for 35–45 days, or even less (REAL Women in Trucking, 2022, FMCSA Public Comment). After this brief period, students are then required to team with another inexperienced driver for up to six months, living and working in a space the size of an elevator. Basic needs—sleeping, changing clothes, and even sanitation—are reduced to makeshift solutions, with drivers often resorting to urinating or defecating in buckets due to lack of access to facilities. These conditions are not only dehumanizing but also foster toxic and dangerous environments.

. . . [The] Federal Motor Carrier Safety Administration's (FMCSA) . . . own studies confirm women truck drivers are more likely to experience harassment than their male counterparts, particularly from trainers within their companies, yet most do not report incidents due to fear of retaliation.

It makes me sick to think that dirtbags are out there debasing my trade by abusing women, and new entrants in general, with this model of training. And that dirtbaggery appears likely to continue. A fully funded and ready-to-go study into sexual assault and sexual harassment (SASH) in trucking that was about to be launched by FMCSA was abruptly canceled in August 2025, with the mealy-mouthed excuse that "the government's priorities have shifted and this project no longer meets our needs." Something tells me the American Trucking Associations may have been involved because it didn't want the public to know about yet another major problem with the team-training model—namely, that it produces on awful lot of sexual assaults. This would have given reformers like Tammie, Desiree, and me yet more ammunition in calling for the whole rotten edifice to be shut down.[9]

》→

I don't want readers to think that all truck-driving schools are bad. There are rule-proving exceptions out there that go the extra mile to teach their students properly and prepare them for life on the road. One of these schools is the Mountain Transport Institute, run by a veteran of the industry named Andy Roberts out of Castlegar, British Columbia. Since the late 1980s, Andy and his team have taught prospective truckers the technical and safety-minded proficiency required to navigate the high passes of the Canadian Rockies safely and without burning the brakes off your truck and winding up in a runaway lane—or worse. Andy's training methods are so effective and produce such good rookie drivers that he has partnerships with numerous trucking companies throughout BC and Western Canada. Even companies in the U.S. send their experienced drivers to him for extra training.

Andy supports, in theory, the idea of a graduated licensing system for truckers. Like me, he understands that exemptions must be made for guys in rural areas, as those who were raised around farm tractors or trucks would only be held back by the system. Those people are few in number compared to the hundreds of thousands churned through truck-driver training systems as they exist now, and the guys who have the competency to bypass any graduated system are those more likely to stick with the business.

Encouragingly, there are moves afoot in Western Canada to bring graduated truck licensing to Canadian roads.

Kim Wylie and Trent Lalonde are truckers from Saskatchewan who are behind an organization called "Make Trucking a Trade," which advocates for reforming how licenses are issued. Kim Wylie has some particularly personal reasons for his efforts: over and above a lifelong career in the business, he hails from Humboldt, Saskatchewan, home of the Humboldt Broncos hockey team that was involved in an infamous truck-and-bus collision in 2018. That tragedy saw most of the team killed in a totally preventable collision between its bus and a truck at an intersection near Armley, Saskatchewan. The driver of the truck had very little experience, and if a graduated licensing system had been in place, he would not have been behind the wheel of the combination he was driving.

In the immediate aftermath of the Humboldt tragedy, Kim made a video that went viral in which he discussed how this situation came to be. "In my video," he says, "I called for making trucking a trade, and I went through all the mentors I had over the years that steered me in the right direction. Three people really stood out: my Dad, my Uncle, and Butch Webber, a guy I worked for for about six years and who was probably my biggest influence. . . . When we moved back to the farm when I was nine years old, my Dad put me behind the wheel of a tractor. . . . These short license courses don't teach you what takes years of experience to learn."

Trent Lalonde has also been active in advocating for increased safety on the roads of his home province, including lobbying the government to build more parking areas for truckers to rest. These oases are very hard to come by on the windswept prairie.

It seems their efforts are beginning to bear fruit, at least in the next province over. Alberta's provincial government has recently made a $54 million investment in the commercial-trucking industry that will strengthen training standards. Devin Dreeshen, Alberta's minister of transportation, said, "Our goal is to have 'truck driver' designated as a trade and to ultimately seek a Red Seal designation for this critical profession." The Red Seal program sets "common standards that assess the skills of various trades across Canada. Skilled workers who pass the Red Seal examination are given an endorsement to their trade certificate."[10]

One would think it common sense to have trucking recognized as a trade—or, at the very least, some level of skilled labor. Why, after all these decades of this critical job keeping the North American economy alive, has this designation not been made? Why is it that training standards are so abysmal? Should truckers not undertake an apprenticeship like the *Wanderschaft*?

We'll get to that.

As for my German journeymen friends, I ended up giving them another ride, this time from Karratha to another remote Ozzy town called Carnarvon, where they helped a homeowner who was still plugging away at fixing his house four years after the Gascoyne River had flooded. Last I heard, they had made their way back to Germany and are building houses that will stand the test of time.

3

The War Begins

There is unrest in the forest
There is trouble with the trees
For the maples want more sunlight
And the oaks ignore their pleas

—Rush, "The Trees"

The Motor Carrier Act (MCA) of 1980 divided truckers and the industry like highway medians divide our interstates.

Consider the experience-formed opinions of two high-caliber trucking people I've had the pleasure of working with over the years. When Nicky Lombard, co-owner and at one time lead driver of the venerable Connecticut-based Lombard Brothers, first heard about the MCA, he exclaimed, "They're going to let any motherfucker do this?!"

On the other side of the median, Scott Paddock praised the deregulation introduced by the MCA for opening "new markets and opportunities, which led to a growing economy." When the scions of two marquee names in the business have such radically divergent views on a policy, it raises more than a few questions, particularly about who stands to benefit and who stands to lose.

Speak with any driver who has been around the trucking industry long enough, even if he or she wasn't a trucker or even alive yet when it passed, and chances are any discussion about the problems we face will eventually come back to griping about deregulation. What they mean, even if they don't know the name of the legislation or the specifics of the problems the legislation was meant to solve, or don't even know if it solved them, is the MCA, a seminal piece of legislation in the age of deregulation, signed into law by Jimmy Carter on July 1, 1980.

Though not the only source of truckers' problems today, the Motor Carrier Act of 1980 is certainly a major mile marker on our long road to perdition. It fundamentally rearranged the economics of the business in such a way as to be an underlying cause of nearly every other problem seen since. And although it was regarded at the time—with some justice—as a necessary corrective to inflationary forces, the pendulum has now swung so far in the opposite direction as to threaten the very existence of trucking as a functional and profitable industry. Numerous companies have gone out of business since 2023, and the steady pace of this decline shows no signs of abating. These bankruptcies and closures have been so regular that the freight-industry online magazine *FreightWaves* devotes an entire section of its website to nothing but.[1]

Trucking was a different universe in the 1970s, when it still operated under the rules of another Motor Carrier Act, this one enacted in 1935 during the presidency of Franklin D. Roosevelt. The 1935 act regulated the trucking industry in myriad ways, including setting freight rates and controlling the issue of "authorities," which you might think of as taxi medallions, a sort of license from the government permitting you to be in business as a trucker at all. New entrants into trucking were required to apply for a "certificate of public convenience and necessity" from the Interstate Commerce Commission. In practice, these were extremely difficult to obtain. The MCA of 1935 effectively restricted entry into the trucking business, which is one mark of a cartel.

An interesting fixture of the original act, which lasted until its replacement in 1980, was that agricultural commodities were exempt. In 1935, the average household was spending approximately 25 percent of its disposable income on food. (The number today is about 10 percent.) FDR, attempting to shepherd

America through the Great Depression, was looking for ways to reduce the cost of groceries and address the failure of his predecessor, Herbert Hoover, to deliver on Hoover's promise of a "chicken in every pot." Reducing the cost of food transportation was one way to do that, and therefore agricultural truckers were exempted from the regulatory regime of the MCA on the correct assumption that an open trucking market in that sector would help keep prices low.

But, as is usual with a large piece of legislation, there were unintended consequences.

Forty years later, the exemption for agricultural truckers created a new update on an ancient American archetype—the outlaw trucker, a cowboy on eighteen wheels who would haul regulated freight on the sly from his position outside the regulated market, helping customers who were being screwed by regulated carriers whose rates were too high and who had become lazy and provided substandard service because they were protected from competition by the federal government. Outlaw truckers used the agricultural-commodities loophole to haul anything they damn well pleased. Yeah, they were outlaws, but they were as American as bootleggers and Underground Railroad conductors.

One such outlaw trucker was a gentleman named Theldon Thornburgh, who in the course of a legendary career traveled over five million miles without a chargeable incident. Theldon was interviewed by my friend—himself another legend of the road—"Long Haul" Paul Marhoefer: trucker, singer/guitarist, writer for *Overdrive* magazine, and host of the popular podcast series *Over the Road*.

Paul has been trucking since the year I was born (1979) and has accrued the kind of experiences and deep understanding of the industry that earned him his nickname. He is also a much-sought-after "trucking troubadour," playing his soulful folk tunes about trucking and its drivers at truck shows around the country.

His interviewee Theldon Thornburgh, who died in 2022, was a free soul. "He didn't want to punch a time clock or join the Teamsters," says Paul. "He would take loads other truckers wouldn't take, go down roads other truckers wouldn't go. And he had no interest in being regulated in any fashion."

"I got fired three times from dispatchers," Theldon told Paul. "I've always hated the union. You can't do what you wanna do, you gotta do what they want you to do. . . . Throw them damn logbooks away."

In the 1950s and '60s, Paul explains, "Theldon was one of those independent truckers . . . but he didn't just haul agricultural products, he was a true wildcatter, meaning he'd haul steel, paper, dry goods, anything he could get in the wagon, and he would give an under-the-table discount to the freight rates set by the Interstate Commerce Commission. That's what wildcatting was."

As Theldon says, "Back in them days there was quite a few wildcatters and we didn't haul anything that was legal. Everything was illegal, but you could make good money; the ICC had high rates on stuff but you hauled it for cheaper."[2]

Outlaws like Theldon were heroic fixtures in the heyday of American cinema and television, the 1970s, with its recurring theme of protagonists fighting a corrupt and depersonalizing system. Truckers and trucking influences such as CB radio were all over such massive hits as *Smokey and the Bandit*, *White Line Fever*, *Convoy*, and *The Dukes of Hazzard*. The characters and aesthetic of this cultural output embodied the spirit of wildcat truckers, which is an awful long way from the realities of truckers—and their perception by the public—today.

But while certain aspects of popular culture of the 1970s were busy duking it out with "The Man," the Man himself was busy trying to figure out ways to fight another fixture of the 1970s: the long-running period of economic doldrums dubbed "The Great Inflation," which economist Jeremy Siegel called "the greatest failure of American macroeconomic policy in the postwar period."[3]

Lasting from the late 1960s into the early '80s, the Great Inflation saw some legendary interest rates. Mortgage interest rates exceeded 10 percent in the late 1970s and peaked at a Third-Worldish 18.63 percent in October 1981. The vibes were bad enough in the late 1970s that President Jimmy Carter organized a team along the lines of FDR's famous "brain trust," except that instead of visiting Mussolini to learn the finer points of corporatism from Il Duce, Carter's crew huddled up to try and nerd their way out of the mess.

One of Carter's main nerds was Cornell economist Alfred E. Kahn, whom Carter had appointed as his "inflation czar." Kahn was responsible for a sweep of deregulatory reforms, most notably in airlines, banking, and trucking. Though President Carter didn't necessarily place a priority on bringing outlaw truckers into the fold through these deregulatory measures, he gave them a nod during a speech to Congress when the Motor Carrier Act of 1980 became law, saying, "I am also particularly pleased that the bill will improve truck service to small communities and enhance business opportunities for independent truckers."[4]

Among those outlaw truckers were a great number of legitimate businesses, many of them small, and many of them having operated for years under the shadow of the regulated system. Large companies, including many manufacturers, had their own fleets of trucks only on paper; more often than not, those trucks were owned separately, but because the owners of the trucks had a lease arrangement with the larger manufacturer or producer whose products were being hauled, they did not require their own authority. As a result, those truck owners were barred from hauling the products of other companies without a lease arrangement. This didn't necessarily stop them: many a trucker back then carried a typewriter in the truck to peck out fake lease arrangements lest they be inspected by the authorities. This was technically illegal, but hey, that's what outlaws do. These were free-enterprise outlaws.

Those truck owners had a legitimate case that the regulated nature of the industry stymied their growth by preventing them from competing fairly against entrenched carriers, who were shielded against competition thanks to the extremely difficult, really almost impossible, process of obtaining authority. Many entrenched carriers had grown lazy and delivered lousy service.

So there was a case for reform, and that case is made well by Scott and Marty Paddock. Having grown up in the family business pre- and post-deregulation, Scott and Marty have nuanced insights into what it was like to operate on both sides of that divide—and what it took to acquire their own authority. Though they are based in Canada, where deregulation came a few years later than in the U.S., their experience is much the same, as they operated in both markets, hauling steel and other goods into the U.S. from Canada.

Marty describes the pre-1980 regulation as "nothing more than a protection racket put together by the haves to ensure that have-nots were never allowed to challenge their grip on the industry. I was there. I lived it. There was nothing good about that style of regulation."

The haves fought tooth and nail to keep the have-nots from getting authority, which is to say government permission to operate. Scott tells me, "We did actively pursue getting authority in Canada just before deregulation. We spent a lot of time and money and had all of our good customers in court lobbying on our behalf, with opposition from every licensed carrier in Ontario."

Adds Marty, "Every application we ever made was opposed by other carriers, but also by the Ontario Trucking Association as well, 'on behalf of its members.' It really was a very dark time in trucking history."

So the hyperregulatory regime was no trucker utopia. It needed fixing. But not the way Alfred Kahn & Company went about it.

One of the main gripes about deregulation was the immediate rate-cutting that resulted from competition, which forced many companies to slash expenses, including driver pay. Dr. Michael Belzer, an economics professor at Wayne State University, is a former trucker who was employed as a driver at the time. He eventually transitioned into academia and wrote what is considered the first major investigation into the effects of the MCA, *Sweatshops on Wheels: Winners and Losers in Trucking Deregulation*.[5]

In *Sweatshops on Wheels*, Belzer describes several key rule changes effected by the MCA, one of which allows virtually anyone with a pulse to start his own trucking company: "Individuals or businesses seeking to enter the interstate trucking business 'need only prove a "useful public purpose" rather than public convenience or necessity.' Carriers must apply for and receive operating authority, demonstrate they are able to provide the service they plan to offer, and prove insurance coverage."[6]

Unfortunately, this provision is vague enough, and the registration cost for a motor carrier number is low enough, that essentially anyone can start a trucking business, whether or not he has the experience or capacity to deliver on his promises. The impact of this change on trucking was felt right away, almost like the industry had been hit by one of its own trucks at speed.

Dr. Belzer was a Teamster working for a liquid-tank firm in the Chicago area. His pay was almost immediately cut by 30 percent in the wake of the MCA. This issue is no abstraction to him; he lived it behind the wheel, not up in an ivory tower. The central thesis of *Sweatshops on Wheels* is that the cost-cutting of trucking rates in the absence of regulation essentially froze truckers' wages and caused a host of other problems, including higher accident rates due to truckers working harder for less. I asked the Paddock brothers if they saw the rate problem the same way in the immediate aftermath of deregulation.

"No," replied Scott, "there was more freight than trucks at that time, and industry growth was being held back due to lack of service and uncompetitive rates by the regulated carriers." Marty, too, says that regulation hamstrung the family company's ability to grow, and deregulation enabled its later success. "In the regulated days," he tells me, "we never had access to overdimensional permits or the customers that require them. We never had access to the big multinational corporations and manufacturers." In the twenty-five years prior to deregulation, the company went from one to forty trucks in spite of regulation; in the second twenty-five years, the Paddocks "went from forty to over one hundred with the help of deregulation."

While the Paddocks have experienced great success downstream of deregulation, it gutted many carriers who could not compete with a new market-driven pricing regime, even if those carriers were run thoughtfully and had built up a reputation for responsive service and safety. One of those carriers was Lombard Brothers Incorporated, a family-owned freight concern that at its height had operations along the Eastern Seaboard stretching from Maine to Maryland and employed hundreds of drivers. Originally based in Waterbury, Connecticut, and started by two brothers with horse and wagon, Lombard Brothers incorporated in 1924 and began using the earliest iterations of diesel-powered delivery trucks. Lombard Brothers was a multigenerational family concern that saw all three phases of American trucking: pre–Motor Carrier Act of 1935, the regulated period from 1935 to 1980, and then the deregulated period from 1980 until the company was sold to North Penn Transfer in 1984.

Contra the idea that carriers such as Lombard benefited from the protection of a regulated market that was closed off from competition and thus delivered shite service, Lombard was the kind of company whose customers sung its praises and whose drivers made a career out of working there. Its turnover rate was extremely low, and Lombard developed a proactive and pro-family company culture. Drivers distributed the printed company newsletter, *Tail Lites*, to all its terminals, keeping everyone abreast of Lombard's internal news. It's hard to imagine a megacarrier doing that today outside of perhaps a private Facebook group or some such digital, less tactile, less human format.

The quality of Lombard Brothers and its customer service can be glimpsed from a letter, featured prominently in *Tail Lites*, from a customer called Caloric Appliance, a brand name still in business today but now owned by Maytag. Caloric district manager George Howland wrote: "After twenty years of hit or miss effort by many of your competitive carriers with poor attitudes, mis-deliveries, denial of justifiable freight claims, and all around bad relations, it is refreshing for me to be associated with your firm."

Perhaps it was those with "poor attitudes" and their "hit or miss efforts" that caused Nicky Lombard to cry out in profane despair upon hearing about the MCA's passage in 1980. Years later, when asked why, after selling the company, he didn't get back into trucking, Lombard said, "The government got involved. . . . They ruined it, they let anybody in, it's full of bottom feeders."

One man's bottom feeders are another man's persecuted innovators. Marty Paddock—sounding a bit like Ayn Rand—for the defense: "Deregulation was the best thing that ever happened to the North American economy. It reestablished the law of nature, and the weak and lazy became prey to the strong, aggressive, innovative group that had always been oppressed by regulation. It brought forth and developed a better, more efficient transportation industry to support North American industry and allow it to grow and prosper."

Marty has his own explanation for the existence of bottom feeders, who I think everyone agrees are a bane of the existence of everyone else in trucking:

The real truth of the matter is the government was never capable of regu-lating the trucking industry. The true regulators were always the banks, the equipment-finance companies, and the insurance companies. If you couldn't demonstrate the knowledge and wherewithal to convince the equip-ment-finance companies to loan you the money to purchase the equipment you needed, the banks to provide the credit you needed to operate, and the insurance company to insure that equipment, you weren't going anywhere in this industry. Unfortunately, all three of those regulators got greedy and no longer vetted any of the people the way they used to.

Later, we'll examine equipment-finance companies and see that between the 2008 financial crisis and the Great Freight Recession of 2022–26 they seem to have had a change in heart with regard to their lending practices.

I've kicked things off with a minidebate over the merits of deregulation and the Motor Carrier Act of 1980 because fairness demands we hear both sides of that debate, and because both are correct in their own ways. The regulated market, while it provided for higher average driver wages and kept riffraff out of the industry, or at least consigned them to operating as "outlaws" if they could get their tire in the door at all, also kept freight rates artificially high, stymied competition, and was, to a point, a drag on the overall economy. The deregulated market allowed many a smaller operator, like the Paddock family, to grow and expand and provide decent jobs to generations of truckers.[7]

But the opening of the market to just about anyone, combined with a lack of market regulation by financiers and insurance companies, has led to a stream teeming with bottom feeders, and forty-five years after the MCA neither government nor market forces have done anything to clean up the water. Most attempts at reform have left the bottom feeders alone while making life a lot more difficult for competent, law-abiding truckers, dragging down our wages and waging war on the healthy aspects of trucking culture. Although deregulation is not the only cause of the War on Truckers, it is certainly where the first shots were fired, and the rest of this book will detail the various battles that have raged against us since.

4

Welfare on Wheels

It's time to end welfare as we know it
Let's get those greedy chiselers off the dole
It's time to end welfare as we know it
Teach them a little self-control
For far too long we've allowed these corporate hogs
To belly up to the public trough
No more welfare as we know it
No more handouts! Cut them off!

—Anne Feeney, "The Corporate Welfare Song"

In early 2016 my wife and I moved to the town she grew up in: Ithaca, New York. Born in Pittsburgh, Jenna moved to Ithaca when she was eight years old, her parents having decided to connect with other families to start an "intentional community." My in-laws wanted to have more of a say in their kids' education, as did a number of people they knew, so my wife was homeschooled with a group of other kids in her parents' living room until high school. Even then she went to the hippie, "democratically run" Alternative Community School. I don't think she ever had a number grade or percentage slapped on a report card until she moved on to university. The community of which my wife and her family are a part, as well as much of the wider population of Ithaca and Tompkins County, consists of progressive Bernie Sanders types. I remember my in-laws having a "Fight for $15" sign on their front lawn when we left our life on the road and moved to town. They've been doting grandparents, with a long history of proactive thoughtfulness toward kids, which is one of the main reasons we moved there. (Dad is still on the road, and my mother is no longer with us.) In addition to Jenna's parents, we had a prefab community and social network in Ithaca, so our move made sense.

Before we got into the business of having children, I tested the trucking waters—oil?—and began looking around for work, only to discover that I had entered a Twilight Zone that time and modern economics had left behind by a few decades.

I was put in contact with a small logging contractor located in a town not too far from Ithaca. It had a truck empty and needed someone with experience, and I needed a job. At that point in my life I'd been trucking for nearly twenty years in four different countries and had done a fair bit of logging. It seemed like a natural pairing, and when I went to meet the man behind this small outfit—we'll call him Travis—he expressed optimism.

"I think you'll like this old Kenworth we've got here," said Travis. "My uncle was driving it until he got sick, and we've been having a hell of a time finding a decent driver for it. The last two clowns we had didn't work out: one guy wouldn't show up for work every day—I think he might have been a meth-head—and the other guy kept running into shit and breaking things."

The unit happened to have a load on it, and I offered to run it to whatever mill the wood was bound for.

"Nah, let's go for a little drive around the neighborhood with it on. I can't take it anywhere yet, but it will work for now to let me see you handle a load."

So away we went. Driving along, moving through the gears with the grace and oneness with the machine I had developed over two decades of driving, I discussed with Travis my experiences; the differences between Canada, Australia, and the United States; and the nuances of harvesting softwood lumber in New Zealand versus harvesting the hardwoods most of the Northeast U.S. is known for. After a while, we returned to his yard and parked the truck. "When should I book you for a pee test?" asked Travis.

"I mean, I can go whenever you like. We haven't discussed any other terms or money or anything though."

"I'll have a discussion with my business partner about that this evening, and in the meantime, I can get you in for a urine test tomorrow morning. Sound good?"

I agreed and left it at that.

The next day, as I was heading to a clinic to "produce a sample," my phone rang. It was Travis.

"My partner and I have decided we can start you at $14 an hour and revisit this number in the new year."

It took me quite a bit of constraint to not burst out laughing. Could this guy be serious? It turned out he was.

"Um, no offense sir, but that's not enough. I'm making $16 an hour cash under the table now helping my contractor buddy schlep gear and run a chop box. I have to be able to at least move laterally, not backwards."

"Well, what did you expect? You're just a truck driver. We can revisit in the new year but I can't pay you more than $14."

"Sir, with all due respect, I just got back from driving road trains in Australia and I was being paid $42 an hour down there. I have twenty years of experience, and that has to count for something."

"You could have been making all of that up."

Despite sending this guy a full list of references, emails and phone numbers of previous employers, and photos of rigs I had driven, this was the offer I got to work at one of the most dangerous and economically critical jobs in the country. It was less than the "Fight for $15" minimum wage envisioned by my Bernie-supporting in-laws. I couldn't believe what I was hearing.

"Well, thanks anyway. And now you know why the last two guys you had didn't work out—$14 an hour doesn't buy what you want it to buy. Good luck."

And that was that.

It turns out that this gentleman wasn't an anomaly. A local gravel quarry that had its own dump trucks and flatbeds for local work was also advertising for drivers. I went to see them, did the drive with one of their old boys, and a few days later a nice HR lady gave me a call.

"Hi there. So we are prepared to offer you $18 an hour as our special summer seasonal rate, but if you stick around and go full time in the fall that drops to $15."

Again, I had to fight back laughter.

"Ma'am, it's awfully difficult to raise a family on the money you guys are offering."

"It is what it is. We usually hire old guys who are retired from driving snowplow or construction for the county or NYSDOT who already have a pension and are just trying to keep busy and out of the house."

Something about my experiences here didn't make sense.

For years we have been told that there is a shortage of truck drivers, and every year the American economy is at risk of total collapse if the American Trucking Associations can't find another 60,000 or 70,000 or 160,000 truckers.[1] Yet the economy never collapses and loads are always delivered while the ATA, and the incurious and utterly decrepit media that amplifies its voice, make these claims, year in and year out.

If there were an actual shortage of truckers, trucking companies wouldn't get away with barely paying minimum wage, would they? If the market for drivers were this hot and this desperate, maybe a guy with two decades of experience and a near perfect driving record would get offers more befitting his profile? In a properly functioning market economy, wouldn't the shortage boost the price of truckers' labor a little higher than what one might expect at a fast-food restaurant, a job often advertised as a stepping stone for teenagers into adulthood, and one not meant to pay that much?

What are we missing here?

In the mid-1980s, when the effects of the Motor Carrier Act of 1980 were first being felt, a new phrase began to circulate courtesy of our friends at the American Trucking Associations: "the truck-driver shortage." We'll get more into the ATA later, but for now just think of it as a corporate lobby that claims to represent the interests of massive trucking companies with thousands of trucks, though it really represents the interests of the customers of those very large carriers—nearly every corporation in America that produces material product. The ATA does not represent a single truck driver, anywhere.

Under the pressure of increased competition, companies sliced driver salaries as a belt-tightening strategy. Many drivers chose greener pastures as a result, and for a brief period in the 1980s there may actually have been a shortage of truckers.

By the late 1980s numerous articles in newspapers across the nation discussed this new phenomenon.

The first public expression of the driver shortage by the American Trucking Associations came in 1987.[2] The media then helped get the message out. A "serious shortfall of drivers is coming," Knight-Ridder assured us.[3] "There will be a 'serious' shortage of long and short distance truck drivers" very soon, added Scripps Howard, whose reporter went on to note that trucking companies would "try to increase their pools of drivers by hiring women, immigrants, and anyone who shows driving competence."[4] By 1990 trucker-shortage stories were appearing in major newspapers. A *Los Angeles Times* article said: "Trucking executives say schools are only part of the solution. A discouraging number of the graduates quit. [Jerry] Moyes, the owner of Swift Transportation, said 35% of his school's graduates quit after a year and go on to different firms or to new occupations. Other trucking companies also report disappointing retention rates."[5]

Thirty-five and forty years later, we hear the same old song. Familiarity, in this case, breeds contempt.

All this discussion in the media didn't help solve the "problem," then or now, and it was never meant to. What it did do was help the ATA and its members figure out a key messaging tool to help them unlock oodles of taxpayer money with which to line their own pockets. In time, they also discovered that constantly recycling this line about a driver shortage would keep the taxpayer money flowing while also stymieing wage growth—to the advantage of trucking-fleet owners and, more importantly, the Fortune 500 companies that are their customers, whose freight prices could be kept artificially low.

A scene in the wildly popular 1986 film *Top Gun*, which details the training of US Navy fighter pilots at a school of the same nickname as the film, illustrates the idea of truck-driving schools entering the culture. After being reprimanded for breaking rules of engagement, pilot Pete "Maverick" Mitchell, played with the signature manicured swagger of Tom Cruise, is further berated by his second-seat radar intercept officer, Nick "Goose" Bradshaw: "Maybe I can learn how to be a truck driver. Mav, you have the number of that truck-driving school we saw on TV? . . . I might need that." Hollywood, only a decade earlier, had venerated truckers in such iconic films as *Convoy* and *Smokey and the Bandit*. But by the late 1980s trucking was portrayed as a job of last resort, a place for washed-up fighter pilots, felons, and luckless losers whom their local unemployment agency needed to move off the rolls.

Though no one knew it back then, nor thought of it as such until recently, the truck-driving schools that were the butt of *Top Gun* humor were a convenient method by which large trucking companies off-loaded the cost of training new recruits onto the taxpayer, if not onto the recruits themselves. In his landmark 2016 investigation into how the trucking industry in the United States managed to attract new and willing entrants, *The Big Rig: Trucking and the Decline of the American Dream*, University of Pennsylvania sociologist Steve Viscelli documented how truck-driving schools work, how they are financed, how they screen people into or out of the seat of the truck, and how at every stage of the process the taxpayer is involved. (Viscelli knows about this process intimately, for as part of his research he became a trucker himself and went through a company-owned CDL mill.) "The cost of training new drivers presents significant risk to firms if they cannot ensure that these drivers will remain with the company long enough to make the firm's investment worthwhile," wrote Viscelli. "In 2007 Ray Kuntz, then president of the ATA, said that the 'biggest problem our industry has always faced is training new drivers.' As ATA president, Kuntz sought to defray the cost to carriers of training drivers by seeking more state and federal funding, such as the $315,000 grant his own firm received in 2007 from the Montana Department of Commerce to train sixty-three new drivers."[6]

Three hundred thousand and change doled out to one company might not sound like much, but an entire system of stealth corporate welfare masked as a jobs program has sprung up around the training of new truckers. And its cost is in the tens if not hundreds of millions annually.

Scratch beneath the surface of the ad copy for any truck-driver training school or local- and state-funded retraining program, and the government grants and subsidies become immediately apparent. From funds doled out by the Workforce Innovation and Opportunity Act to Pell Grants to $47 million in extra funding from the Biden Administration in a 2023 handout, it is clear that the trucking industry is awash in taxpayer largesse, and unless we recognize this corporate-welfare program for exactly what it is, the money will continue to flow.[7]

Viscelli recognized this. "Whether or not they operate a CDL school," he explained, "a few dozen large companies serve as gatekeepers for the industry's labor force, because they are the only place new drivers can complete the last stages of training and initial employment."[8] Even though that statement is not 100 percent correct—some small companies, rare and becoming close to extinct, will take on rookie drivers and get them over the finish line—the dominance of the megacarriers is a fact, and the corporate-welfare scam they are running imposes an artificial wage ceiling and particular standards on trucking as a whole. If truckers want to know who is primarily to blame for their wages being stuck in the 1970s, look no further than the American Trucking Associations and the taxpayer who pumps money into its capacious tank. And the taxpayer ought to ask about the bang for the buck he is getting from paying for all these CDLs, because America sure does produce a lot of them.

In 2021 National Public Radio pondered the question of whether there is a truck-driver shortage, and for once NPR produced a piece of journalism useful to the public and not blatant propaganda. Among the excellent questions and citations in the piece, we find this nugget of information, which ought to have been investigated by Elon Musk's DOGE to see just how much money has been dumped into the bottomless pit of truck-driver training: "According to the American Association of Motor Vehicle Administrators, state governments issue more than 450,000 new commercial driver's licenses every year. A large fraction of those drivers enter the long-haul trucking industry."[9]

Depending on who you believe (the U.S. Census Bureau, the Bureau of Labor Statistics, or the American Trucking Associations), the rough number of jobs requiring a CDL in the United States is about 3.5 million. I've seen numbers showing that between 1.8 and 2.2 million of those are truckers, either local or OTR or both. Of the other 1.3 million jobs requiring a CDL, many are in local delivery or the types of jobs in which having a CDL is ancillary to the primary task: say, a job with an electrical utility that requires the use of bucket trucks for tending to power lines or thinning trees. I've been told it's difficult to capture single-truck owner-operators in any statistics outside of active CDLs.

For the sake of argument, let's assume there are 2.5 million active truck-driving jobs any given year. If the U.S. CDL training and license-issuing system produces roughly 450,000 CDLs a year (setting aside the work of the Biden Administration, which nearly doubled that to 876,000 in 2022), then where are all these drivers going? The system produces 20 percent of the annual number of required CDLs annually; are we completely replacing the entire trucking workforce every five years?

A 2019 study by Stephen V. Burks and Kristen Monaco that was cited by the U.S. Bureau of Labor Statistics demonstrates pretty conclusively that the market for truck drivers functions about as well as any other labor market. If prices rise to signal demand for drivers' services, the market should respond. Burks and Monaco also found that the dysfunction in the trucking labor market is almost completely isolated to the long-haul truckload sector, where turnover is very high relative to other parts of trucking, never mind the markets for other types of labor. And what do you know? That is the market whose players are represented by the American Trucking Associations. "Surprisingly, the occupational attachment of truck drivers is actually a bit higher than that of some other blue-collar occupations," write Burks and Monaco. "This finding suggests that the market for truck drivers works about as well as that for other blue-collar occupations, and that, broadly speaking, *we should expect that if wages rise when the labor market for truck drivers is too tight, the potential for any long-term shortages will be ameliorated*" (italics mine).[10]

The large fleets that have captured a great deal of the American truckload market are not interested in raising wages or adjusting any of the myriad negative conditions of the job that are described throughout this book. They don't give a damn about Big Brother intrusiveness, oppressive rules of operation, or drivers' time being wasted in unpaid detention. What they will do, and have done, is complain endlessly about a shortage of drivers and demand that the government do something to assist them in producing more of them. What a major inconsistency in trucking culture (or what's left of it): so many truckers fancy themselves conservatives, or at the very least believers in the free market, yet major players in their own industry have effectively allied with the state in a mass wage-suppression operation.

Steve Viscelli, with coauthor Eric Balcom, prepared another study, commissioned by the state of California for its agricultural shippers, investigating why prices for shipping produce spiked in 2021. It was thought that the "driver short-age" was to blame, but Viscelli's study put that theory to bed, immediately, and in the process showed us that the trucking industry continuously shoots itself in the foot by doing nothing to retain good truckers while constantly begging the government for money to train new ones. He also found that it was the same old culprits causing the problem:

> We did not find evidence of a shortage of people interested in becoming truck drivers, but we did find strong evidence of a retention problem. That problem is concentrated in the long-haul segment of the industry—the segment that caused shippers the most pain in 2021. Because of this high turnover, long-haul trucking is the primary gateway to the industry for new truckers. Drivers argued that the job was challenging because of long hours and time away from home, but poor-quality training and bad initial jobs discouraged many would-be drivers. In this area, the state has some unique opportunities to foster partnerships that will better utilize state training monies.[11]

And oh boy, are there ever training monies: "California spends millions of dollars from public and private funds to train new drivers each year. Right now, it is likely that much of the money feeds into this suboptimal system and subsidizes high turnover."[12]

As of 2021, California was spending roughly $20 million of its cut from the Workforce Innovation and Opportunity Act on truck-driver training, and there is even more government money sloshing around to these schools, in California and everywhere else, from Pell Grants, veterans' assistance, and state and local programs. In conversations I've had with Professor Viscelli, he has relayed to me how difficult it is to track all this funding. There is—surprise, surprise!—very little accountability, and states are loath to share the intel. We can assume that California's total spending on truck-driver training is well north of $20 million annually.

And what do the agricultural shippers of California, not to mention the California taxpayer, get in return for this corporate welfare masquerading as a jobs program?

Not much, as it turns out, which is why the study was commissioned in the first place. Most of the long-haul refrigerated truckers that the California agricultural-produce shippers claim they require don't stay. This segment of the industry has the highest turnover problem, and Viscelli's conclusion is that this training money is wasted because the training programs start by throwing newbies off the deep end into long-haul trucking before they even know what they're doing.

Even former Secretary of Transportation Pete Buttigieg admitted, "My department estimates that 300,000 people leave that career every year, and we just can't afford that."[13]

Well, Mr. Buttigieg, neither can the taxpayers of California, or those of the United States in general, but we keep throwing money at this problem anyway, because as Viscelli has written elsewhere, "It is cheaper to keep churning through drivers than it is to pay them more."[14]

A significant reason why it is cheaper is that you and I are paying for the cost of constantly training new people. An interesting complaint in Viscelli and Balcom's study was lodged by one of the shippers for whom it was written: "As 2021 progressed, however, shippers increasingly worried that higher shipping costs would cost them market share. As one major shipper reported: 'We are used to rates from California to New York of around $6,500 to $8,000. I swore I would never pay more than $10,000. But we are looking at $13,000 right now. We can't stay competitive for long at that price.'"[15]

I guarantee you that not a single employee driver who worked for a company marking up its rates that much saw a penny of the extra five grand this guy was paying to move his stuff, and that right there is part of the problem. An owner-operator probably made out like a bandit, but one of these kids who works for a megafleet? Not a chance he saw any meaningful increase in pay during COVID, and certainly nothing reflective of what shippers were paying at the time. Cents-per-mile rates for company drivers are almost always locked in, especially at big fleets, where such things as bonuses, at least those derived from hot market conditions, are nonexistent.

Way back in 1996, one megafleet did experiment with paying its drivers more money and eschewing the hiring of recent graduates of trucking schools. For this story we return to Stephen Burks of the University of Minnesota–Morris, who is also the head of the Truckers and Turnover Research Project. Professor Burks, like Michael Belzer, is a former trucker turned academic, and probably knows more about the economics undergirding how America's truckers are paid than nearly anyone else.

"Observing the persistence of high turnover in its industry segment after deregulation," according to Professor Burks and three coauthors,

> one of the largest general freight long-distance truckload motor carriers, J.B. Hunt, in 1996 decided to try to break out of the "run hard, pay modestly, and experience high turnover" pattern. They announced they would raise starting wages by 35%, close their training school for inexperienced drivers, and hire only experienced drivers. They expected the reduction in crashes and turnover to pay for the higher wage costs. They implemented this plan in February 1997. Their results were extensively analyzed. *Investigators found that turnover rates and crash rates were both cut in half.* However, in March of 2002 managers at Hunt unwound this change, cutting their starting pay back to near its earlier level.[16]

The italics are mine, and for good reason, for this statement says so much about the mentality of those who manage the megacarrier portion of the trucking industry. Due to the gravity of their scale, everyone in this segment of the industry has a massive effect on the wage floor and employment structures of every other player in the game and could, if they so chose, improve the remuneration and safety of their drivers, right now. The evidence is right there: if you pay drivers better money, they stay with the industry and get in fewer accidents.

"But what about the other guys?!" I can hear all the fear-driven Boomer types cry. Yes, yes, those other guys. It's always the other guys, and there is something to that. What if "the other guys" are only able to get away with undercutting everyone else because (a) very few in the general freight market are willing to make the bold move J.B. Hunt did, and stick with it; (b) they have off-loaded the cost of training onto the taxpayer and the cost of the collisions that result from a never-ending stream of rookie drivers onto the insurance companies, which ultimately pass it to the rest of us in the form of higher premiums; and (c) they engage in "power only" subcontractor arrangements, which lean heavily into the most recent arrivals in America's labor pool?

Although J.B. Hunt did eventually alter its business model by focusing on building its own intermodal network and reducing the general freight side of the business, what if another similarly sized company did the same today? There are plenty of examples of companies with near-zero turnover, including my boys the Paddocks back home in Canada. Scott Paddock knows the score: treat people the way you want to be treated, pay them well, and they will stick around. Paddock Transport International has possibly the lowest turnover rate in the industry, at less than 5 percent.

Burks et al. compared the long-haul truckload sector to two other areas of the industry—less than truckload (LTL) and private carriers (trucks owned by the shipper)—and found that like the Paddocks and other specialized carriers, LTLs and private carriers had a fraction of the turnover rate of the truckload sector. Through thick and thin, whatever the economy is doing, LTLs and private carriers appear to remain steady at a roughly 17 percent turnover rate. Burks concludes that this disparity is a structural issue. I agree, though I don't need any academic veneer to tell you that the problem is greed, along with the complete and utter disrespect for truck driving as a skilled trade, and thus for truck drivers themselves.

In a 2022 article for *FreightWaves*, journalist Rachel Premack spoke with several politicians and industry insiders, including Bob Costello, the chief economist of the American Trucking Associations. Throughout the article, Premack highlighted boneheaded statements from politicians who repeat the driver-shortage lie, such as Arizona Democratic Senator Mark Kelly, who sponsored the stupidly named LICENSE Act of 2022, which sought explicitly to reduce the barrier to entry for getting a commercial driver's license. Premack wrote, "As Kelly said in his campaign video, the law would ease America's 'truck driver shortage,' helping hardworking Americans and slashing costs for all."

This "hardworking Americans" nonsense is an insult to America's truckers, who are the hardest workers of all, regularly putting in seventy-hour-plus weeks and spending millennia away from home and their families and communities. Flooding the zone with more people instead of fixing the problems endemic to trucking is always the go-to for people like Senator Kelly. Perhaps the former astronaut spent too long in space and forgot about reality on the ground, or else he got American truckers confused with the Space Truckin' exploits of Han Solo.

In fairness to Kelly, of all the people Premack interviewed, Bob Costello ought to come in for the most derision, because Costello revealed quite effectively what he and his colleagues in the professional managerial class think of us truckers. In an email to *FreightWaves*, Costello wrote that high turnover rates represent "the free agency of trucking and the ultimate worker empowerment." What he meant is that truckers are playing a game of musical chairs, moving from one bad job to another, as the rules of the game and the wage floors (and ceilings) for the entire industry are set by the giants who compose the membership of Costello's employers at the American Trucking Associations. You can have the freedom to choose between crappy jobs, but you cannot have more money or a better job.

Costello even argued that higher pay only encourages drivers to work less. He told *FreightWaves*, "With regard to pay, counterintuitively, increased pay rates can lead some drivers to work less in order to be home more often. In fact, almost forty percent of truckload carriers reported to ATA that increases in pay last year resulted in drivers choosing to drive less, make the same amount of money and be home more often."[17]

Oh no! Some drivers might choose to prioritize family if we pay them more; therefore let's *not* pay them more or do anything substantial to adjust or improve the material conditions of the job. I hope Bob Costello doesn't get run over by one of the chumps who churn through his members' CDL mills.

You might be asking: How do we measure the number of truckers out there, or the number of CDLs? What are the baseline metrics for the driver-shortage claims of the ATA, and how did they arrive there?

To buttress the ATA's claims about a driver shortage, the organization retained an outfit called Global Insight, which is affiliated with Northwestern University, to conduct a survey.[18] It asked ATA members: How many trucks do you have sitting? How much work do you think you could have? There is very little specific data about each carrier's actual workload versus its number of trucks. Predictions are difficult given the sometimes volatile nature of the freight market and the economy in general. Claiming you need X number of drivers involves guesswork and predictions about the future that may not, and often do not, pan out. An industry insider tells me that this survey model has been recycled every year since 2005 and is completely unreliable as a method of determining legitimate demand for drivers.

Industry veterans have also accused some larger carriers of overpurchasing trucks as a tax write-off, which they justify by the alleged shortage of truckers. "Oh, I'm sorry Mr. IRS auditor, we need to write off all this expensive equipment we bought because we just can't get drivers!" It sounds ridiculous, but given the complex nature of our corporate tax structure, it is plausible enough, especially when you consider these guys have been lying to everyone about the driver shortage for decades. Congress, media, IRS: everyone got the message and no one questions it.

As regards CDLs, that number is fairly easy to come by. Our friends at the American Trucking Associations gave away their own dishonest game in a 2019 report. You have to dig into this tedious tome, but on page 6, footnote 10, we are given some interesting numbers to ponder: "Of the 7.8 million people employed throughout the economy in jobs related to trucking activity, 3.5 million were truck drivers in 2018. There are over 10 million CDL (Commercial Driver's License) holders in the U.S., but most are not current drivers and not all are truck drivers. There are roughly 3.7 million trucks on the road today that require a driver to have some sort of CDL. The Department of Labor says there are 1.8 million [that] are heavy and tractor-trailers drivers. We are only focused on the over-the-road tractor-trailer drivers."[19]

But most are not current drivers.

Could it be, maybe, that these millions of "not current drivers" were budding truckers that ATA members chewed up and spit out?

The fact that the ATA admits to the existence of ten million CDLs is helpful, as is the rest of the breakdown. The ATA is correct that roughly three and a half million vehicles ("jobs" would be a better way to explain this) in the U.S require a CDL to operate, though many of those jobs are not in trucking, and the vehicles are not even trucks. Coaches, school buses, and the bucket trucks your local utility uses for maintaining electrical lines or cutting back trees all require a CDL. Yet approximately two million jobs are in trucking, and if there are ten million CDLs that means eight million people made the choice to *not be a truck driver even though they went through the process to get a CDL.*

It is difficult for researchers who do not speak directly to ex-truckers to find out why people are not driving. Trucking is not the kind of industry that conducts exit interviews to glean useful information that might prevent the unnecessary attrition we see in trucking.

Churn and burn, baby—we can always get more.

One insidious effect of the bogus driver-shortage narrative is that it begets a real shortage of the deeply experienced and highly skilled drivers sought after by companies in more specialized areas of trucking, such as hauling logs, livestock, hazardous materials, or oversized loads. The constant churn of drivers at the entry level of the business results in a deficit of those drivers who stick around the business long enough to acquire the skills and experience necessary to fill those niche, higher-skill, and much better-paid roles. The entry-level trucker in America, who is not trained well enough, not paid well enough, and not even treated like a human being, eventually gives up and exits the business before moving up in the trucking hierarchy. Real pros in the business often return to the refrain that "there are plenty of steering-wheel holders and not enough professional operators."

Like with that little boy who cried about a wolf who wasn't there, eventually a real shortage did show up, and no one outside the business noticed or cared.

I used to be a member of a small, short-lived trucker advocacy organization called CDL-Drivers Unlimited, the name being a play on "Ducks Unlimited," the conservation group that preserves wetlands for waterfowl and other wildlife. I remember that when I mentioned this to Michael Belzer in an interview, he said, "They're only preserving the ducks so you can shoot them, so maybe think about that."

In 2023 CDL-Drivers Unlimited commissioned an intern to chase down state DMVs and DOTs in order to compile a state-by-state list of the number of active CDLs in the country. We thought this would be helpful in taking on the driver-shortage narrative. The number CDL-DU came up with was 8.8 million, but this was somewhat conjectural, as we had to make our best guess for the sixteen states whose bureaucrats did not respond to requests for information. One of those states was New York, which might have a larger number of extant CDLs than can be "average-inferred" from the other states' numbers.

The team at American Truckers United, a newer advocacy organization based in Little Rock, Arkansas, whose work will appear again later in this book, extracted data from Federal Motor Carrier Safety Administration databases while investigating what appear to be massive anomalies in the issue of CDLs. The ATU team estimated there to be nearly 5.9 million CDLs, which is a big drop from what CDL-DU and the ATA found. That said, we are dealing with the government here, and it is within the realm of possibility that these numbers are incorrect. Or maybe over four million people got the message about how bad the trucking industry is between 2019 and 2025. Given the wild variations, the reluctance of at least sixteen states to play ball with CDL-DU in coughing up numbers, and the questionable issue of CDLs by states cooperating with Biden's 2021 Trucking Action Plan task force, it is probably impossible to know how many CDLs have been issued. The only sure answer is "a lot." Any number you choose is well north of the number of jobs that require one.

Is there a partisan angle to this? Is it merely the Democrats ladling out corporate welfare to trucking companies that wouldn't know what a free market in drivers was if it blasted an airhorn at them? Hardly. The Republicans have been only too happy to help the more generous of their constituents to the trough.

As recently as spring 2025, Republican Congressman Zach Nunn of Iowa introduced legislation that hit all the notes described here. His bill invokes the fake driver-shortage narrative, offers tax credits to trainees, and directs government subsidies to truck-driver training facilities. Per usual, the bill comes with a misleading title: the "Strengthening Supply Chains Through Truck Driver Incentives Act." If passed, it will accomplish the opposite of what it sets out to do—and stick taxpayers with the bill.

Representative Nunn is full of more manure than an Iowa hog pen. "Right now, we're facing a serious shortage of truck drivers," he said, "and it's putting pressure on Iowa families and our nation's supply chains."[20]

Pressure on Iowa families? Hmmmm.

Congressman Nunn went on: "Iowa has approximately 36,000–38,000 heavy and tractor-trailer truck drivers employed according to the U.S. Bureau of Labor Statistics. This large workforce plays a key role in supporting Iowa's agriculture, manufacturing, and logistics sectors—all critical to the state's economy."[21]

Yes, truckers are critical to Iowa's economy, and if you want to support the families of those 38,000 Iowa truckers, maybe watering down the pool of available drivers with inexperienced talent—which by the laws of supply and demand will exert downward pressure on rates and wages—isn't the way to go about this?

By the way, according to OpenSecrets, Representative Nunn received $114,434 in campaign contributions from the "Transportation" sector in the 2024 cycle.[22] This is how patronage politics works.

Another method by which Republicans sought to expand the pool of drivers, rather than let the market bid up wages or the industry actually improve conditions, was a 2019 piece of legislation with yet another misleading title: the "DRIVE-Safe Act." This bill would have lowered the age restriction on interstate commerce. Under federal law, you must be twenty-one years or older to engage in interstate commerce with a commercial vehicle. On its face, this is a silly restriction, as you can apply for and obtain a CDL when you turn eighteen. But due to this restriction, an eighteen-to-twenty-year-old can only drive within his or her home state. This produces absurd situations like an eighteen-year-old driver in Omaha, Nebraska, being prohibited from driving just a mile over the river into Iowa but being allowed to drive over four hundred miles across the Cornhusker State. Imagine the hamster wheel of being an eighteen-year-old trucker in a tiny state like Rhode Island or Delaware.

The problem with this bill, however, is the implication, unspoken but well known to everyone in the industry, that this new potential cohort of drivers would be fresh meat to throw at the long-haul truckload sector, which has a major problem keeping people around. Despite the bill's flowery language about an apprenticeship program, there is no middle step between the minimum number of hours under the watchful eye of a trainer and being thrown into the deep end. If the bill's supporters were serious about an apprenticeship program, they would impose some kind of air-mile radius restriction from home on these new drivers, which is something my bosses did for the first two years I had my license. When you are closer to home, you are easier to rescue if there is a problem, your employers are handy for further training and advice, and you don't have to deal with the stress of being far away from home, family, and community while you are still wet behind the ears. That is not what the DRIVE-Safe Act proposed, so we can safely assume that its unspoken purpose was to throw more people at a problem that requires systemic solutions, not more bodies.[23]

Truckers are, on average, grossly underpaid, and have been for decades. Consider just the last decade. In 2015, industry analyst Gordon Klemp, president of the National Transportation Institute, pointed out in a conference call with investors and reporters that truckers' wages had averaged $38,618 in 1980. Adjusted to 2015 dollars, those wages would exceed $111,000 a year.[24] Yet as *Overdrive* magazine noted, average company-driver pay in 2015 was about $57,000, which is barely over half the inflation-adjusted amount. (I'm not sure how *Overdrive* was counting the beans, since, according to the U.S. Bureau of Labor Statistics, truckers' median pay in 2015 was $40,260.)[25]

After ten more years of terrible government policy and insane spending, the story hasn't changed. In April 2025, industry magazine *CCJ Digital* cited a report showing that truckers' wages have not only remained stagnant; they haven't even tracked with wage growth in other occupations and industries: "BLS data indicates that from 2019 to 2023, the average truck driver's annual earnings rose [from] $46,850 to $55,990. However, despite wage growth in the trucking sector, average earnings across all occupations increased even more significantly from $53,490 to $65,470, which is nearly a $3,500 difference in annual growth."[26]

A minority of trucking jobs in niche sectors pay over $100,000 a year, but averages are what they are, and the big players in the industry set the wage range for everyone else. And they are able to keep wages as low as they are by suckling on the taxpayer's tit.

Though it is nearly impossible to cut off wards of the state from a pipeline of "free" money once that pipeline is laid, there is proposed legislation out there that seeks to balance the scales—with zero taxpayer funds. It should come as no surprise that this piece of legislation has, at the time of this writing, been stalled for over three years and not yet made it out of a congressional committee.

Introduced in 2022 by Democrat Andy Levin of Michigan—who was primaried and lost his seat that year—the Guaranteeing Overtime for Truckers Act (GOT) contains just one line. All it does is remove the overtime exemption for truckers in the 1938 Fair Labor Standards Act. No pork, no new regulation, no taxes.

One might wonder at the bipolarity of FDR, who regulated the trucking industry with the Motor Carrier Act of 1935 and three years later effectively prevented truckers from being paid the overtime every other worker is due. But the fact remains that for nearly ninety years truckers have been rendered second-class citizens where it concerns pay, which might also help explain the retention problem.

This reform seems simple enough, doesn't it? Remove the exemption, and then it's up to trucking companies and their customers to figure out how best to deal with it. Maybe customers stop holding drivers up at their facilities, which means the trucks are more time-efficient and make more money, and thus trucking companies will be better able to absorb the cost of overtime. If not, trucking companies pass the marginal cost on to their customers. Some might say the marginal costs associated with paying drivers overtime would end up being absorbed by the Almighty Consumer, but the people who usually complain about that don't say anything about the taxpayer footing the bill in other ways. And are not truckers consumers themselves?

The GOT Act has been reintroduced in Congress by New Jersey Congressman Jefferson Van Drew, one of Levin's original cosponsors and, thus far, the only Republican to officially endorse the bill. Republicans might say they're the party of the free market and private enterprise, *but by their fruits ye shall know them*. Most of Van Drew's colleagues would rather the trucking industry remain a socialist parasite on the body politic.

As for the Republicans' clients at the American Trucking Associations? What a surprise: they oppose the GOT Act.

ATA President and CEO Chris Spear hands down the party line:

This proposal is nothing more than a thinly-veiled attempt to boost trial attorneys' fees. It would reduce drivers' paychecks and decimate trucking jobs by upending the pay models that for 85 years have provided family-sustaining wages while growing the U.S. supply chain. Truckload drivers today are earning nearly $70,000 on average plus benefits, and wages across the board continue to rise at historic rates year-over-year. . . . The bill would not affect owner-operators, who, as independent contractors, are not covered by the Fair Labor Standards Act.[27]

Trial attorneys' fees? What? Oh, right—Chris Spear's members would uniformly refuse to pay and therefore end up in court. I appreciate the honesty, Mr. Spear.

As for his claim about reducing drivers' paychecks, I would suggest Mr. Spear look in the mirror—or, at the very least, at the receipts for the campaign donations the ATA has made over the years. According to OpenSecrets, the ATA spent $2.8 million in 2024 on political lobbying, which is pretty good bang for the buck, given the exponential returns its members get in all that taxpayer money funneled to driving schools.[28]

Mr. Spear's claim about independent contractors is only partially true. The Owner-Operator Independent Drivers Association, America's largest association of those contractors, supports the GOT Act. OOIDA Executive VP Lewie Pugh told me: "A rising tide lifts all boats; if these megacarriers have to set their rates upwards, we would be fools not to do likewise. They already set the floor for everyone else, and that floor would rise if drivers' time was accounted for under the law."

It ought to be noted here that OOIDA released a white paper on the driver-shortage narrative, and its opening paragraph could read as a condensed version of this chapter:

> In the U.S. trucking industry—particularly in over-the-road (OTR) long-haul trucking—one observes a seemingly paradoxical situation. For years, trucking companies have warned of a "driver shortage," yet the industry experiences extraordinarily high annual turnover rates among drivers, often exceeding 90% at major truckload carriers. In a typical free market scenario, a labor shortage would trigger market corrections: rising wages, improved working conditions, and other incentives to retain workers. As any basically competent economist might point out, persistent shortages should not exist if prices (in this case, wages) are allowed to adjust freely. Why, then, has the trucking sector seemingly failed to self-correct in the face of chronic driver attrition? The answer lies in a web of systemic and structural factors that have entrenched a high-churn labor model as the status quo.[29]

To OOIDA's great credit—well, I give them great credit—their white paper quoted my handy phrase, which describes the whole rotten edifice: *"stealth corporate welfare disguised as a job training program."*

The American Trucking Associations and its members, recipients of so much of this corporate welfare, are a major cause of the driver-retention problem and the lagging of truckers' wages. You have 3.5 million people in America being grossly underpaid for the work they do, a situation exacerbated by a 1938 law that artificially limits truckers' wages. Many of America's truckers live where rural decay and wage stagnation are eroding American communities. Paying these people properly, as everyone else is supposed to be paid, would go some way to boosting the broader economic prospects of those communities. The American Trucking Associations and its puppet politicians employ the rhetoric of "good-paying American jobs," but more often than not this is but noise justifying corporate-welfare projects that produce the exact opposite.

Truckers deserve better than this.

5

The Trucker as Indentured Servant

I owe my soul to the company store.

—Merle Travis, "Sixteen Tons"

For most of my life, I wanted to go to Australia to drive road trains. Maybe it's the Freudian thing about size. Or maybe it's the little boy in me who, inspired by his father's *National Geographic* magazines with all those photos of kangaroos, wanted to drive the biggest Tonka trucks in the world. For as long as I can remember I have had an obsession with the Land Down Under.

As I left high school and undertook my trucking career, I learned that about seventy countries had bilateral agreements with other nations to issue "working holiday visas" to young people as a sort of exchange program. Each of these countries made available a small number of visas to people like me who were happy to pass through for a year, carrying a backpack and undertaking incidental work along the way.

There were conditions, of course—to receive a work holiday visa in Australia you had to have (at the time) five grand in the bank to prove you weren't a bum

Kiwi timber: Me in Kaingaroa Forest, North Island of New Zealand, 2003.

and wouldn't become a burden on your host's welfare system. You also needed proof of onward passage in the form of a flight out of the country, or the means to buy one, and you had to pass a basic background check to establish that you weren't a criminal. Easy enough.

Twenty-year-old me saw this as a pathway to trucking in Australia. I had already been pulling "heavy" with B-Trains and Michigan Sleds in Canada for two years, which I thought would endear me to Ozzy operators, and I spoke the language. (Well, sort of—I still had to learn a lot of Ozzy slang.) I didn't have a girlfriend at the time, and to be honest, both the trucking lifestyle and my young-man awkwardness weren't helping. Maybe I could both go trucking in the Outback *and* be regarded as exotic enough to sweep a young Australian lady off her feet. What did I have to lose?

And so it was that in 1999 I obtained one of these visas and headed to Australia, still soaking wet behind the ears. The trip did not go exactly as planned. But I did learn quite a bit, the main lesson being to do more homework before traveling halfway round the world.

Arriving in Sydney with nothing but my backpack, I immediately went about the work of looking for a job and figuring out how to get my Ontario license converted to a New South Wales trucking license. This is when I discovered that Australia had a graduated truck-licensing system—and their version of the local DMV was about as helpful and pleasant to deal with as those back in North America. No one I spoke with at NSW's transport authority knew what I needed to do, nor did people in trucking. Plus, members of the latter group seemed a little skeptical of hiring some twenty-year-old kid fresh off the plane from Canada. Various of these gents indicated that hiring people under twenty-one was off the table regardless of where I was from, and one fellow asked me if I'd had any practice driving on the "correct side of the road."

After several weeks of this sort of thing I had grown despondent. So I decided to lean into the backpacker part of the deal and just be a tourist for a while. I took a bus to South Australia and ended up spending about six months in the Flinders Ranges, working for a four-wheel-drive tour company and an associated hostel accommodation. I shelved the trucking and just had fun. I did appear exotic enough to a young lady from Melbourne named Rachel, if only briefly. We spent New Year's Eve of the new millennium camping under the stars somewhere along the Oodnadatta Track deep in the Australian Outback. So my first trip wasn't a total loss.

I left Australia before my visa expired (without, it should be noted, the kind of protest lodged these days by thousands of Indians in Canada, who demand that their temporary visas be regarded as permanent).[1] But my dream of road-train driving in Oz remained alive, and a few years later, in 2004, I returned to Australia, this time on a tourist visa that I was hoping I could upgrade to a work visa after I got the licensing and job parts figured out. I now had a year's worth of experience driving big trucks on the wrong side of the road across the Tasman in New Zealand, and I had done a lot more homework on how to navigate the Australian truck-licensing system. I had a plan, and the Australian trucking industry, like trucking industries everywhere else, was whining about a shortage of truckies. Why not me?

So it was that with the help of a transplanted Kiwi named Errol Parkinson of Mount Barker, South Australia, I found myself enrolled at a trade school in Adelaide to upgrade my New Zealand Class 5 license to an Australian Class MC or road-train license. It cost me a couple grand and several weeks of my time, but at least I would be brought up to snuff on the Australian regulatory side of things and could leverage this knowledge in attempting to get a job. You might say I was going about things correctly and above board—legally, even.

There was a hitch. Despite its claim of a truckie shortage, the Australian trucking industry had not yet convinced the government of said shortage. The Australians may have had a legitimate claim at that time, contra the decades-long fake-driver shortage psyop in the U.S. brought to us by the American Trucking

Associations. But this did not translate to my qualifying for any work visas. I spoke with companies all around Adelaide, traveled to Perth, and then hitch-hiked my sorry ass all the way to Darwin to speak with a company up there. This was the equivalent of traveling from New Orleans to Los Angeles and then up to Minneapolis in search of work, which was plentiful. The problem was getting a visa, or anyone to sponsor me for such, and I kept running up against the same obstacle: there was no visa specifically for truckers, and I did not qualify for any visas that were available. Failing once again to realize my dream, I went back to Canada with my tail between my legs and my wallet a lot lighter. At least I had a new souvenir: a South Australia–issued Class MC road-train license, something few people had back home.

It was nearly another ten years before I had the chance to go back to Australia and see if the third time was, indeed, the charm. Having been hooked up with a small and specialized company out of Perth by my Kiwi mate Gavin, whom I'd worked with on the Ice, it seemed like this time I might actually realize the dream. Gavin spoke highly of the company, which seemed pretty keen on hiring people and was impressed with my résumé, especially my time hauling fuel into remote oil-development projects in Northern Alberta. After a number of emails back and forth, and dealing with various firms to help me navigate the work visa and everything that comes with that, the company in Perth agreed to bring me to Oz.

I was no longer seeking to appear exotic to a mythical Australian lass, for I was married by this time—to an American girl—and I brought my wife along with me. Alas, our long-distance relationship would continue while I was in Australia. For the first few months after her arrival she worked in Melbourne, and when she did make it out west, I was always on the road. I might see her once every two weeks, if we were lucky.

Upon arriving in Perth, I had to play a little catch up, which included contending with the fact that my expired South Australia road-train license would not be recognized in Western Australia. Thus I had to take yet another road test in a truck through a private but state-recognized driving school. That cost me $800. I also had to contend with a couple of other things that were going to make my time in Perth with this company short. One was that as I was in the process of getting a visa, the company was beginning a transfer to new ownership in the form of the aforementioned energy-services company from Scotland. The other was that things were no longer, as the Australians put it, "casual."

For example, in the past, Western Australia, along with the Northern Territory, had not enforced any law regarding logbooks, or what Ozzy truckies call "work diaries," which supposedly enable the authorities to measure what they call in Australia "fatigue management." Although Western Australia has remarkably loose hours-of-service rules, its government was now requiring us to carry a logbook, which I had hoped to avoid, based on my idealistic notions of being left alone in the Outback. As I was to discover in time, especially through the capricious and sneering attitude of the Scottish-owned company's health and safety manager, this was only the beginning. Western Australia, whose economy was dominated by the mining and oil and gas sectors, had become Californicated in micromanaging the working class.

One particular customer to which we were hauling was an under-construction onshore natural-gas processing plant near the tiny remote town of Onslow, about eight hundred miles north of Perth. It was comanaged by the American construction giant Bechtel—and the Bechtel guys were a huge pain in everyone's ass.

Before leaving Perth with a load bound for Onslow, every driver had to sign off on half a dozen sheets of paper acknowledging that, among other things, he understood Western Australia's hours-of-service rules and knew the route from Perth to Onslow. (There's only one road, so I don't know how anyone could get lost.) What was the point of this? Were truckers at risk of forgetting all this after each trip? Had the Australians imported the American managerial fetish for endless amounts of paperwork? Even the dispatch personnel at my company understood it as a farce, but they had to play along. Not a single driver was under any illusions about the purpose of these redundant reminders: it was simply about control and insulting our intelligence.

One arrived at the Onslow site only to encounter more of Bechtel's micromanagement. The check-in guys would come out to inspect the load on your trailers. Never mind that the loads had already made the journey of eight hundred miles from Perth and arrived safely—if the Bechtel guys didn't like how you tied it down, they would make you do it over again to travel the final few hundred yards into the construction site. They would also get very picky about the clothes you wore. One started a fight with me because of a small hole in my work boots. I didn't take kindly to being told I had to buy a new pair of boots by people who weren't going to pay for them, so I didn't. On my next trip to Onslow, the same dude inspected my boots again and wrote me up for failing to adhere to Bechtel's safety standards. The safety guy back in Perth had a field day with this. He was overjoyed at the opportunity to feel useful by belittling me for not buying a new pair of boots when there was nothing wrong with the pair I was wearing.

Another clothing-related issue might not seem like a big deal but is revealing about the nanny-statism animating certain Australian workplaces. Even when working outside in heat exceeding one hundred degrees Fahrenheit, you must wear a long-sleeved shirt for any job, regardless of the task. The stated concern is that you might get skin cancer at some point in the future, and the assumption is that you, a grown adult, are not to be trusted to apply sunscreen. "It's for your own good, mate," was the near universal reply whenever I spoke with Australians about this. Nanny statism runs so deep in their society that it's like talking to the proverbial fish about water. It is inconceivable that you may have legitimate agency, as an adult, to make your own decisions about the clothes you wear or whether to apply sunscreen.

The new Scottish managers had very much the same approach to management as these False Dinkum Ozzies. Our general manager told us about a new contract the firm was pursuing with a waste-management company and regaled us with stories of the eight hundred pages of documents that had to be produced outlining safety procedures and redundancies simply in order to bid on the contract. This was before anything was signed or guaranteed. No doubt the process was rife with additional needless friction.

Our new Scottish overlords were also behind the policy that prevented my wife from coming trucking with me. This was half the reason I had brought her along. Every other place I had ever worked tolerated my proclivity for picking up hitchhikers or taking friends and family trucking with me; my little brother has been a regular passenger in past trucking trips, as have friends and various girls. If these managerial demons thought I was going to stick around while they mandated loneliness for employees who spent weeks away from home, they were out of luck.

Like many of his contemporaries, the Australian poet, philosopher, and

The road warrior: a man, his road train,
and the big sky of Western Australia, 2015.

comedian Clive James found himself living abroad, seeking fame and fortune as an expat. Mr. James, who had quite a career as a satirist, critic, and TV personality in the UK, memorably described his homeland in a way that explained so much of my own struggle in not getting along with these people: "The problem with Australians is not that so many of them are descended from convicts, but that so many of them are descended from prison officers."

Though I am Canadian, I spiritually identify as an Appalachian-American and am a devotee of the small-L folk libertarianism that enlivens so much of American culture. It seemed like my issues with this company in Perth, its new Scottish managers, and the obey-nanny attitude of so many Australians were going to doom this final stage of realizing my lifelong dream. The folksy 1980s Ozzie tourism campaign that featured Paul Hogan, aka Crocodile Dundee, putting "some shrimp on the barbie," and the Australian national saying, "She'll be right, mate," both of which have come to stand for the entire country's self-perception, are advertising scams built on a mountain of bullshit and internalized as a way for the descendants of convicts to deal with the descendants of prison officers who have never stopped viewing their role in society as heartless and cold administrators rather than the shepherds of a new polity. Look at what happened to Australia during COVID—politicians like "Dictator" Dan Andrews, the Premier of Victoria, made Justin Trudeau look like Ron DeSantis.

That said, physical escape from the attitudes of certain of my hosts, if not digital and managerial escape, was possible, at least temporarily, in the Outback. I regularly slept on the side of the road in the middle of nowhere, cooking my own dinner on a small butane stove behind the bunk of my truck under a million stars. I also carried beer in the fridge of the truck and communed with the universe by firelight while hanging out next to my parked road train, an experience not available to most of the world's truckers. I shared many evenings in communion with Ozzy truckers, sharing stories of our respective exploits and lives. Despite the prison officers, Ozzy truckers are devotees of the same folk libertarian "Don't tread on me, thanks" attitude that I am. These memories salvaged an otherwise negative employment experience.

After other incidents of management failing to manage properly and generally making my life difficult, I gave the company my notice. Sixteen months of trying to deal with them was enough. I had to move along.

That was easier said than done. I was married to this one company under the conditions of my work visa; I was not permitted to work for anyone else. I knew from speaking with truckers who hauled cattle through the Outback that they, like their American livestock-hauling cousins, enjoyed a much more hands-off atmosphere, but there was no legal way for any of those companies to take me on. Once again, I folded up my tent and made my way back to North America.

Did I experience servitude in Perth? Technically no, but knowing that I was stuck with one firm and couldn't shop my services elsewhere in Australia sure tempered my agency as a worker and limited my range of responses to their insulting and micromanaging ways. How many other truckers around the world have found themselves in similar situations? As it turns out, plenty, especially right here in the United States. Some are migrants being indentured by their coethnic homeboys, who take full advantage of loopholes and lack of enforcement of the law; some are the economically precarious who have been sold a bill of goods about buying their own trucks in lease-purchase arrangements; and some are convicts, who, having done their time for the crimes they have committed, are preyed on by trucking companies who know that options for convicts are limited and thus that they are ripe for exploitation.

One particularly egregious story of indentured servitude in trucking appears in Benjamin Lorr's popular 2020 book, *The Secret Life of Groceries: The Dark Miracle of the American Supermarket*. Lorr's was one of those works of pop journalism that pull back the curtain on some industry or aspect of American life, not unlike Eric Schlosser's wildly popular *Fast Food Nation* (2001), which looked at the underside of the fast-food industry. Lorr went on an extended trip with a trucker named Lynne Ryles, a fourteen-year veteran who is a lease-operator under the Cargill banner. To really get into the lifestyle, Lorr spent multiple days with Ryles on the road, bunking in the top bed of the sleeper unit in her Peterbilt. Though Lorr is a journalist who came into this experience knowing nothing about trucking, and although his observations will sound pedestrian to my fellow truckers, what he revealed to his non-trucking readership ought to have shocked them about the degradation of American truckers—the men and women who keep our grocery shelves full. It's often said that our modern distribution system works "as if by magic," but in reality it is fueled by grinding, punishing servitude and exploitation.

After meeting Lynne and giving his initial and almost snobbish impressions of her, how she lives, and the accommodations inside her rig, and then offering praise for her skill at coping with the terrible driving of "four-wheelers" who must be managed like children, Lorr goes on to describe her debt peonage. Lynne puts in incredible hours and overcomes daunting adversity only to keep treading water.[2]

For hauling a three-stop load of dairy products over 1,050 miles, Lynne grosses just $1,231—a laughably cheap $1.16 per mile—which Lynne tells Lorr is "pretty decent."[3] Lorr notes that while the shipper grants Lynne a $368.50 fuel surcharge for just two or three days of work, she faces what he calls a

> blizzard of deductions: 28 percent of the gross and 10 percent of the fuel is snatched off the top by Cargill for the privilege of driving in its fleet. Then there is a $300 weekly payment for leasing the truck she drives. There is the $300 she has to pay for the week prior, when work was slow but the truck payment was still due. Then there are the lumper fees, heavy-usage taxes, costs for various federally mandated fuel additives [Lorr probably means diesel exhaust fluid, which is not a fuel additive but a necessary input for the mandated emission control system] . . . and [trailer washout]. So without any other expenses [she is] below $500 for the entire trip.[4]

Add in taxes, insurance, and an accountant and lawyer, and Lynne—who works seventy hours a week—nets less than $17,000 out of an annual gross of $200,000. Lorr speculates that she exaggerates her net income as a matter of pride. Like Tennessee Ernie Ford, she's another day older and deeper in debt.

There is a certain type of trucker who will scoff at Lynne's situation and blame her for her problems: "She signed up for this, bro. The government shouldn't do anything to interfere in the contract opportunities of people who want to get in the business." I get it. But it's a lot easier to avoid the situation Lynne Ryles and so many others have found themselves in if you grew up in and around trucking. Because every *experienced* trucker on the road knows about this scam, and how the washout-to-success ratio is so very lopsided.

When I was eighteen years old, I attended an industry trade show with my old boss, Scott Paddock, in Toronto. As we toured the exhibits of products, new trucks, and recruitment scammers, we happened upon a display from one of Canada's megacarriers that promised to hire rookies off the street and turn them into "owner-operators" in three months. Scott leaned over to me and said, "These guys are just crooks. They're taking people for a ride. There is no way you can learn everything you need to know in such a short amount of time." Experienced truckers call these "Never-Ever-Never" plans. What this means is that you should *never* sign up for one of these because if you *ever* do sign up you will *never* do it again.

The lease-operator arrangement that Lynne Ryles found herself tied up in has been a pervasive fixture of the North American trucking industry for years, and it is no coincidence that this system has tracked with the growth of CDL mills in the wake of deregulation. CDL mills and the lease-operator scam are related in many ways. Downloading cost and risk onto unsuspecting people chasing the dream of self-employment and financial success was the subject of Steve Viscelli's previously mentioned *Big Rig*, which describes how those new entrants to the industry who survive the first few months of life on the road are solicited to become lease-operators. The program is predatory from the start, as it charges desperate people hard money just to apply and holds them in debt from the word go. This is a far different system than the one that paid a kid like me to learn from the bottom up, as the Paddocks did.

Viscelli's eyes were opened on the first day of training at "Leviathan," his pseudonym for the CDL mill at which he enrolled: "Despite the fact that the students were all there because they were recruited for the job and the training was required, it would become apparent within a couple hours, when school staff explained the terms of the training contract, that the company had no intention of hiring all or even most of us. [And yet] . . . we could owe the company more than $4,000 if we didn't work for them for a year."[5] Viscelli took this training in 2005, when four grand was a much bigger deal than it is today.

Viscelli describes the oppressive mood that descended upon his fellow trainees. They were under "constant surveillance" and were evaluated dozens of times, though no one ever showed them these evaluations or told them exactly what was being assessed. Soon, "the sense of insecurity among the students was palpable whenever we gathered as a group. Underlying it was the threat of failure combined with the steep price of training."[6]

That price was not refundable, which was "the only thing keeping some of the students there," writes Viscelli. "Only about half of the workers I trained with would complete the initial training and be hired by the company. . . . A few were forced to leave because of drug or criminal histories not disclosed to the company. A few others were advised to leave because of poor performance operating the trucks. The atmosphere was so intimidating and coercive that several students snuck away in the middle of the night, as if escaping some kind of forced labor camp. . . . On graduation day Leviathan hired about half of the original fifty-eight trainees."[7]

Half of fifty-eight is twenty-nine; twenty-nine times $4,000 = $116,000. That's a tidy six-figure sum for washing out dreamers and some folks who probably had no business being there in the first place.

Friend and fellow trucker Justin Martin tells me a similar story. On his first day of training for Schneider National at one of its facilities in Green Bay, Wisconsin, there were eighty-seven budding truckers. Twelve months later, Justin was the only one of those eighty-seven still behind the wheel.

Viscelli concludes his tale of Leviathan, "The trainees who did not complete the initial training had wasted their time and gone into debt to *apply for a job*. The firm had weeded out undesirable workers and foisted much of the cost onto them or the government programs paying for their training. It had also indebted the workers it hired with a high-interest loan for a year, which would deter them from quitting. This is how most new long-haul truckers are introduced to the truckload industry."[8]

Like the thousands of people who wash out of these exploitative programs every year, the twenty-nine Leviathan rejects were most likely ill-equipped to afford that four grand. Unsavory elements of the trucking industry are now four decades into running every scam in the book to try to find drivers, and over the years the pool of potential employees has dwindled as many people have wised up to the scam and avoided it like a speed trap. The industry has responded by digging ever further into the bottom of the human-resources barrel to find recruits, hoping that they are unwise to what their chances of success will be, or precarious and desperate enough to try anyway. Benjamin Lorr is incisive on this point:

> There are some jobs where it is almost impossible to succeed because they are very difficult. Then there are jobs where you are designed to fail. Lease to own programs in OTR trucking seem like both to me. . . . I came to see the trucking industry as structurally vampiric. I don't say this to be dramatic. It is an industry that creeps along the margins of society and seduces the vulnerable. . . . Debt is the financial instrument that best expresses hope. . . . I hear repeatedly about trucking recruiters who cruise for drivers from homeless shelters, soup kitchens, recovery wards, prison work release programs . . . [and] from several tours of duty overseas.[9]

A job training and placement agent from the state of Maryland who wishes to remain anonymous told me of the incentives that push the marginalized into trucking—whether or not those folks are capable or skilled enough to deal with the demands of the job. In his capacity as a placement agent, he said, the only two considerations were "labor-market demand" and if someone on unemployment, or simply a job seeker, wanted a job. Asked if he, who had no particular knowledge of the trucking industry, was capable of screening a potential driver trainee, he replied, "God no. We would make people get a driving record [abstract] from the state. We certainly never saw them operate a vehicle." The more job placements the better—for the bureaucracy, that is. Once they are placed, it doesn't really matter if people stick with trucking. Simply getting them off unemployment is more important than the success of those placed. Many wind up back at the placement agency when the trucking industry spits them out.

"Nobody above me was asking if we were meeting labor demand," the Maryland job training and placement agent told me. "They were tunnel-vision focused on [certain] metrics. . . . Nobody answered the question of how we get truck drivers without CDL mills, which are not the only way to produce truck drivers."

At heart—or at heartless—the lease-operator scheme is a way for companies to download costs and risks associated with capital (the truck) onto workers. It's a sort of inverted socialist scheme where the worker doesn't own the means of production but merely owns the payments and maintenance costs on the means of production. As Viscelli explains, the economics of the post-deregulation era left trucking companies paddling to stay afloat and keep the freight moving. Early on, many benefited from using owner-operator contractors. Eventually that changed.

The problem was twofold: first, owner-operators in the late 1980s and early 1990s had the same problems fleet owners had with financing equipment and operational costs in an environment of cutthroat competition and low rates, but without the economies of scale that fleets enjoyed with regard to purchasing power. Second, owner-operators were, as a rule, unwilling to tolerate inconsiderate treatment from dispatchers who did not distinguish between owner-operators, who are independent businesspeople, and company drivers, who are not. In short, owner-operators tended not to take any shit, and as a result they did not meet some carriers' requirements for "control and reliability." So carriers "began consciously transforming labor market institutions to create a new kind of contractor that would fit their needs."[10] The owner-operator was too independent a soul; the lease-operator model was born.

Viscelli lists four main advantages to using lease-operators rather than employing drivers directly. First, they are legally self-employed and thus do not receive employer contributions to Social Security, Medicare, worker's comp, or unemployment insurance, which can save trucking companies roughly 30 percent. Second, a great deal of capital cost is shifted to the contractor—paying for, maintaining, and fueling the truck. Third, despite "independent contractors" being legally required to have choice over their work, the lease-operator model locks the contractor into an exclusive relationship with the carrier. Because of the pressures to pay off the truck, lease-operators are less likely to reject loads or say no to work, which is much easier to do for an employee driver, who can always quit if the carrier acts like the firm I worked for in Australia. And fourth and finally—though this is less of a concern now that the Teamsters only represent about 5 percent of truckers—contractors are less likely to unionize.[11]

Viscelli found that much of the trucking industry has adapted to the idea that they don't have employees anymore and that any person, regardless of skill, training, or business acumen, can be a contractor. He related the story of a driver named Claudio, an immigrant from Mexico. Married and with a bunch of kids to feed, Claudio was talked into a lease-operator arrangement with a flatbed carrier in Texas. Working weeks away from home but getting short-haul loads that didn't pay very much, Claudio sometimes ended up owing the company money at the end of a work week. He worked harder and harder, staying a month away from his children at a time, but the carrier still gave him low-paying loads or otherwise jerked him around. He lamented: "I am going to quit. I got $41.58 in pay last week [a seven-day work week]. That is not going to put food on my family's table. It's not going to pay for my home. Every time that I call [the carrier] they are too busy to talk."[12]

This entire system is what Viscelli refers to as "debt peonage." Stories like those of Claudio or Lynne Ryles are more common than not, and they are also happening in sectors of trucking other than general freight, refrigerated, or flatbed. In one of the key subdivisions of trucking, "drayage," or hauling shipping containers on and off ports, the lease-operator model is now the dominant mode of employing drivers, at a far higher percentage than with over-the-road freight. These indentured servants are also more likely to be recent arrivals in America.

In a 2017 three-part *USA Today* series, journalist Brett Murphy dove into drayage operations at Long Beach and Los Angeles, the biggest port facilities in America. Buttressed by stories of immigrant truckers taking home starvation wages despite moving goods for corporate giants such as Target and Home Depot, Murphy's series delved into the world of "port truckers—many of them poor immigrants who speak little English—[who] are responsible for moving almost half of the nation's container imports out of Los Angeles' ports. They don't deliver goods to stores. Instead they drive them short distances to warehouses and rail yards, one small step on their journey to a store near you."[13]

Murphy's investigation revealed that for the previous decade or so, trucking companies in the Los Angeles area had been "forcing drivers to finance their own trucks by taking on debt they could not afford. Companies then used that debt as leverage to extract forced labor and trap drivers in jobs that left them destitute." He continues:

> If a driver quit, the company seized his truck and kept everything he had paid towards owning it.
>
> If drivers missed payments, or if they got sick or became too exhausted to go on, their companies fired them and kept everything. Then they turned around and leased the trucks to someone else.
>
> Drivers who manage to hang on to their jobs sometimes end up owing money to their employers—essentially working for free. Reporters identified seven different companies that have told their employees they owe money at week's end.[14]

Trucking companies were abetted in this appalling behavior by the government of California in the form of yet another state mandate. Murphy explains:

> For decades, short-haul truckers at the nation's ports relied on cheap clunkers to move goods to nearby warehouses and rail yards.
>
> With little up-front investment, drivers—most of them independent contractors who owned their own trucks—could make a decent living squeezing the last miles from dilapidated big rigs that weren't suited for the open road.
>
> In October 2008, that changed dramatically in southern California, home of the nation's busiest ports, Los Angeles and Long Beach. State officials, fed up with deadly diesel fumes from 16,000 outdated trucks, ordered the entire fleet replaced with new, cleaner rigs.
>
> Suddenly, this obscure but critical collection of trucking companies faced a $2.5 billion crossroads unlike anything experienced at other U.S. ports.
>
> Instead of digging into their own pockets to undo the environmental mess they helped create, the companies found a way to push the cost onto individual drivers, who are paid by the number and kinds of containers they move, not by the hour.[15]

Port truckers, in my own personal experience, have always been the worst treated. When I rode with Mark "Mouse" Williams one summer, hauling cans from the old Kodak plant in Rochester, New York, down to the Port of New York and New Jersey, he had to use a "can chassis," a trailer that is custom-built specifically for hauling shipping containers. There was a massive pool of them on the dock, but they were all junk. Mouse spent hours looking for a unit that didn't have flat tires or inoperative lights or twist locks missing—just something fit for service. We were always delayed and ended up in huge lines. Mouse was not paid for these lengthy delays.

This initial impression of these facilities stayed with me as I got into truck-ing. Occasionally, I would have to go to container-handling facilities such as empty storage yards, rail intermodal facilities, or the ports themselves, and it was always the same story—some level of chaos that proper investment and management could have addressed. Perhaps that has always been off the table for international shipping lines, which didn't get to the point of generating quarterly profits in the multiple billions of dollars by being generous or thinking about the suppliers who interact with their facilities.[16]

Many truckers know the score and simply refuse to work with these corpo-rations. Maybe that's why the firms turn around and hire subcontractors who in turn convince the unknowing to sign up for indentured servitude.

In 2020 and 2021, the term "supply-chain crisis" entered our vernacular, as many people were stuck at home, laid off from closed businesses, or otherwise had a lot of time at home to scroll through their newsfeeds. As the worldwide shipping industry went through stages of this crisis, either in "whiplash" or "accordion" fashion, depending on shipping cycles from China and elsewhere, Americans were afforded images of over one hundred massive container ships at anchor off the coast of Los Angeles, unable to dock and unload due to the massive backlog of containers. Companies of every description around the United States were experiencing shortages, whether in manufacturing, retail, or some other sector. To an extent, they had the high-living and obscenely compensated exec-utives of the international shipping industry to blame—cloud people whose riches came at the very human cost of bankrupting a bunch of migrant workers who didn't understand the scams in which they found themselves trapped.

To be trapped is, in essence, to be a slave. That word does a fair job describ-ing the situation in which many recent immigrants to Canada and the United

States find themselves. And these drivers are responsible for a shockingly disproportionate number of road tragedies.

On a windswept corner in the center of the Canadian Prairies, a haunting roadside memorial has for eight years been weathered by the northern summer sun and the dark, icy prairie winters. Crosses and hockey jerseys stand as sentinels, an analog to the rows of crosses one might see in a similar field in Belgium or France, though the battle that these jerseys mark is economic, and the shots fired silent and mostly unheard by the wider world.

This roadside memorial, despite symbolizing a serious problem with Canada's immigration system and its regulation of who and how one becomes a trucker, seems not to have disturbed the consciences of Canada's smug politicians. They have done nothing to honor the young people who were killed. They have done nothing to reform the system that led to these sixteen deaths— and the deaths of so many others across the continent in the eight years since.[17]

On April 6, 2018, the lives of sixteen people were snuffed out. Jaskirat Singh Sidhu, a Punjabi native of India with a degree in commerce who had been a permanent resident in Canada since 2014, blew through a stop sign and crashed his truck into a northbound bus carrying the Humboldt Broncos of the Saskatchewan Junior Hockey League. Investigations later revealed that Mr. Sidhu didn't touch his brakes and had an unobstructed view of the road and all the warning signs leading up to the intersection. He was pulling a Super B-Train.[18] One might think that Canadian federal or provincial authorities would have separate training requirements for drivers of these much larger trucks, but they don't.[19] Mr. Sidhu reportedly had about a month of trucking experience before he caused this crash and took sixteen lives.

What was a guy from India, carrying a degree in commerce and with so little training, doing driving one of the heaviest truck combinations on North American roads? What possessed him to go trucking in the first place? Sidhu is one of nearly two million immigrants to the country from India. Though Indian migration was slow through most of the twentieth century, composed mostly of Sikh men headed for the lumber mills of British Columbia, over time that migration accelerated, especially under the policies of Pierre Elliott Trudeau.

In 1971, the elder Trudeau, then prime minister of Canada, announced that multiculturalism was heretofore to be official government policy.[20] In time, this announcement would have far-reaching consequences. Though not made law until 1988 with the passage of the Canadian Multiculturalism Act, Trudeau the Elder's announcement set into motion dramatic demographic change. As it concerns trucking, things really got interesting, in a very negative way, when Trudeau the Younger gained power in late 2015.

Because Mr. Sidhu had a degree, he was probably eligible for permanent residency under the points system that used to be a hallmark of the Canadian immigration system. Many of his fellow countrymen who come to Canada explicitly to be truck drivers, however, enter with what's called a Temporary Foreign Worker (TFW) permit. The TFW system, implemented in 1973, was originally meant only to allow highly skilled foreigners to come to the country to fill necessary vacancies in medicine and engineering. Over time, and over several changes in government, the plan expanded in both the jobs and the number of people eligible for TFW status. Corrupt employers began taking advantage of a captured market in Third World labor to undercut Canadian workers.

A 2014 report revealed that under Prime Minister Stephen Harper, thousands of workers in the province of Alberta had been brought in under the TFW program, many from the Philippines and India. Documents obtained by the CBC revealed that rules of the program were "being bent and broken, and . . . thousands of temporary foreign workers were being underpaid." Truck drivers were among the list of affected occupations.[21]

Though Harper, the leader of the Conservative Party of Canada, lost the election late in the following year to Justin Trudeau and the Liberals, the change in prime ministership and government did nothing to fix this broken system of insourcing "temporary" labor to Canada. In a 2022 interview with *The Canadian Bazaar*, an Indo-Canadian online news website, a Punjabi immigrant named Nachhattar Singh Chohan claimed, "We Punjabis control more than sixty percent of all trucking operations in Canada. There is a perpetual shortage of truck drivers and mechanics and new Punjabi immigrants fill this need."[22]

Setting aside the cojones it takes to brag about taking over the majority of an industry in someone else's country, it is notable that Mr. Chohan justified this takeover by using the driver-shortage lie, which is as big a humdinger in

Canada as it is in the United States. His claim about Punjabis controlling a significant stake in Canadian trucking is, however, correct. Everyone can see it on the roads—or in the ditches, where many of these drivers end up after rolling their trucks. As far back as 2016, the Ontario Trucking Association published statistics showing that, in 1996, "just 1.8% of Canada's truck drivers were from South Asia. . . . By 2016, almost one in five (17.8%) of Canada's truck drivers had South Asian backgrounds. One in three drivers in B.C. (34.6%) were from the demographic group, as were one in four (25.6%) of Ontario drivers. In Vancouver, South Asian immigrants now account for the majority (55.9%) of drivers. The share in Toronto is not far behind at 53.9%."[23]

Whatever one's views on immigration and its effect on labor policy, this massive spike in Punjabi penetration of the Canadian trucking market ought to raise a few eyebrows. Given that the driver shortage is and always has been a lie, one has to ask how much wage arbitrage is going on here, and is wage arbitrage the only explanation?

Though its editors may not have had my exact question in mind, in 2019 Canada's largest newspaper, *The Globe and Mail*, conducted a major investigation into the surge of immigrants into trucking. The *Globe and Mail* editors, much like everyone else in the country, had seen and heard about immigrants taking over whole industries, Canadian kids not being able to get summer or part-time jobs, recent arrivals being abused by their employers, Canadian truck-crash statistics going in a bad direction, and so forth, and naturally they had questions. In its series on the abuse of the Temporary Foreign Worker program, *The Globe and Mail* revealed that Punjabi penetration into the Canadian trucking industry relied heavily on indentured servitude, which is the polite way of saying modern-day slavery.

Among those profiled was Mahan Singh, a twenty-six-year-old rookie driver with minimal training who was tasked to drive a semi-trailer "through treacherous mountain passes." Mr. Singh, who was sent out on the road under a temporary work permit, confessed to "feeling terrified he would lose control on an icy highway and kill someone." A native of Amritsar, India, he "had never experienced ice or snow," according to *The Globe and Mail*. Nor had he ever "considered being a truck driver . . . but *Canadian immigration consultants told him that getting experience in trucking could help him qualify for permanent residency*" (italics mine).[24]

The manager of a Greater Toronto area truck-driving school told *The Globe and Mail* that "a lot of these guys are only getting into trucking to help them get permanent residency, they're not in it to be truckers." *The Globe and Mail* discovered that

> young foreign nationals like Mr. Singh are routinely steered into trucking by some immigration consultants, in collaboration with particular trucking firms. Both take cash payoffs from recruits in exchange for jobs—even though that practice is illegal.
>
> That has spawned an entrenched, lucrative and dangerous immigration scheme, centred in Surrey, that is exploiting newcomers and putting lives at risk across the country.
>
> In audio recordings obtained by The Globe, consultants told one international student a trucking job costs $35,000 to $55,000—an astonishing sum for aspiring immigrants, who often borrow the money to pay the fee.[25]

Mr. Singh told the reporter that he had to shell out $10,000 for his job, and he promptly racked up two accidents in his first four months.

Fifty-five grand is a lot of cake to buy a job that—supposedly—nobody wants, in a country where you may not speak the language, have no knowledge of the driving culture, much less the culture at large, and have never had to navigate the Rocky Mountains in wintertime. But as *The Globe and Mail* discovered, the scummy companies operating in this sector don't care. Nor do their bureaucratic enablers. "[Our] investigation has revealed that immigration authorities let trucking companies hire newcomers through the Temporary Foreign Worker Program, even when the carriers have a proven history of multiple-injury accidents, serious safety violations or exploitative labour practices. . . . Marginal operators were granted permits to hire many more foreign drivers than they had trucks, raising questions about whether they actually needed the labour. *Several people in the industry say small companies can profit more from cash paid by recruits than they do from hauling loads.* Many of those businesses operate out of private homes, sometimes under more than one name. Often they have just one truck, according to government records" (italics mine).[26]

On the American side of the border, the use and abuse of migrants in the American trucking industry shows no signs of slowing down. While researching this book, I was alerted to several scams. When I followed one of these leads and posted on Twitter/X about it, a firestorm ignited that soon implicated the secretary of state and governor of Nebraska.

The kindling was an interesting article sent my way from an online outfit called "Kenya Insights." Despite the ambiguous phrasing of the title—"Kenya Secures American Jobs Deal for Truck Drivers Through Nebraska Partnership"—my curiosity was piqued. American jobs? A Kenya-Nebraska partnership? *What?* The first few paragraphs were eye-openers:

Kenya has entered into a groundbreaking labor mobility agreement with Nebraska State that will open doors for Kenyan truck drivers to work legally in the United States, officials announced this week during a joint press conference in Nairobi.

The deal, signed on Tuesday between Principal Secretary for Diaspora Affairs Roseline Njogu and Nebraska Secretary of State Robert Evnen, specifically targets licensed commercial drivers amid a significant shortage of truck drivers across America. Evnen confirmed the high demand for skilled drivers in his state and emphasized that the agreement provides an organized, legal pathway for Kenyans seeking employment opportunities in the US.

"We began with labor mobility with commercial driver's license [sic]; these are skilled truck driving positions. We have a need for that in the United States, we have the need for that in Nebraska, and we have training available in Nebraska," Evnen explained during the announcement at the Kenya-Nebraska Beef Trade and Investment Conference.

The timing of this agreement is particularly significant given President Donald Trump's administration's heightened restrictions on illegal immigration to the US. The Nebraska deal ensures that Kenyan drivers will follow proper visa procedures and legal channels to enter and work in America, with participants required to meet all visa conditions and return to Kenya upon contract completion.[27]

America is going through a protracted freight recession, thousands of companies have gone tits up, and many thousands of drivers have been rendered unemployed, and these guys are bringing in potential truckers from Kenya? What is going on here?

I found another article in the Kenyan media making the same claim. This time, a company was implicated: one of the biggest trucking companies in America, in fact—Werner Enterprises out of Omaha, Nebraska:

Werner Enterprises is one of the largest logistics companies in the United States, and has been a key player in the industry for decades. Their discussions centred on exploring avenues to engage Kenyan truck drivers overseas and support the Kenyan diaspora in securing more opportunities for employment and enterprise development.

The truck driver shortage is no secret.

"There are tens of thousands of truck driving jobs that are open at any given time," said Nebraska Secretary of State Bob Evnen. . . .

[Principal Secretary, State Department for Diaspora Affairs, Ministry of Foreign and Diaspora Affairs, Roseline K. Njogu] further extended an invitation to the Werner Enterprises team to visit Nairobi with the aim of further solidifying the engagements and allowing the team to witness the hardworking spirit of Kenyans firsthand. Additionally, it would provide an opportunity for the company to train prospective Kenyan recruits on the requirements needed to qualify for positions at Werner Enterprises.

"Kenya is open to sharing its excellent talent with the world, and we think Nebraska would make a good home for our people," stated PS Roseline Njogu.[28]

I took to Twitter with screenshots of these articles, and boy did that light the internet on fire. Between my own tweet and those made by colleagues about the same issue, reaction to the story was swift, with responses from Derek Leathers, the CEO of Werner, and denials from various bureaucrats within the state of Nebraska.[29] The media picked up on it immediately, with stories from *Freight-Waves*, Land Line Media, and even local mainstream media.[30]

There was enough going on with this "memorandum of understanding" and the inclusion of trucking company Grand Island Express in a 2024 trade mission to Kenya that the denials fell flat. So flat that the governor of Nebraska threw the secretary of state under the bus: "The MOU is exclusively between Secretary Evnen and the Kenyan government. The Secretary of State is an independent state constitutional office and is [not] accountable to the Governor," a press release emphasized. The Nebraska DMV even felt compelled to state that at "Governor Pillen's direction and pursuant to federal law, we will continue to diligently ensure only individuals with lawful status in the United States receive Nebraska driver licenses of any type."[31]

What can I say to wrap up this chapter, dear reader, except that we North American truckers have targets on our backs? If they aren't trying to indenture us through lease-operator arrangements that make drivers into debt peons, they're trying to indenture budding immigrants (or allowing immigrant communities to indenture their own people). Whether you blame Wall Street, the value-scrapers of private equity, the government, or corporate America in general, it sure seems like the goal is to replace us—first with the indentured, and then with robots.

6

Panopticons of the Interstate,
or The Hitchhikers You Don't Want

ICC is a checking on down the line
I'm a little overweight and my logbook's way behind
But nothin' bothers me tonight, I can dodge all the scales alright
Six Days on the road and I'm a gonna make it home tonight.

—Dave Dudley, "Six Days on the Road"

There's nothing like that first cold beer on a Friday afternoon to mark the end of the week, be it at the pub on the way home or maybe as a sneaky road soda from the gas station.

Fridays, however, are not as much of a cause for celebration for truckers as they are for the average working man with a Monday-to-Friday gig. Many drivers are away from home for weeks—or months, if they haul seasonally for specific industries, as I did as a younger man.

In the last trucking gig that required me to be away from home, I was on a Monday-to-Friday schedule: leave the house at two or three in the morning on Monday and get home Friday somewhere around seven p.m. Four nights in the truck and weekends off is actually something of a deal in trucking, given that many companies want you to stay out for two or three weeks at a time. Regardless, when Friday comes around after four nights away from a beautiful wife, getting your ass home and back to her is about the only thing you think about all day.

Thoughts of my own bed and the woman I shared it with were front of mind one particularly unremarkable late fall afternoon, when I crawled out of the coffin bunk of a T-800 Kenworth parked at the Blandford Service Plaza on the Massachusetts Turnpike, otherwise known as Interstate 90. I had arisen at about two p.m. after sleeping roughly six hours, having parked the truck that morning after completing an oddball overnight run that involved taking a food-grade liquid tanker to a small farm near Duanesburg, New York, where a chap had set up a used vegetable-oil collection facility in his barn. The gentleman in question would roam the countryside in a small truck with a vacuum-equipped tank used to clean out the grease traps of restaurants or hospital kitchens and other such facilities. He would perform preliminary filtering and upgrade of the oils, and when the tanks in his barn had a full truckload he called us, and we would take it away to be refined into biodiesel.

I had started the previous evening at six o'clock, left the yard near Syracuse, rolled over to Duanesburg, loaded, and then trucked the roughly 7,400 gallons of fine-smelling slop to a biodiesel refinery in Newport, Rhode Island. By the time I had pumped off into one of the storage tanks and begun the trip back home empty (there's not much in the way of backhauls for a trailer that has been filled with waste-oil sludge), I ran out of hours on the Mass Pike. In the United States you are only allowed to drive eleven hours in a maximum shift of fourteen hours, and I was being tracked by an electronic logging device (ELD) in my company's truck, even though that mandate wasn't set to become law for another couple months. The primary customers of the company in question were energy companies whose truckers hauled a lot of gasoline and diesel to gas stations. Energy companies, believe it or not, are more anal about safety and compliance than nearly any other industry, given their risk exposure and the decades of media attacks they have endured. Thus, they have forced their many contractors to be early adopters of this surveillance technology.

There isn't much of a line at Starbucks for its gruesome coffee at two on a Friday afternoon, so I got a cuppa and went back out to the truck fairly quickly.

I looked at my ELD: I had nearly four hours until I would be allowed to put the truck in gear and head back to Syracuse. That meant sitting for four hours of unpaid time, then spending another four or so hours on the road, an hour to post-trip inspect the truck and trailer, fuel it, file paperwork, clean my stuff out for the weekend, and then an hour and forty-five minutes driving my personal vehicle home. I'd be getting home around one in the morning, long after my wife would have gone to bed, having spent a Friday night without me, and me without her.

This was the first job in which I had dealt with an electronic logging device, and after a little over a year working for this company out of Syracuse, I had just about had enough of it.

There had been other things during my employment by these cats that had driven me wild. Being sent out to Minnesota or Wisconsin to pick up brand-new trailers for their trailer-sales business usually resulted in me hitting Chicago right when my eleven hours was up. It would be pointless to sleep on one side of Chicago only to wake up and then be caught in the infamous traffic that paralyzes the Windy City, so I often kept on driving and would park somewhere an hour or so west of the city. Of course, these thoroughly reasonable exercises of my agency, which were meant to save me hassle and time and the citizens of Chicagoland yet another trucker clogging up their commute, were met with reprimands from the safety guy I had to report to in Syracuse. (He got to sleep with his wife every single night of the week, if I remember correctly. Maybe that's why he had so many kids.) If there were no ELD in the truck, my stretching of the rules would never have been noticed.

Sitting in that parking lot choking down Starbucks sludge, I got to pondering. I had nearly twenty years of trucking experience under my belt and had never been involved in a collision nor hurt anyone nor wrecked a truck, but due to the whims of safety bureaucrats, who were worried about compliance or being sued should an accident take place, I was being denied my agency as a professional and yet another night at home with my wife. I decided against sitting on the Mass Pike with my thumb up my ass and took action. I quickly texted another driver I knew. He had been let go by the same company. I asked him what his login credentials were for the company ELD system.

"What are you up to?"

"Going home on a Friday night. Just send me your login and your PIN."

"Good luck. Don't blame me if you get canned."

And away I went. Not long after I put the truck in gear and got rolling, my phone started lighting up with text messages.

"WHAT ARE YOU DOING?"

Well, I'm not allowed to touch my phone while I'm driving, and there's also a driver-facing camera in the truck, so I ignored it.

A few minutes later the phone rang.

"Mr. Magill, what do you think you are doing?"

"Going home. It's Friday."

"You weren't allowed to leave for another four hours."

"A few years ago, before you adopted these goddamned ELDs, you wouldn't have cared and done the same thing yourself, sir."

"That doesn't matter. Pull the truck over and wait your time out."

"No sir, I'm going home."

"Hey man, you've got a kid on the way. Are you out of your mind?"

It was true: my wife was pregnant with our first daughter, Vivian. Part of the reason I had agreed to be on this company's "regional" board and out all week was to advance myself up its weird seniority system for local jobs.

"No, I'm not sitting on the Mass Pike and twiddling my thumbs because Uncle Sam says I have to. Pretty insulting when there is no regulation on car drivers, who cause the vast majority of the collisions out here. You guys know how to backdoor; rearrange the time."

"Clean your truck out when you get back. We can't take risks like this."

We can't take risks like this.

It was in this moment that I realized the trucking business had entered a different phase. A once humane and laissez-faire approach to letting grown men manage their own time had been obliterated by some outside force, with not a shred of logic. Even Canada, the frozen gulag camp whose guards are soulless bureaucrats, used to have a "Friday heading home" logbook exemption. You were permitted to take a shorter sleep and make up those lost resting hours in your own bed by adding them to the total you needed for your weekend reset. Eventually the authorities took that away—not because of any particular incident, but presumably because they lack basic humanity.

By the time I got back to Syracuse, all the managers had left, typical of the nine-to-fivers on a Friday, and that was that. To his credit, the head shop mechanic stuck around, saw me off, and bid me the best of luck.

Electronic logging devices are a communications technology that tracks the movements of big trucks and the hours that a trucker puts into driving them. They are meant to enforce compliance with what are called "hours of service," the bureaucratic rules meant to keep truckers from being overworked and a danger on the roads. Because many drivers are paid by the load or by the mile—and have been since forever—a concern has arisen that drivers, their wages dependent on production that is often hampered by frequent delays, are incentivized into dangerous driving. You've probably heard or seen the stereotype about highways full of "tired truckers." This stereotype has lodged itself into the collective psyche of America's governing institutions.

However, there are contradictions built into this concern with compensating the poor guy behind the wheel for all his hours away from home, and these have been with us for a long, long time.

The Fair Labor Standards Act (FLSA) of 1938 instituted standards of employment for workers that we now take for granted: the forty-hour work week, minimum-wage laws, a ban on child labor, and mandated overtime pay of time and half for any hours worked over that forty-hour benchmark. Passage of that legislation took a whole lot of cajoling with many groups and constituencies—a fascinating story outside the purview of this book—but what is relevant here is that eighty-eight years later, we are still governed by an exception to the overtime component applying to transport workers, specifically truckers.

The language is as follows:

> Thus, the 13(b)(1) overtime exemption applies to employees who are:
> 1. Employed by a motor carrier or motor private carrier
> 2. Drivers, driver's helpers, loaders, or mechanics whose *duties affect the safety of operation of motor vehicles in transportation on public highways in interstate or foreign commerce* and
> 3. Not covered by the small vehicle exception.[1] (italics mine)

This section of the act immediately raises questions. For instance, a driver or his assistant or a mechanic whose job duties directly affect safety of operation is exempt from overtime. Does that mean that the people we rely on to keep our highways safe are not due the extra pay that all other workers are entitled to? Wouldn't you want to adequately pay the people responsible for safety? Wouldn't making them second-class citizens grate on them, and perhaps create a needlessly antagonistic situation when they are asked to work overtime with nothing extra in the bag for them?

This same weird logic was applied when the FLSA was first drafted. It was believed that if truckers were incentivized to work longer hours by being paid overtime, they would present a safety risk to other motorists. The only problem with this logic is that truckers are prevented through hours-of-service regulations from working over . . . seventy hours a week. That seventy-hour max has become the de facto expectation of most truckers, creating a situation in which they are denied overtime pay—because we don't want them working too many hours—yet are expected to work *seventy* hours, week in and week out. As the kids say these days, *make it make sense.*

This strangely incoherent and contradictory arrangement has survived since 1938 and has become an ingrained component of the trucking industry. The incoherence and contradiction, however, have taken on new and punishing levels of absurdity in how truckers' lives are governed.

The electronic logging device mandate came into effect in December 2017. The ELD was meant to supersede many decades' worth of truckers keeping track of their hours with paper logbooks. These logbooks have been the subject of scorn and derision by truckers for as long as they have been the law of the land, as the economics of the business and the vagaries of the job meant that, for the most part, it was nearly impossible to stay in compliance with hours-of-service regulations and the schedules demanded by the customers whose freight the truckers hauled. Though the demands and deadlines of the job may have been difficult to keep up with (depending on who you hauled for), the benefit of paper logs was that it was a lot easier to massage the accounting. This is not the case with a government-mandated satellite tracking device. Yet it turns out that America's supply chains, like drivers' paychecks, depended greatly on the massaging that was previously possible.[2]

Created by the MAP-21 Act signed into law by President Obama in 2012, the ELD mandate took time to come to fruition. It was pushed by the corporate lobbyists of the American Trucking Associations and the usual safety groups, such as Parents Against Tired Truckers, which later became CRASH (Citizens for Reliable and Safe Highways). It faced lawsuits from the likes of the Owner-Operator Independent Drivers Association and massive, if unsuccessful, opposition from working truckers.[3] In the popular (with NPR-type nerds—and me) podcast *Over the Road*, hosted and narrated by Long Haul Paul Marhoefer, the widespread reaction to the ELD mandate was expressed by a trucker named Mike Landis of Lititz, Pennsylvania:

> It counts down every second of your day. Whereas before on a paper logbook, if you're five minutes past your time pulling into a truck stop, nobody knew the difference, no harm no foul. But now, I've seen people backed halfway into a parking spot in truck stops because if they finish backing up the ELD is going to put them in violation to back another fifty feet into a parking spot. . . . To me, it's a slap in the face; driving a truck at eighteen years old, I'm now thirty-three, closing in on two million miles, I have a clean driving record. To me, that all comes down to the way I was taught, that comes down to the responsibility of knowing you're operating an eighty-thousand-pound machine. The fact that they're going to tell me that I need this thing in my truck to keep me safe on the road? Doesn't sit well with me at all.[4]

In late 2018, after the ELD mandate was implemented over the objections of nearly all of America's truckers, a bill introduced by former congressman and now Senator Kevin Cramer (R-ND) called for the Transportation and Infrastructure Committee to "conduct a study to determine how many 'employees' who must comply with the electronic logging device requirement . . . have ceased being operators of a commercial vehicle . . . as a result of such requirement."[5]

Unfortunately, this resolution died in committee when the 2018 midterms rolled around, but the regulatory scrambling continued in the wake of the predictable consequences of the ELD mandate. Later in 2019, FMCSA set up a series of listening sessions to hear from those affected by the mandate, though one might have asked if they were listening at all when truckers told them that it was going to be a disaster during the earlier (not) listening sessions in 2017.[6] In September 2020, hours-of-service rules, which the ELDs are meant to monitor, were overhauled again, as the device—a veritable (and no less intimidating) miniature "Eye of Sauron"—made it impossible for drivers to get anything done, over and above the chaos already being caused by COVID.

In the meantime, what were truckers doing to get around this? "Gaming the system" is a feature of human behavior as old as time, and given that drivers' incomes were being directly affected by the ELD mandate, as it cut into their driving time, the gaming did everything possible to maximize that driving time. Something all of us did and continue to do is log all detention and waiting time as "off duty," though that only works so far as your maximum daily window and weekly accumulated hours will go. Still, it is a widespread practice and was predicted to happen by everyone, including Michael Belzer, author of *Sweatshops on Wheels*, who noted during a discussion before ELDs became law:

And so the Fair Labor Standards Act rule says, okay, you got to pay minimum wage, but it's averaged over all hours.

What are the hours?

Well, they use what's on that logbook. Even worse, they use what's on the electronic logbook and drivers pop that over to line one or line two instantly when they stop.

As soon as they stop, they're not getting paid. That was the change that happened when the exempt sector rolled into the common freight sector, the common carrier sector in 1981.

So that fundamental thing that happened then, you had unionized drivers who were always paid for all their time, loading, unloading, breakdowns, everything was paid.

Whether you were an owner-operator, who was a Teamster, and you could be, or you were an employee driver, it didn't matter. You're always going to pay for your time. That's the contract.

All of a sudden, that changed.

So the exempt sector rolls in. They don't pay for time. You haul corn. You can wait in that line for twelve hours before they load you.

And you can haul that a couple of hundred miles. And you can go back and get another load. But you're never going to get paid for your on-duty, not-driving time.

So you're going to log it off-duty. The Fair Labor Standards Act suggests, well, it says here that they only work forty hours a week. They actually worked 120 hours a week, but they were paid for forty and that's what's logged. That means that there is a disconnect between the Federal Motor Carrier Safety Administration's rules that allow you to log all that time off duty and the Department of Labor rules which say you have to be paid for all your time.[7]

Something Belzer mentions here has been a problem in trucking since basically forever: *"You can wait in that line for twelve hours before they load you. . . . You're never going to get paid for your on-duty, not-driving time."*

This problem is called "detention" and it is the bane of a trucker's existence. While the law prevents drivers from overworking to compensate for the time we lose waiting in lineups or sitting at docks, the law also prevents us from being paid any overtime—which we might not have to work if we were actually trucking instead of sitting. This problem is so pervasive and touches on so many other problems in the industry that a team of researchers led by former MIT data scientist David Correll has released a number of papers analyzing it and proffering solutions.

Correll's research has been highly regarded—if not by the industry itself then at least by those of us who pay attention to such things. Correll was asked to submit testimony to President Biden's 2021 Trucking Action Plan task force, and what he presented is so staggering that it will make you wonder how anything in this country ever gets moved:

My student teams and I have analyzed the working hours and pickup and delivery experiences of approximately 4,000 OTR truck drivers employed by one midsized and one large national carrier in snapshots from 2016 to 2020. We have also analyzed thousands of freight pickup and delivery appointments using data provided to us by shipper and broker companies. We supplement this analytical work with frequent conversations with truck drivers, their management, as well as the shippers and receivers who hire these drivers' services.

First, I believe that the American truck driver is chronically underutilized, and has been since at least 2016 when our data begins. Based on our analysis of electronic working records, I estimate that American long-haul, full-truckload truck drivers spend, on average, 6.5 hours per working day driving their vehicles. Yet, according to hours of service regulations, they are allowed to drive for a maximum of 11 hours per day. *This implies that 40% of America's trucking capacity is left on the table every day* [my italics]. This result is especially troubling in times of perceived shortage and crisis like we find ourselves today. To put my argument in the context of the "driver shortage," the American Trucking Associations estimates the national driver deficit at 80,000 drivers. By my calculation, this represents about 4.4% (conservatively) of the US Census Bureau's estimation of 1.8 million employee Class-8 freight truck drivers in the United States. Adding 4.5% back to a long-haul truck drivers' working day of 6.5 hours would mean adding only 18 minutes. Seen this way, an 18-minute improvement to the daily average utilization of America's existing cadre of truck drivers could be equivalent in effect to recruiting new ones and then similarly squandering their time too. My research leads me to see the current situation not so much as a headcount shortage of drivers, but rather an endemic undervaluing of our American truck drivers' time.

As a lifelong trucker, I could write another entire book filled with nothing but stories about the centuries of unpaid time I have waited to be loaded or unloaded at customer facilities, so Correll's numbers ring particularly true for me. That said, I learned early in my career which parts of the trucking universe were notorious and incorrigible black holes for my time, a commodity that no human can create more of and that is the most important resource any of us has, and I have avoided them accordingly. The secret sauce, for the most part, is to never pull trailers equipped with doors; you will thus never have to deal with the worst offenders, overwhelmingly found in the general freight and refrigerated markets, who operate the distribution centers and freezer/cooler warehouses where so much human potential is wasted. Ironic, isn't it, that the system that feeds most of us is fueled by the dead and unpaid time assessed against truckers who are just trying to do their jobs?

For example, when I was working local delivery, an over-the-road driver for the Paddocks brought in a multidrop load, all the way from Arizona to the Toronto area, of organic peppers, green, red, and orange, the kind you cut up for a salad or a snack tray. I took the load for the first three deliveries to various locations in the city, and then the balance of the load went to a warehouse/ distribution center owned by Loblaws, a national grocery store chain—which is where the trouble started. I arrived on time, but they made me wait outside their gates for a couple hours. When they finally put me in a door, they made me wait the rest of the day and still did not take the dozen or so pallets of peppers out of the trailer. As I was a local driver and did not have a bunk to sleep in—I only lived an hour's drive from this facility—I was told to drive the truck back to our yard, go home, and try again in the morning. I did as instructed, returning first thing in the morning. Again I spent an entire day waiting, and they still did not take their peppers. So I went home again.

I came back for a third day of trying to unload these damn peppers. They finally began to unload me just before lunchtime. After the pallets were removed, I went to the receiving office to get my paperwork. The personnel had all disappeared for lunch, so I went back and double-checked my trailer to see that it was empty, swept it out, pulled the dock plate and undid the dock lock, got back in my truck and pulled it out, shut the doors, parked next to the office, and went back inside to wait for my paperwork.

When the staff returned from lunch, the head receiver, a giant bald man of about 6'5" who was dressed like a cop, thundered at me, "You're not allowed to park there or pull out until we tell you!"

I replied, with equal vehemence, "You are not allowed to waste three fucking days of my time or my employer's truck for the sake of twelve pallets of peppers."

"Oh, Mr. Attitude. We can have you banned from here!"

"*Excellent*! Where do I sign up? If I never have to come back here again it will be too soon."

I never did, and the damnable place was eventually closed; gee, I wonder why?[9]

I came to find out that this particular distribution center was so notorious for wasting truckers' time and receiving the kind of response from drivers that he had gotten from me that they had a stamp made that said "Driver Not To Return," which they placed on shipping bills to make it clear that any driver who stood up for himself was no longer welcome at their facility. I should have grabbed it for the many other joints that operate just the same.

It feels an awful lot like that's how this industry, as it is currently constituted, treats nearly all truckers.

Back to David Correll.

He was ignored, along with pretty much everyone else who testified before that task force. The McKinsey consultants working under Transportation Secretary Pete Buttigieg must have been pulled into a secret meeting with the American Trucking Associations and told not to act on Correll's findings, as the solutions would cost the ATA's members, and more importantly its members' customers, a marginal amount of money. Obviously, I have no idea if such a meeting took place, but the results speak for themselves. Instead of increasing the efficiency of America's trucking fleet during the supply chain "crisis" that took place during COVID, the Biden Administration flooded the market with more truck drivers, seemingly by grabbing migrants off the street and convincing certain states to hand them CDLs.

Correll's observations have implications for the wider issues involved with how truckers are paid and regulated and how their lives are ultimately governed in the age of surveillance technology.

If your average trucker is paid by the mile but limited to driving only roughly half the available hours in his day because of the intransigence of the facilities operated by his customers, then it stands to reason that the trucker will do whatever is necessary to make up for that lost time, be it in the form of "on-duty, not-driving" time—or by much more dangerous methods.

One of the more insidious claims made by those who pimped the ELD mandate was that having all of America's trucks equipped with these tracking devices would give trucking-company managers fine-grain details on detention and irrefutable evidence to prove its existence, in which case they could negotiate higher rates to cover the pay of drivers' waiting time. They were only looking out for us! Of course, this never happened. Drivers are still, for the most part, not paid for their detention time, and detention time remains one of drivers' top concerns according to surveys conducted by the American Transportation Research Institute (ATRI).[10]

Another claim made by boosters of ELDs was that they would enhance safety. None of that advertised safety has materialized. In 2022, *Overdrive* magazine, in conjunction with a sister outfit called RigDig, compiled data on truck crashes and citations and tickets issued to truckers for their bad behavior since the implementation of the ELD mandate. It turns out that truck crashes went up rather than down in the first four years after the mandate came into effect (in late 2017). Those latter four years included 2020 and 2021, when traffic took a nosedive during COVID. From 2014 to 2017, the researchers found 504,214 truck-involved crashes in the United States; the total from 2018 to 2021 was 565,043. This translated to an annual increase of more than 15,000 injuries and nearly 1,700 fatalities.[11]

Another study, this one analyzing citations against truckers post-ELD-mandate implementation, found that while hours-of-service violations went down, speeding tickets went up.[12] The lesson from this ought to have been that tracking truckers as if they were convicted sex criminals is a much less effective policy than addressing the economic incentives at play.

ELDs are not the first piece of surveillance technology to be imposed on truckers in the name of safety or keeping them "honest," as is explained in an excellent book exploring the history of the movement toward monitoring the men and women who move our economy. Karen Levy's *Data Driven: Truckers, Technology, and the New Workplace Surveillance* is a broad inquiry into how truckers are surveilled from afar, what the effects of that surveillance are, and what this means for other groups of workers. *Data Driven* represents a decade-long study of the lives and work of truckers and looks all the way back to the first iteration of this technology, which first served as a communication, rather than monitoring, tool. Though Levy acknowledges and describes the "interoperability" of early systems put out by companies like QUALCOMM, these earlier systems were out of the hands of the government and not necessarily used as disciplinary or punishing tools. No more.

In time, other technologies were added. These include cameras used to monitor the driver—even some that measure the rate at which your eyes blink as a prediction of fatigue—and technologies that track a driver's braking and acceleration patterns, measuring them against other metrics so as to guess when a driver might be thinking about quitting a company.

How, you ask, do braking patterns indicate whether a driver may be thinking of quitting? Levy writes: "The proprietary Omnitracs Driver Retention Model analyzes hours-of-service data in order to identify 'drivers suspected of flight risk'—which it does by looking for 'patterns and subtle changes in driver habits and work activities that serve as indicators of voluntary terminations.'"[13]

Levy offers a history of the ELD, from early proposals in 1988 to recent studies conducted in the years after the mandate came into effect. Confirming the suspicions of every driver who is paying attention, Levy demonstrates that none of the stated objectives of the mandate have been met: truck crashes, as well as speeding and other incidents of dangerous driving, have increased. Nevertheless, the mandate remains.

The Owner-Operator Independent Drivers Association has been fighting the requirement for these sorts of surveillance systems every step of the way. A 2016 court challenge argued that these devices, installed in a long-haul truck in which the driver spends weeks and months of time, infringe the Fourth Amendment rights of the drivers who basically live in their rigs; effectively, having an ELD is like having Uncle Sam in their living rooms. The Seventh Circuit Court of Appeals thought otherwise, citing the "pervasively regulated industries" exemption, which sounds an awful lot like circular reasoning—this industry is already regulated, so the fact that it is regulated means we can regulate it some more.

The court's acknowledgment that trucking is a pervasively regulated industry only highlights the deep ironies of deregulation, including the fact that economic liberalization laid the foundation for an increasingly intrusive surveillance apparatus. Levy, to her credit, brings us back to Michael Belzer's observation about the transfer of regulation: "Another key concern that truckers brought to the fore was that the ELD addressed the wrong problem. . . . Focusing on truckers' log fudging treated a symptom of the problem, not its root cause. Truckers weren't tired because they were able to falsify their logbooks; they were tired because the industry is set up in ways that necessitated them breaking the rules."[14]

Levy has made this salient point in numerous interviews, arguing that no amount of surveillance technology can fundamentally alter the economic incentive structures at play, which force drivers into regular and frustrating delays beyond their control and for which they do not get paid while their main source of income is based only on driving. And she is correct.

Another trend in trucker surveillance that has gained a worrying amount of traction in the past decade is the employment of driver-facing cameras, which we are always told have been placed there for "safety and training purposes" and not to "spy on us." On both counts, these claims are utterly false and insulting.

I've only worked for one company that had a driver-facing camera in the truck, and it was the same guys I opened this chapter with. When they hired me, the owners pitched the camera as a safety measure, claiming that it only recorded a loop from which a twelve-second snapshot would be recorded if an incident took place and that it would only be used against me if I hit someone. Though I bristled at the idea of being subject to such a thing after twenty years of experience and a nearly perfect driving record, I needed the job and let my naïveté get the best of me.

The problems with these cameras are manifold. For example, the "incident" triggers that take those twelve-second snapshots are *hair triggers* that will go off from the most minor bump in the road or from a deceleration to avoid a driver who cuts in front of you. It was one of these drivers who caused me to be pulled into the safety guy's office. While sitting there, I noticed he had a flat-screen TV showing a square for every driver camera in the fleet, and nearly all of the cams were on or displaying a cycle of all those twelve-second clips running together. I could watch any guy in the company—and so could the people who claimed they would never do that.

A video from a female trucker-TikToker with the handle "Original Trucking Barbie 2.0" went viral a couple of years ago. Slowing down to accommodate drivers cutting her off had led to reprimands from her safety department. Those reprimands escalated into creepy sexual abuse: "It has a sensor on it, it knows when your eyes leave the road for any reason, it knows when you are following too closely to the car in front of you. . . . If someone moves over in front of me, I am not gonna slam on the brakes. . . . I will slow down. . . . As soon as I notice that they are too close to me, I look at my camera, and it's gone red, which means it's already caught me."

Damned if you do the right thing, damned if you don't.

It seems like the cameras might just be a jobs program for the type of jerks who get off on harassing employees. The female trucker continues:

I've only had my camera for about six months, and I have had five phone calls from the safety team, three of which were telling me that I need to pay attention to what I'm doing, two of them were to congratulate me on seeing improvement, and one of those bad calls was to give me an award because I avoided someone trying to fling me off the road . . . and then they proceed to tell me I have a one-day suspension. . . . They are telling me that no matter what I do I'm going to get disciplined. . . . I talked to my dispatch about it. . . . I heard I am being targeted, that they're watching me super close. That makes me feel violated. . . . I know that that camera is still on even when I'm in my sleeper. . . . They're watching me while I'm undressing.[15]

This follows a pattern of drivers feeling like they're being watched no matter what they do, especially female truckers. A 2023 report from ATRI notes: "Females rated the technology's ability to protect their privacy 24% lower than male drivers. Some female drivers complained they have experienced '*voyeurism, unwanted comments about their appearance, and even sexual harassment from employees tasked with reviewing DFC footage*'" (italics mine).[16]

Surveillance technology comprises more than just those Palantirs that can be fitted to a truck. Nor is it unique to the United States. In many ways, other countries are ahead of America in this insidious and demoralizing curve. Our friends Down Under seem only too happy to treat their own citizens as if they are all criminals; they have been monitoring truckers from roadway cameras for decades.

In 1985, the Ozzy state of Victoria began trials of what later became known across the country as "Safe-T-Cams." These are cameras mounted above the highway, not unlike the toll-collection cameras we see on so many interstates. These cameras take photos of the license plate on the front of Ozzy big rigs and then store that information in a database accessible to all police and enforcement officials. By the 1990s the cameras were being installed across Victoria and the neighboring state of New South Wales; they are now fixtures in most populated areas of the country. They can measure average travel time between two points and generate speeding tickets automatically. In recent years the Safe-T-Cams have been upgraded to spy on drivers, who receive a ticket in the mail if the software that analyzes the photos determines that you were holding your mobile phone or did not have your seat belt on. This is no longer limited to truck drivers; these cameras are spying on all Australians in all types of vehicles. Who needs to hire more police officers when Big Brother can simply look into your vehicle from afar? I catch a lot of flack from my Australian friends for stating the simple fact that they've regressed back to the penal colony from which they started; there is no escape from the state on their Cursed Island.

Mike Williams is a lifelong trucker from Australia and host of the popular *On the Road Aussie Trucking Podcast*. He recalls that, for example, "coming out of Sydney you would get to Marulan, the biggest truck checking station in Australia . . . [and get] thirty-five checks on you from the time you go under the first camera to the time you cross the first weigh in motion plate. . . . Sometimes they're not even marked as Safe-T-Cams." Australia has a graduated licensing system and mandated truck-speed limiters, which contribute to it having two-thirds fewer accidents per person than the U.S. trucking industry, but that's apparently not enough. Williams continues: "We've got seat-belt cameras, mobile-phone cameras . . . cameras cameras cameras, we've got bloody cameras everywhere now. . . . They love to be able to issue these tickets. State governments consider them a voluntary tax. . . . If you're a well-endowed girl and the seat belt is obscured to the camera, well, that's a fine now."[17] Williams says that the truck he is currently driving has three—count 'em, three— different camera systems on board, two of which are watching him while he drives. Even a prison cell doesn't have three cameras.

Another point missed by nearly all commentators is that the imposition of modern surveillance technology follows the same track as the effects of deregulation—or as Belzer has accurately described it, a *transfer* of regulation from the government to the marketplace. In *Sweatshops on Wheels*, Belzer noted an increase in "social regulation," which is to say that the cops and state DOTs have been chasing down speeding or aggressive truckers more often as those truckers attempt to balance the scales of the Catch-22 upon which their paychecks are built. I would argue that these enforcement efforts have also increased because as the effects of deregulation took hold, and driver pay, on average, either flatlined or did not keep up with most other jobs, the churn and retention problem worsened, and poorer-quality drivers flooded the roads. This phenomenon is whispered quietly by dispatchers and managers but can be heard quite loudly from old-timers who take pride in their jobs and are forced to compete with those whom Karl Marx referred to as the *Lumpenproletariat*. Lower-skilled people are going to do the things that lower-skilled people do, thus necessitating further intrusions by law enforcement or Big Brother into everyone's trucks.

Surveillance technology, working in tandem with rampant maternalism and the micromanaging of truckers, creates something of an Ouroboros, the infamous snake that ate its own tail. This treatment really pisses people like me off, so we refuse to work for the companies that engage in it, and then those companies have to resort to hiring people who are either desperate or don't know what they're getting into. Sooner or later a point is reached where the pool of potential candidates who will voluntarily get in a truck is winnowed down to those who shouldn't be allowed to do so. It's not for a lack of decent truckers. The system has chased out decent truckers because it refuses to treat them with decency.

Matthew B. Crawford is a philosopher, physicist, motorcycle mechanic, and *New York Times* bestselling author of three books, two of which are germane to trucking. His work often speaks to the debasement and disregard for the value of work in the physical realm. His book *Shop Class as Soulcraft: An Inquiry into the Value of Work* delves into the question of what has happened to modern society as the result of shifting our focus from the material to the world of information and screens. Crawford examines what we lose when we forget the value of making and doing things in the real world.

In a passage describing the frustration of working on modern cars, whose sensors and superfluous technological impositions have vastly overcomplicated the job of the mechanic, Crawford asks, "What sort of personality does one need to have, as a twenty-first century mechanic, to tolerate the layers of electronic bullshit that get piled on top of machines?"[18]

I pose the same question about trucking. What sort of personality must you have to tolerate being minutely surveilled and having your constitutional rights abridged? The trucking industry, and the government it grovels to and cooperates with, want compliant automatons—human "RoboTruckers," in the words of Karen Levy—who will sit there in that truck and take their shit.

Not me.

The technology with which the tech companies monitor drivers is the same one they use to render skill, craft, and years of experience and local knowledge supposedly "obsolete." Over and above the surveillance of the driver, trucks now come equipped with mandated lane control and front-crash avoidance systems. Many companies have been slowly increasing the use of automatic transmissions over the past two decades, not because they are cheaper or easier to maintain, but because they further lower the bar to entry. What is the point of having a trucker behind the wheel when so many aspects of the job have been automated? Most likely it is for the human driver to take the blame when these electronic systems malfunction and the truck crashes anyway.

Crawford describes the fate of the Black Cab drivers of London, who have been marked for obsolescence by Google. Black Cabs are an almost legendary fixture of life in London, their signature black-painted Austin FX4 model going back many decades. Crawford references a *New York Times* story about a budding Black Cab driver and the training he underwent, juxtaposing this against the incentives and marketing of tech companies that seek to supplant his entire industry: "In 2012, Matt McCabe was studying to become a London taxi driver. The process takes four years, on average, for those who devote themselves to it full time." (If only truckers were subject to these minimum training requirements, something like heaven might dawn.) Crawford continues:

> McCabe logged more than fifty thousand miles on a scooter during his period of study, a distance equal to traversing the North American continent sixteen times, but almost entirely within the city center. And such a curriculum is typical for those who seek the Knowledge, as it is called. For the sheer cognitive accomplishment it marks, it has been called the most demanding professional test of any kind, comparable to those that control admission to the legal and medical professions.
>
> It is largely a skill of visual memory that the "Knowledge boys" develop; in plotting a route in their minds' eye they will alternate between a street-level view and the aerial views that they absorb by poring over maps for many hours every day. According to Rosen they "speak of a Eureka moment when, after months or years of doggedly assembling the London puzzle, the fuzziness recedes and the city snaps into focus, the great morass of streets suddenly appearing as an intelligible whole."

I have received directions and been downloaded wisdom from older truckers whose decades of experience crisscrossing North America give them an understanding of this continent in the same way that Black Cab drivers possess an intimate recall of London. It's like knowing the feel of your woman's curves in the darkness of the bedroom. The description of mountain grades, where scales are and how to get around them, the warmth or coldness of various customers, precise directions on how to get into facilities, all from memory, forged through years of the windshield and the prism-like beam those years of experience have blasted into their minds . . . all to be replaced by Google Maps!

This Crawford passage resonated strongly with the old trucker in me:

In much commentary and reportage, several unrelated developments get mixed up together: driverless cars, electric vehicles, and ride hailing. I believe this fuzziness is deliberately cultivated, as it imparts a sheen of technological progress to the ride-hailing firms when in fact their core business is one of labor arbitrage. *Their "innovation" is merely to exploit the deskilling effect of GPS for this purpose.* The main divide across which they practice labor arbitrage is time of residence in a city, which corresponds to the acquisition of knowledge held independently in a person's head, without reliance on GPS. Continued high levels of immigration guarantee a persistent gradient—of personal knowledge—along which to conduct this labor arbitrage. *And in fact, the majority of Uber drivers are recent immigrants. Here is one instance where the "humanitarian" mindset of maximum migrants happens to line up with the interests of a small number of corporations.* It is an alliance that gets covered over by the mystifications of "tech."[19] (italics mine)

The "deskilling effect of GPS" works a little differently across an entire continent than it does within one major city. It has produced both comedic and tragic consequences along the American interstate.

One such incident in Tennessee took place after the rains from Hurricane Helene had famously flooded much of the eastern portion of the state. A driver named Ankit Ahammitt, who either ignored or could not read highway closure signs, missed his truck detour exit and wound up jammed inside narrowing concrete barricades along the damaged interstate. When questioned by police about what he was doing there, Ahammitt simply kept stating "GPS," an indication that he probably could not read English and was just doing as he was told by a formless tech instructor—"vaporware," as the kids say—not unlike some migrant to London who simply follows mapping software rather than relying on the hard-won knowledge received after years of training.[20]

In similar fashion, a gentleman licensed in California named Harjinder Singh found himself in quite a pickle in Arkansas after getting lost by following his GPS, and then following it some more, right onto a bridge that was not built to accommodate his fully loaded forty-ton semi. He promptly collapsed the bridge, sending his truck into the river below. Mr. Singh either ignored or was unable to read the signage indicating the bridge's weight-rating capacity of only six tons.[21] California is one of those states where the DMV hands out licenses to various groups of prospective truckers without requiring a test.[22] It is unknown if California handed out millions to the state of Arkansas to pay for craning Mr. Singh's truck out of the drink and rebuilding the bridge.

Social media is full of such photos and reportage, with "truckers" being found on closed mountain passes or backroads, often having gone catty wampus and requiring the assistance of heavy tow trucks. The problem is so pervasive that the federal government—via the United States Space Force, interestingly enough—has a reporting website where locals who live along routes where truckers shouldn't be—but where certain truckers show up anyway because of GPS-issued directions—can contact mapping software companies and have their systems updated.[23]

Alas, the North American trucking industry doesn't want to pay or respect the kind of driver who doesn't collapse bridges and has the agency and judgment to tell a dispatcher or other manager to get bent when asked to drive past the point of being dangerously tired. And so the industry has come to rely on insourced labor, throwing poor saps with no language skills and almost nothing in the way of training into the deep end. The industry is also forcing these guys to work like dogs. The companies get away with it by abusing the technology that was sold to the public as a way to make trucking safer: the ELD.

ELD "backdooring" has been a concern since the mandate was proposed. Any device connected to the rest of the world is at risk of being hacked in numerous ways, but this hacking is a feature, not a bug. It allows for editing by management personnel at companies that use these devices to monitor and record their drivers' time so as to be in compliance with hours-of-service regulations. The problem is that this editing has become standard operating procedure. Reporter

Clarissa Hawes spoke with truckers working for companies operated by Russians and Ukrainians. These drivers had received text messages from their managers telling them that their ELDs had been altered and that they could keep driving, despite having exceeded legal hours of service.[24] Stories have subsequently appeared online describing how companies owned and dispatched by offshore management use encrypted texting apps like Telegram to give drivers explicit instructions on how to speak with enforcement officials. These drivers are given the names of "ghost" co-drivers who aren't in their trucks and the locations where they ostensibly pick up and drop off those ghost drivers. These "ghosts" are probably real people with CDLs whose names are simply being used to fill in for the indentured servants being forced to work way past the hours that ELDs were meant to prevent.

Danielle Chaffin is the daughter of a multigenerational trucking family. Her father and grandfather, like mine, were both truckers. Danielle carries on the family tradition, though in the technology field, working for a Transport Management System (TMS) software company. On the side, Danielle applies her skills and knowledge of the industry as a kind of online sleuth, alerting the public to suspicious carriers and their activities by using publicly available online databases provided by government enforcement agencies. She has been bumping into an awful lot of this ELD backdooring nonsense.

Danielle told me:

I've reviewed dozens of FMCSA-certified ELD providers. Most are foreign-owned or run their operations outside the U.S., with virtually zero cyber-security oversight. That means foreign entities could be sitting on a gold-mine of real-time data about freight, drivers, border crossings, and supply chains.

These devices don't just log hours. They track every move. And many ELD apps allow full access to a driver's phone: contacts, camera, files, and location. There is absolutely no reason for that, unless you're interested in surveillance or shady data harvesting.

With backend access, tech teams can reset logs on command. That means dispatch can override reality and push drivers past legal limits, all while keeping a clean digital paper trail. It's coercion disguised as compliance. And it's dangerous.[25]

Chaffin has referred to these ELD backdoor operations as "Trojan Horses," an apt though not totally accurate description. The drivers being abused by these systems are more often than not recent arrivals to the U.S., often talked into working here for paychecks that would be higher than wherever they came from, though not higher than an American truckers' pay. But the administration of this backdooring is always done overseas, where those who ought to be held accountable for it are beyond the reach of the law.

Just as the GPS system is built on fragile and aging satellites, the ELD system is also a risk, not just for the kind of abuse that overworks truckers but also for the theft of the loads they're pulling down the road.

No doubt this correlates with the increase in freight and identity theft. Danielle Chaffin explains how it works:

1—A dispatcher sends shipping details, including pickup location, delivery address, and cargo contents, directly to the driver's ELD.

2—That data flows through the ELD's backend, often to servers run by third-party tech firms, many of which are overseas or operate without proper oversight.

3—Not long after, a specific truck carrying $1 million worth of Nintendo Switch consoles is hit in a targeted cargo theft.

Sure, it *could* have been someone watching the warehouse. Maybe a tip-off. Maybe pure luck. But let's not kid ourselves. When shipment details, GPS data, and driver communications are flowing through third-party tech platforms, many of which are hosted overseas, it would be naïve to assume those data centers are operating with airtight security and zero unauthorized access.[26]

This systemic abuse is new enough that there is almost no reporting on it, though USDOT has been alerted, and surely digital forensics teams are looking into recent incidents. But the larger point is extremely hard to ignore: born-and-raised American truckers are being forced to compete with insourced truckers who are then given an hours-of-service advantage by the very device that treats American truckers like management risks, with the implied insults to their honor, skill, and professionalism. These same devices are being used by organized crime to assist in the theft of millions of dollars' worth of products; in 2024, cargo theft in North America resulted in losses to the tune of $454 million.[27]

Is it OK that American truckers are treated like convicted sex offenders, tracked in their homes by ELDs, driver-facing cameras, and other Fourth Amendment–erasing technologies, while being forced to compete with a flood of insourced labor whose managers are using that very same technology to give insourced labor a competitive advantage? Are we to understand that a highly skilled and well-trained American driver is of the same quality as some person who showed up here yesterday and therefore typically lacks the same skill, experience, training, and culturally relevant knowledge?

Some of the companies that work with the scammers insourcing labor are getting pretty damn bold about what they are up to. *Overdrive* magazine reports that they are now advertising ELD backdooring online and through cold calls to various trucking companies. Reporter Alex Lockie writes:

> Dispatcher Hector Adrien Esquivel Rodriguez got an unsolicited call from a company called Logbook Hub that advertises on Facebook that it can "FIX your logbook" for $30 a week. Rodriguez posted a video to YouTube that featured him asking this question to the company: "Let's say I don't have any more time, I already used my 14 and my 11, and I need to run one more hour. Can you help?"
>
> "Yes, totally," the voice on the other end of the line responds, saying they have a number [that] drivers can text and a team [that] will edit the logs for them "24/7, no holidays."[28]

This is a bad deal, and a major safety, security, and economic risk not worth taking, whatever savings the value-scraping class believes it is receiving.

7

Interstate United Nations?

—Harry Nilsson, "Everybody's Talkin'"

Like many high schools, mine had a wonderful cast of characters, including the teachers, who ran the gamut of school-teacher stereotypes. One such instructor was Madame Waite, who taught French. Like most Anglophones, who are referred to by certain Québécois as *têtes carrées*, or blockheads, I only took the minimum required single French credit to obtain my Ontario Secondary School Diploma. I can't even remember who the teacher was, but it wasn't Madame Waite; although I never took one of her classes, I will never forget her.

With tightly curled silver-gray hair, glasses, and a somewhat diminutive figure cloaked in the unassuming and boring wardrobe one associates with a librarian, Madame Waite didn't cut the profile that you might think would occupy the mind of a horny teenage boy. She occupied mine for a different reason, however, and only after I dared to make fun of her with a newly learned Québécois slur.

One of the cultural exchanges I was privileged to experience before many of my peers was regular interaction with *les camionneurs*, or, as my Anglo trucker friends referred to them, Frenchmen. As part of my duties after school, I regularly went into the two big steel mills of Hamilton, Stelco and Dofasco, to assist the evening-shift drivers with chaining down and tarping loads of steel coils. While the loads we picked up were typically bound for points in the United States, *les camionneurs*, being truckers from Québec, were taking their loads back home, or possibly points further east.

A fixture of truck driving is the amount of time one spends standing around at various facilities, yakking with other truckers who, like you, are also waiting to be loaded or unloaded. Stelco and Dofasco were no exception, and it was in these convivial hangouts that I was first exposed to Québécois culture, not having yet set foot in La Belle Province.

By this time I had taken a fair bit of French instruction: all eight years of elementary school and mandatory grade-nine French in high school. But it was not enough to enable me to competently hold court with my garrulous new trucker associates at the mill. They repeatedly used a word I had not been taught in school: *tabarnak*. They used it with the same frequency with which a certain type of young working-class guy drops the F-bomb. *Tabarnak* was one of those words that could be a noun, verb, adjective, or expression of surprise or dismay, sometimes all at once. Like the many *sacres*, it was versatile and profane, a Catholic liturgical term that had been weaponized as a vulgar expression in Québécois society.

One day I thought I would impress my friends and get a rise out of Madame Waite by yelling *tabarnak!* at the top of my lungs when I saw her coming down the hallway. Needless to say, she was not impressed, and with a mixture of mortification and the death stare one can only get from a true schoolmarm, Madame Waite exclaimed, "You can't say that! Where did you learn to say that? Certainly not in any classroom here!" My friends, ignorant of *les sacres*, laughed at me for being the object of Madame Waite's fury, and they moved on as I was interrogated by her. I told her the truth: "I learned it from truckers at Stelco!" Madame Waite rolled her eyes. A teacher who had overheard the exchange reminded me that this was not Stelco, and that I had better carry on to my next class and not repeat this new word.

"Cette prof a une branche au queue tabarnak!"

Later in life I came to regret not taking an additional three years of French while in high school (for free, no less). My trucking adventures took me to Montreal and eventually all over La Belle Province (or through it en route to the Maritimes). It would have been helpful to have the ability to communicate with the many folks I met in rural and especially Northern Québec who did not speak English, though my rudimentary understanding of the language allowed me to read road signs, order a coffee at Maison Tim Horton, or tell staff when arriving at a lumber mill, "Je suis un camionneur ici pour récupérer une chargez de bois à destination du Michigan," or some other location.

It is the same for many French truckers who operate in Anglophone North America. They are surrounded by people who speak English, so typically they either are bilingual or have picked up enough English to get along when they inevitably haul product into the rest of Canada or south into the United States. Stories of *les camionneurs* causing trouble on the roads of English-speaking Canada or in the United States are nevertheless rare to nonexistent because of the self-regulation that was for a long time practiced by trucking-company owners in Québec. These folks were wise enough not to send drivers into the rest of the continent who had no hope of communicating with staff at shippers or receivers or being able to read road signs warning of construction, high winds, or chain-up advisories for mountain passes. U.S. Customs officials at border crossings are not required to speak French, and it has been the law of the land in the United States since 1937, when Federal Motor Carrier Safety Regulations were first outlined, that anyone who holds a commercial driver's license "read and speak the English language sufficiently to converse with the general public, to understand highway traffic signs and signals in the English language, to respond to official inquiries, and to make entries on reports and records."[1]

Over the years, this rule's enforcement may have been massaged with latitude and interpretation in those parts of the country where French- or Spanish-speaking truckers are often found (the Northeast and Southwest, respectively). In general, however, English has been the official lingua franca of the interstate if you want the privilege of driving a truck, and it was enforceable by roadside testing, which, if failed, could place a driver "out of service" (OOS), no longer legally permitted to operate a commercial motor vehicle and forced to leave the truck in need of rescue. Imagine the logistics and cost involved of a Québec-based carrier having to send another driver to Arizona to rescue a truckload of lettuce parked by the cops because the driver couldn't communicate to the level of federal requirements.

A curious change to the enforcement of this regulation took place in 2016, nearly eighty years after it was first outlined. In the waning days of the Obama Administration, the Federal Motor Carrier Safety Administration sent out a memorandum creating a substantial loophole—large enough, you might say, to drive a truck through any Big, Beautiful Walls. The memorandum, dated June 15, 2016, reads: "This policy removes the requirement to place drivers out of service for English Language proficiency violations and changes the agency's standard for determining non-compliance based on . . . direction from Office of the Secretary and the Department of Justice." The memorandum also informs us that the Commercial Vehicle Safety Alliance, a group comprising trucking-enforcement-agency members across Canada, the U.S., and Mexico, had an internal vote among themselves and, rather than following the rules as written, would "remove 49 CFR 391.11(b)(2) from their out of service criteria because they could not substantiate the safety impact."[2]

Unfortunately for everyone other than road bureaucrats, almost immediately after enforcement of this regulation ceased, America's highways became more dangerous, for the less scrupulous members of the trucking industry figured out ways to employ insourced labor illiterate in the English language—and perhaps ignorant of the fact that they were being taken advantage of to undercut the wages of American truckers. (Though I am sure there are more than enough insourced truckers who give not a whit for the Americans whom they are displacing; the remittances they earn generally go a long way wherever they came from.)

Data from the National Highway Traffic Safety Administration shows a reduction in truck-involved collisions and resulting fatalities on American roads up to 2009, but they have been on the rise ever since.[3] As an aside, the FMCSA's annual truck and bus crash data reports are stalled at 2021 because the agency changed the methodology used to measure crashes, discounting less serious crashes in what some call an attempt to skew numbers. The number of fatal crashes, however, has been rising every year since 2016, with only one blip in 2020 due to COVID.[4]

A particularly grievous example of "new" truckers as a public-safety hazard occurred on August 12, 2025, when a tractor trailer attempted to pull an illegal U-turn through a small access point in the median of the Florida turnpike near

Fort Pierce. As the driver of the truck executed the turn, he pulled in front of a minivan, which ran into his trailer at high speed. All three occupants of the minivan were killed. Initially, the crash didn't draw much attention beyond the online trucking commentariat and local media. Then driver-facing camera footage of the truck driver showed up on the internet, and the tragic incident dominated the news cycle for two weeks straight—something that never happens with trucking.

The driver, Harjinder Singh, is seen pulling the truck off the shoulder without bothering to look behind him first, and when the minivan crashes into his trailer, he doesn't appear to register any shock or much in the way of concern. In a photo of him standing outside the truck a few minutes later, he continues to hold an emotionless expression, despite having just killed three people.[5]

This video, combined with the facts surrounding Mr. Singh's presence in the United States, which were revealed by the Florida Department of Highway Safety and Motor Vehicles, fanned flames of outrage across the country. Singh was discovered to have entered the country illegally and to have been issued not one but two different CDLs illegally: the first by the state of Washington and the second by California. He had been considered for deportation but was ultimately allowed to stay and was even issued work permits by both the Biden and Trump administrations. It was later revealed by FMCSA investigators that Mr. Singh failed an English proficiency test, which may have been why he ignored the sign seen in crash photos saying in capital letters OFFICIAL USE ONLY beneath what ought to be the universally understood symbol for No U-Turns.[6]

Another horrific incident took place on the evening of March 13, 2025, in Austin, Texas, where a commercial transport traveling at high speed crashed into a number of stopped vehicles along a stretch of Interstate 35 that was under construction. The driver was moving so fast that it took his rig running into seventeen vehicles before it came to a stop. Five people were killed, including an entire family—mom, dad, an infant, and a very young child—and another eleven people were sent to the hospital, many with critical injuries.

The driver of the truck, a man by the name of Solomun Weldekeal Araya, was a very recent migrant from Ethiopia who had had his commercial driver's license a scant four months. Officers investigating the crash found that Mr. Araya had some difficulty communicating in English and had racked up numerous hours-of-service (HOS) violations and a previous speeding ticket. When arrested, Araya was suspected of intoxication and seemed not to understand what he had just done. Nor did he express any empathy. He was later cleared of being under the influence, but he has been indicted on twenty-two charges, including five counts of felony manslaughter. The legal case is ongoing at the time of this writing, though the HOS violations, matched with the appearance of intoxication and apathy in the immediate aftermath of the crash, tell me the obvious: Araya was overworked and shouldn't have been behind the wheel.[7]

In March 2024, a deadly trucking incident took place in Nevada, where a man named Claude Rafiki, driving a commercial transport truck, crossed into oncoming lanes of traffic and hit three motorcyclists head-on, killing all of them instantly. Mr. Rafiki, though he had a Michigan-issued CDL, hailed from the central African country of Rwanda. Court proceedings for this incident were delayed due to Mr. Rafiki's inability to speak English and the difficulty in locating a translator who spoke his native tongue, Kinyarwanda. Perhaps the new colonial project is to bring Africans here in a more acceptable form of slavery, but instead of picking cotton, these guys drive trucks at a discount for companies like Amazon.

A man in West Virginia was killed when his car was pushed off a bridge by a truck driven by Singh Sukhjinder, who when finally apprehended and arrested required an interpreter to communicate with police and investigators. The century-long British rule of India does not guarantee that everyone hailing therefrom speaks English.

One of the most horrifying of all these incidents involved a crash between a truck driven by an Ethiopian refugee and a large van in Alabama. The truck driver in this incident failed to slow down for stopped traffic on Interstate 65 near Pruitt, Alabama. His truck crashed into a van carrying the members of the Tallapoosa County Girls Ranch, pushing the van into other crashed trucks and igniting a deadly inferno. Ten people were killed; eight children were burned alive while one of their mothers fought like mad to try and rescue them from the twisted wreckage.[8]

As reported by Rob Carpenter at the trucking-industry investigative Substack *Talking Wreckless*, it appears there were significant attempts to cover this story up.

The NTSB investigation found that [Mamuye Ayane] Takelu [the driver of the truck] was traveling at approximately 60 to 73 mph when he encountered the traffic jam on the wet bridge. Instead of maintaining control, he veered left across lanes, struck the bridge rail, plowed through the median, and crushed the children's van between his truck and the first commercial vehicle. Investigators found no evidence of impairment or cell phone use, but Takelu's actions suggest either fundamental incompetence or complete disregard for basic safety principles.

Here's what investigators never bothered to ask: What was Takelu's immigration status at the time of the crash? How did he obtain his CDL, and were proper procedures followed? What was his English proficiency level, and could he actually understand American traffic regulations and safety requirements? Were translators used during post-crash interviews? These aren't academic questions, they go to the heart of whether a qualified driver was operating that commercial vehicle and should ever have been placed on the highway.

Recent federal enforcement data reveals the scope of the problem investigators ignored. Violations for "Driver cannot read or speak the English language sufficiently to respond to official inquiries" have skyrocketed across multiple states. New data released by the FMCSA via Trucksafe Consulting indicates that violations and enforcement have skyrocketed.

Today, Takelu runs his own single-truck operation in GA. No criminal charges were filed against the driver who killed eight children. The system that enabled him to kill children continues operating exactly as it did in 2021.[9]

Another high-profile incident highlights the importance of the requirement that truckers be able to read English and was cited as such by Transportation Secretary Sean Duffy in a news release from the FMCSA. A Cuban immigrant named Rogel Aguilera-Mederos lost control of his rig while traveling down a steep section of Interstate 70 near Lakewood, Colorado, and crashed into traffic, killing four people and setting multiple vehicles ablaze from the impact. Investigations into the crash, along with Mr. Aguilera-Mederos's own testimony, reveal that he had difficulty getting his truck back into gear while navigating the grade and didn't properly perform a pretrip inspection on his equipment, which tells us he probably wasn't trained adequately and therefore didn't foresee the brake failure that led to the incident. More importantly, however, Mr. Aguilera-Mederos couldn't read the multiple warning signs along Interstate 70 advising of dangerous downhill grades and corners, or of the runaway ramps available for trucks should a situation like his develop.[10]

Mr. Aguilera-Mederos was famously sentenced to 110 years in prison, though this was later commuted to ten years by direct intervention from Colorado Governor Jared Polis, who called the sentence "highly atypical and unjust."[11] Maybe, but the fact remains that there are quite possibly hundreds of thousands of people driving trucks on America's roads right now who have no idea how to read the warning signs telling them about steep grades, runaway truck ramps, construction zones, high winds, chain-up laws, or any number of safety-critical communications that truckers and other members of the motoring public are expected to heed. When is the next truck-crash inferno going to take the lives of children?

Prior to the waiving of English-proficiency requirements, many of the drivers involved in these incidents would likely have been taken off the road and placed out of service by state DOT inspectors. Perhaps this would have given these gentlemen the necessary introspection and incentive to take a course in English as a second language, thus making them safer drivers and offering them another skill as they navigated the American job market. That detour might have cost them a little bit of time and money but would have ultimately saved lives and made the world a better place.

As reported in *Overdrive* magazine in August 2025, a study conducted by MC Advantage found that truck drivers who don't communicate well in English are involved in significantly more crashes than even those English-speaking drivers who are regularly caught speeding or have drug and alcohol violations.[12]

The data is clear: truck-involved collisions on American highways started ticking up in 2016, which is when English language proficiency enforcement was waived. So what is the argument for this waiver? Who benefits? Major corporations, that's who, for which this simple requirement is a hurdle to incremental increases in shareholder return. One such corporation that comes up again and again in these incidents is Amazon, which you may have possibly used to purchase this book. Mr. Araya, the Austin trucker, was pulling a trailer for Amazon. There have been so many incidents involving contractors working for Amazon—who obtain loads through Amazon's internal freight board, Amazon Relay, a kind of Uber service for finding trucks to move trailers around—that both the *Wall Street Journal* and CBS have done their own investigations into just how poor some of these contractors are.[13] Their work highlights how carriers contracted through Amazon Relay regularly ignore orders from the DOT to repair their equipment and how Relay has been repeatedly warned of the poor performance of its contractors—and has often ignored these warnings. Cumulatively, as of 2024, contractors pulling Amazon's trailers have been involved in incidents where over 140 innocent motorists have been killed.[14]

The fact that it is contractors pulling the trailers insulates Amazon from liability when damages are assessed. Nor is Amazon the only player in this game; many of America's largest trucking companies, such as J.B. Hunt, Werner, and Knight-Swift, now advertise directly in the "power-only" market. Under this arrangement, they hire contractors to pull loads using their trailers through their own internal load boards, much like Amazon Relay. With this system, these massive companies can wash their hands of having their own trucks or drivers, and if questioned about the insourcing of labor, they can claim not to be involved.[15]

What a bummer that the wage floor and rates of other truckers are not insulated from Amazon's (and others') proclivity to engage low-quality contractors. Amazon appears to target those recently arrived in the United States, most of whom are also recently arrived in the world of trucking and haven't got a damn clue what they are doing or how to drive properly. If Amazon owned its own fleet of trucks with employee drivers, those drivers might recognize some common cause and demand better pay and working conditions. But if you employ thousands of subcontractors from all over the world who not only do not speak English but also do not speak each other's languages, it is extremely difficult for workers to build solidarity and agitate for better rates and treatment. The more libertarian-minded and free-market-oriented among us might suggest that freedom of contract and direct negotiations would achieve better rates, but why would Amazon bother if it has easy access to a pool of labor the size of the entire planet?

Amazon is named in a suit being brought by an injured party in the Austin crash, and as of this writing that suit remains outstanding. The same parasites sucking taxpayer money from the body politic to finance their CDL mills appear to be behind the flooding of American interstates with insourced labor of dubious vetting and training standards, perhaps because those CDL mills just weren't throwing enough bodies at the churn problem.

In 2021 and 2022 the COVID regime brought to America yet another curious policy, this one formulated by a task force convened by those holding up the walking corpse of former President Biden.

When the COVID lockdowns hit in 2020, the trucking industry went through very brief and wild demand fluctuations as businesses closed and people lost their jobs. At first, the rush for groceries and toilet paper caused a demand spike. That quickly dissipated. At the same time, people with "email jobs" began working from home, and the government started handing out "free" money to those out of work.

This is when online shopping exploded and long-delayed home-improvement projects were undertaken with gusto; all at once, truckers were more in demand than ever. Rather than letting the market do its thing and letting rates signal to truckers to get back in the game, the usual suspects got into Biden's ear, and you can guess their mantra.

Late in 2021, the White House released a document outlining its plan to tackle one of America's longest-running psyops and nonproblems: the truck-driver shortage. The title alone shows the administration was starting from a false premise: "The Biden Harris Administration Trucking Action Plan to Strengthen America's Trucking Workforce." Was it weak and in need of strengthening? By whose metrics and standards? What was the goal of this plan, and who did it serve? The contents and consequences of the plan, like many a government program, achieved exactly the opposite of what was advertised, though what was actually intended by the people who requested this plan was delivered on schedule and without incident.

Let us first examine this plan by critiquing its premises. It declares:

Trucking plays a critical role in the U.S. supply chain and economy. America's truck drivers have been on the frontlines of this pandemic, delivering goods to every corner of this country. Seventy-two percent of goods in America are shipped by truck, and in most communities, trucks are the only form of delivery. A strong, stable, and safe trucking workforce that offers good-paying jobs to millions of truck drivers is a critical lifeblood of our economy. But outdated infrastructure, the COVID-19 pandemic, and a historic volume of goods moving through our economy have strained capacity across the supply chain, including in trucking.[16]

A strong, stable, and safe trucking workforce, you say? Perhaps Biden should have reenforced the English language proficiency requirement waived by his former partner in crime, President Obama. But that is not what happened. In a rare moment of clarity, the plan's authors give us a shot of truth: "The pandemic exacerbated longstanding workforce challenges in the trucking industry, including high turnover rates, an aging workforce, long hours away from home, and time spent waiting—often unpaid—to load and unload at congested ports, warehouses, and distribution centers." The authors go on to cite the research of David Correll: "According to one estimate, long-haul full-truckload drivers only spend an average of 6.5 hours per working day driving despite being allowed to drive a maximum of 11 hours. That means about 40 percent of their capacity is not being used."[17]

Yet the real problem, in the eyes of the people using their connections to Biden and the Democrats, is revealed further down in the announcement: "At the same time, the industry reports historic demand for its services. Reflecting that demand, *wages for employed drivers in all trucking segments have increased 7–12% in the last year alone*, but employment in some segments is still below pre-pandemic levels" (italics mine).[18]

Correll was not the only expert called to submit testimony to this task force, which happened to be run in conjunction with Secretary of Transportation Pete Buttigieg's old pals at McKinsey & Company, where Buttigieg worked for three years before serving as mayor of South Bend, Indiana. McKinsey has something of a reputation for sociopathology, such as in the advice it gave to Purdue Pharma when people started noticing that a hell of a lot of people were dying of overdoses from its infamous product, OxyContin: "McKinsey laid out several options to shore up sales. One was to give Purdue's distributors a rebate for every OxyContin overdose attributable to pills they sold."[19]

What a surprise, then, that McKinsey, and thus this Biden task force, ignored testimony from numerous trucking industry insiders and experts who told them that there was no driver shortage and that the industry was plagued with many problems easily solved via policy changes or tweaks. These experts included Steve Viscelli, author of *Big Rig*; Craig Fuller, FreightWaves CEO and scion of the U.S. Xpress trucking dynasty; and Raman Dhillon, CEO of the North American Punjabi Trucking Association, who was invited to meet President Biden at the White House. Dhillon told *Overdrive* magazine that a number of problems were relayed to representatives of FMCSA, the U.S. Departments of Transportation and Labor, and others, over a meeting that went four and a half hours.

"There's no driver shortage. It's just made up," said Dhillon. "We have the problem that the big trucking companies are not taking care of their drivers, and drivers leave the industry within the first year of their joining." Dhillon referenced big fleets with their own training programs, which might bring "100 people in, get funding for their schools and all kinds of things to do that, and out of those 100 people, within the first year 90 leave."[20]

Dhillon recalled telling Biden Administration officials that a "person crossing the border with no experience . . . gets a work permit in two months, and within one month gets their CDL. Well, they never even drove a car in this country, so why are we doing this? This is not even an issue [just] for the trucking industry. This is a national security issue."[21]

That warning fell on deaf ears. At the White House, surrounded by all manner of trucking interests, from big and small business to the various associations, the message didn't get across. Mr. Dhillon lamented, "Seriously, I'm saying there was no attention paid to it. I repeatedly met with FMCSA administrators" to point out that states are handing "licenses out left and right. States are issuing licenses without even taking a test first."[22]

During the pandemic, truckers were venerated as the most essential of essential workers—working-class heroes—while also enduring some daunting challenges to their typical operations. Governors in many states closed highway rest areas, truck-stop restaurants ceased operations or otherwise limited hours and services, and many shipping and receiving facilities across the country treated drivers as potential vectors of disease, telling truckers to stay in their trucks or otherwise barring them from access to facilities, including washrooms.

And when truckers' wages started to go up, the people in charge of our society decided that this was the problem, not any of the other myriad challenges truckers faced.

The real purpose of the Biden-Harris Trucking Action Plan was to once again unnaturally increase the pool of available truckers in the American market. This time, however, the candidates relied on to become "truckers" were decidedly not Americans.

A group of small- and medium-sized trucking company owners in Arkansas had been paying attention to fluctuations in the trucking market. They saw the fortunes of their own companies suffer downstream of the Trucking Action Plan and began collecting data. Shannon Everett, the son of a trucking family in Arkansas, is their leader. Everett spent many years behind the wheel, starting out as soon as he could get a CDL at eighteen, and later moved into management. Like me, he has spent his entire life in the industry.

"In 2019," Everett told me, "I was losing a lot of contracts to these fleets using noncitizen drivers. I had gone around speaking to some of our legislators. . . . We had laid off 450 drivers from losing these contracts. . . . I was surprised at how much no one seemed to want to support any action . . . and then the freight recession came . . . and my friends were saying 'What's going on? What's different here?.' . . . If there's no cap on how many of these guys are coming into the United States, I'm sure it's spreading into the other verticals now."[23] What really lit a fire under Everett and his associates, however, was news of a horrific truck crash in Colorado that had killed an off-duty trucker on his way home from work.

Scott Miller was in his personal vehicle and he was driving home when an out-of-control truck hit him with a flatbed load, and the load came off the truck, landed on Scott Miller's cab and . . . killed him. Come to find out that the driver of the truck was not a citizen, had been deported sixteen times, was under deportation orders at the time of the accident. . . . God had really been doing a mighty thing in my heart. . . . His kinda mission for me in life was loving people and serving people and when I saw that, with my background in trucking, I thought man, I could really help those people. . . . I immediately started doing research.

Working with business associates and trucking industry veterans Cliff Bates and Harvey Beech, Everett founded American Truckers United (ATU). This new group started investigating how insourced labor was affecting drivers' wages, as well as the horrific crashes they kept reading about in the news. What they found correlated almost exactly with what the White House was advertising with its Trucking Action Plan, along with the loophole opened up by the waiver on enforcing English proficiency created by the Obama Administration. An April 2022 fact-sheet update that was later scrubbed from the White House website included a stunning figure that ought to have raised eyebrows. Thanks to "cutting red tape," the USDOT helped states "more than double new commercial driver's license issuances in January and February 2022 compared to January and February 2021. States have issued more than 876,000 CDLs since January 2021."[24]

Those numbers do not sit well with anyone who knows and understands the industry. Typically, between 400,000 and 450,000 new CDLs are issued every year in the United States. How did the Biden plan manage to double that in twelve months? Did the number of truck-driving schools double? How did they pull this off in the middle of a pandemic when the government was paying everyone to stay home and employers were having a hell of a time attracting anyone to actually show up for work? From what ether did they manage to summon double the number of state driving examiners overnight?[25]

Everett and his team scoured data from state DOTs about the issuance of CDLs, as well as information publicly available from the Motor Carrier Management Information System (MCMIS), which is a data aggregator operated by the FMCSA. When they crunched numbers, what they found was revealing: at least ten states had registered enormous increases in the number of CDLs issued, and these ten states, along with Puerto Rico, had managed to issue over three-and-a-half times as many CDLs as the other forty states combined.

To take just two examples: Oregon added an additional 98,872 truck drivers into the system in 2022, a staggering seventy-seven times the normal yearly number. South Carolina counted 77,580 new truckers in 2021, versus only 1,765 in 2020. Some of those states have pushed back on these numbers, claiming that the numbers spiked because companies moved around or because drivers came in from other states, or that other unusual circumstances drove the increase. Everett and his team claim to have seen available data removed and the original numbers changed after ATU's findings drew media attention. Shannon posed a question about these numbers online: "Is it even possible to test, train, and qualify 43 times your normal throughput? . . . Did FedEx and UPS move all of their operations to South Carolina?"[26]

These increases in CDL numbers are simply too high for existing truck-driving schools and technical or community colleges to have accommodated. There aren't nearly enough driving examiners, and claims on the part of state officials that such a high number of drivers have moved around the country are unbelievable and impossible to back up. Everett points to incidents such as the crash in Colorado, and similar crashes in Texas, Nevada, West Virginia, and his home state of Arkansas, and comes to a different conclusion.

The ATU found that states like Arkansas and Texas changed their domicile requirements. It used to be that in order to get a CDL in those states, you actually had to live there and provide proof of address. The removal of those requirements, like the waiving of English proficiency rules by the feds, has made it possible for states to issue a massive number of CDLs to migrants, refugees, and other foreigners, with a whole lot less vetting than would normally take place. Updates from the Biden White House on the Trucking Action Plan essentially admitted as much.

One of the stated goals of the original 2021 plan was to open up "more seamless paths for veterans and underrepresented communities, such as women, to access good driving jobs." No mention was made of refugees or migrants, but in a 2023 update the administration announced that resources would be directed to "increase [the] capacity to train veterans and their family members [and] individuals from underserved and refugee communities."[27] Similar language appears in a 2024 update, which pledged to "increase the training opportunities for candidates from rural, refugee, and underserved communities."[28]

Though it is unclear how much cooperation took place between the Biden White House and various states, it is abundantly clear that when truckers were the most essential of essential workers in a time of national crisis, the government abused their work ethic and undercut their wages. Truckers were considered so essential that the FMCSA issued an hours-of-service waiver allowing many to work beyond their normal time limits, and that waiver lasted for two-and-a-half years, from March 2020 until October 2022. When drivers' pay started to creep up, instead of letting the market do its thing and naturally add capacity, the government, working on behalf of America's biggest corporations, flooded the market with often untrained recent arrivals in a blatant wage-suppression operation that abused many of the new drivers, who often wound up in predatory employment arrangements. The whole scheme screwed American truckers and trucking companies, who have been feeling the pain ever since.

Once the COVID demand spike subsided in 2022 and freight markets returned to normal, a protracted slowdown in freight took hold of the industry and has lasted until time of this writing (summer 2025). It was dubbed the "Great Freight Recession" by certain industry commentators. The problem with this designation is that it obscured a rather inconvenient fact only discussed by the likes of Shannon Everett or more realistic industry commentators like Freight-Waves CEO Craig Fuller, which is that there wasn't necessarily a severe or protracted period of less work. Rather, Biden's Trucking Action Plan added massive numbers of new truckers, and freight rates in many areas of the market have therefore stayed in the basement. Many players in the industry have been shaken out as a result, including a disproportionate number of legacy small- and medium-sized American trucking companies that have largely been replaced by what Everett and other commentators have called "Ghost Carriers" or "Chameleon Carriers"—small no-name trucking companies often run by recent arrivals who employ their coethnics.

Until Donald Trump issued his Executive Order on English Language Proficiency on April 28, 2025, and enforcement of the rule began to ramp back up, these companies, often managed through layers of LLCs and shell corporations registered in the hundreds at a time to residential addresses, running old junk for equipment and paying drivers far less than what Americans would work for, easily held on through this period of overcapacity. The enforcement of the old rule, welcome as it is, is but to take a cigarette lighter to an iceberg that is perilously close to sinking the entire industry. It's also a cat-and-mouse game in which the cat, in this case the FMCSA, is ill-equipped to do anything about the mouse.

Industry investigative researcher Danielle Chaffin explains:

A chameleon carrier is a trucking company that shuts down, often due to safety issues, legal problems, or fraud, and then reincarnates under a new name to avoid consequences.

They have a stack of new U.S. Department of Transportation (USDOT) numbers, change the numbers on the same trucks, and keep moving freight.

. . .

Think of them like someone getting kicked out of a bar and walking back in wearing a different hat and t-shirt.

Imagine a trucking company with a long history of safety violations, crashes, or outright fraud. The government shuts it down. End of story, right? **Nope. Wrong.**

Next week, **the same company will be back on the road.** New name, new address, new USDOT number . . . but it's the same trucks, the same people, and **the same horrible operations.**[29] (boldface in original)

This is the type of garbage that established American companies are expected to compete with.

As noted earlier, *FreightWaves* has an entire section of its website, and some full-time journalists, dedicated to nothing but covering "layoffs and bankruptcies." For the past four years, that section has been humming, documenting tens if not hundreds of thousands of truckers being laid off and companies going out of business. So much for that driver shortage, eh?

Trump's decision to enforce the English language proficiency rule appears to be showing early signs of fruit, with rates on the spot market slowly making very modest gains, some freight brokers demanding English-speaking drivers in the rate agreements they make with carriers, and signals coming from various ethnic trucking enclaves that they are now feeling the pain their very presence had imposed on others. Some of those enclaves are in the Chicago area. The nerve center appears to be the Chicagoland suburb of Elk Grove Village, a heavily industrial area adjacent to O'Hare International Airport. This enclave has been operating for so long that it has earned a nickname from truckers, "The Chicago Volvo Mafia," which notes their location, preferred make of rig, and perhaps some of their business practices. The Chicago Volvo Mafia is composed mostly of companies run and staffed by Serbians, Ukrainians, Russians, Georgians, Poles—basically everyone in the neighborhood from the Balkans on up to Moscow.

A trucking business YouTube channel called "Trucking Made Successful" is run by a young Ukrainian-Georgian-American lady named Miranda. In a video released about a month after Trump's Executive Order on English Language Proficiency, Miranda explained how the Eastern European trucking community actually operates. Miranda starts off by telling us that many Eastern European trucking companies "just don't insure," and that most of their drivers are "independent contractors, there are no W-2s." These companies, she says, only hire other Eastern Europeans, which is to say they discriminate against American drivers, because they expect their fellow Eastern Europeans to operate with their "different mentality" and to "run like maniacs," which is to say break HOS regulations and work themselves to near death.[30]

These practices have been confirmed by Clarissa Hawes, who in a 2021 article describes some pretty gross abuse of Ukrainian and Russian truckers at the hands of their homeboys:

> The average yearly pay for a truck driver in Russia is roughly equivalent to $4,700, according to Salary Explorer. Truck drivers earn even less in Ukraine—about $3,100.
>
> So when the drivers saw the YouTube and Facebook ads offering to pay them up to $3,000 per week to transport cars in the U.S., they jumped at the opportunity to make a better life for their families and achieve the American dream. Others wanted to earn money to help support family back in Russia and Ukraine.
>
> However, once in America, the drivers told *FreightWaves*, they found themselves trapped in an alleged human trafficking scheme, forced to drive seven days a week and up to 20 hours a day and getting paid a fraction of what they were promised.[31]

Twenty hours a day? How are they pulling this off with an electronic logging device in the truck? *FreightWaves* revealed a practice discussed in hushed tones by these Eastern European and Balkan truckers. That practice is the "backdooring" of ELDs. The truckers' actual working hours are manipulated, most often by ELD service providers located in their home countries, safe from any oversight by American authorities. A driver named Chris told *FreightWaves* that he was forced to drive fifty hours straight to meet customer deadlines, and those hours disappeared on his ELD. Fifty hours is an incredible amount of time for the human body to try and stay awake, even with chemical assistance. Hawes reports:

> Chris said he didn't want to do this, but he felt trapped and feared reprisal from the owners if he refused to drive because he was tired. Instead, he found himself working illegally through an alleged immigration scam for little pay. He said he wasn't alone.
>
> "There are hundreds of guys out there just like me," Chris said. "We worked hard and drove long hours, but we weren't paid close to what we were promised."
>
> When he was running out of hours he could legally drive on some of his trips, Chris said he would receive a text message from a number in Ukraine. "OK, I see you are close to the limit," he said the text messages read. "Stand by and I will adjust your [electronic logging device] time."
>
> Other drivers confirmed to *FreightWaves* this happened to them as well.

In another piece for *FreightWaves*, Hawes found that insourced labor is often abused and overworked in ways that would have made some antebellum plantation owners blush, and all of this is possible through manipulation of drivers' ELDs by agents located offshore, conveniently out of the reach of enforcement authorities. (Not that they're doing much of anything about it here in the U.S.) She writes:

> At the time the U.S. driver contacted the ELD Rider representative in Serbia. The driver, who didn't want to be named for fear of retaliation, had no drive time left on his clock and only 12 hours remaining on his 70-hour cycle before he was required by FMCSA to take a 34-hour reset.
>
> The video, which was reviewed by *FreightWaves*, shows an alert being sent to the engine control module (ECM) connected to the driver's truck. The alert notified the driver that a representative was logging him off and taking over to edit his logs.
>
> He later received a call from ELD Rider confirming that the representative had edited the log to add a co-driver, often referred to as a ghost driver. The video then pans to the driver logging back into his device, showing that he now had almost 10 hours of drive time left in his day and around 68 hours

remaining on his cycle before he must take 34 consecutive hours off duty before driving again.[32]

With a touch of a button, "Strong Solo Sergey," who has just completed an eleven-hour shift of driving, is now good to go for another ten hours of immediate driving and another five days of driving after that before requiring a day off to recuperate.

Funny, we were all told back in 2016 that the electronic logging device mandate would put an end to this abuse. Perhaps the FMCSA did not foresee the gutting of the American trucking industry by foreign entities who could not care less about the strictures of our safety regulations and would only be too happy to have offshore offices make the "necessary adjustments." Easier than spending an hour reworking a week's worth of your logbook like in the old days, I guess. Friend and fellow former trucker Justin Martin likes to put it this way: "Paper logs were an IQ test— you had to make it look good, and you had to be good enough at math so that your times and locations were plausible and believable to a DOT Officer. ELDs, once again, reduce the barrier of entry into trucking to a much lower common denominator."

Trump's English language proficiency enforcement order appears to be scaring some of these assholes into (possibly) going straight. Miranda describes what she is hearing from associates in this particular trucking community: "The business model of these companies . . . relies on Eastern European drivers . . . folks who are not proficient in English. . . . What they are experiencing is that they are losing a percentage of their workforce. . . . Many of these companies relied on the lax immigration policies. . . . A lot of work authorizations are not being renewed. . . . Those who have freshly financed equipment, it's only a matter of months before they have to shut down."

On behalf of American truckers everywhere, especially those laid off in the past few years of the Great Freight Recession, let me break out a tiny violin for the Russian and Serbian gangsters and other parasites who are about to lose their shirts. The Serbs have made massive inroads into America's trucking industry, sometimes without even being here. They have become a big player in the world of brokering freight, with many offices hustling loads in America and taking their own cut in Belgrade.

This cottage industry has grown to such proportions that it became the subject of a feature documentary for the trucking industry news website Freight Caviar. From the documentary, "Inside Serbia: The Hidden Hub of U.S. Freight Outsourcing," we learn that organizing loads on American interstates pays much better than the average wage in Serbia. Shortly after the beginning of the documentary, the host, Freight Caviar founder Paul-Bernard Jaroslawski, is being driven under a huge billboard across the road leading out of Belgrade's airport. The billboard advertises Super Ego Holdings, a massive trucking company that operates out of Chicago but has headquarters in Belgrade. Later in the documentary, Jaroslawski mentions, on his way to Super Ego, that "they have thousands of trucks, and they know their reputation is not good."[33]

The reason Super Ego's reputation is not good might have something to do with the multiple lawsuits filed against the company, including a class action filed in Illinois that is ongoing. Every one of these suits alleges that SuperEgo altered rate confirmation paperwork and underpaid its contractors. From the class-action suit website: "Super Ego has a companywide practice of underpaying drivers by skimming off the top of the load price. . . . Super Ego regularly lied to truckers about the price of the load by secretly altering the brokers' rate confirmation sheets to make the load price appear lower than it actually was. Super Ego then paid truckers a percentage of the lower, secretly altered price, and pocketed the difference."[34]

The lawsuit also claims that Super Ego misclassified truckers as independent contractors, made illegal deductions from their pay, withheld their pay, and even paid them less than the federal minimum wage during some pay periods. Plaintiffs seek damages for fraud, breach of contract, violations of the federal Truth in Leasing Act and Fair Labor Standards Act, and violations of the Illinois Wage Payment and Collection Act.[35]

Though Super Ego is based in Belgrade, its American operations do not exclusively employ insourced labor, as a number of the defendants are Americans. You could say the Super Ego folks are "diverse" and approach their abuse of truckers with an equal-opportunity mindset. Like so many other operators discussed in this book, they heavily rely on the independent-contractor model: directly employing truckers, whether you are an American company owner or a Serb immigrant company owner, is far too much hassle. TikTok and other social media sites are awash in reports directly from truckers about the company, and I would invite the reader to go and have a listen.

The Super Ego people aren't the only Serbs attempting to cash in on America's trucking industry, as a website called Balkan Truckers will attest. Balkan Truckers hosts, among other things, advertising for various trucking service providers, and the home page prominently features advertising for drivers to buy their own trucks, which they will then ostensibly lease with one of the ninety-odd different Serb and other Balkan-based carriers on the site.[36] I've been told by some that many Serbs hate Americans, a historical animosity that stems from the 1999 NATO bombing of their country. I guess they don't hate the U.S. so much that they can't stomach the idea of setting up massive companies from which to extract value out of the U.S. economy.

Forty-five years of squeezing every last penny out of the American trucker has resulted in bringing in non-American truckers to see if the squeeze can be kept going just a little bit longer. And it is not like American or Canadian truckers have anywhere to go—the only other economies where drivers make remotely similar salaries are Australia and Europe, and Australia has the same problem with insourcing labor from India that Canada has, while the European trucking industry has been dealing with cheap labor flooding over its borders for much longer than North America. The American trucker has nowhere to go, and I dare you to find me an American working in the Punjab or the Balkans who is taking a job away from the locals while also crashing trucks all over their turf at great frequency.

What do our friends at the American Trucking Associations have to say about this?

When I wrote about the connection between the increase in traffic fatalities and the flooding of the trucking market with insourced labor by President Biden for Blaze Media,[37] a day later the ATA responded in a lazy blog post that did not address the problem of increased traffic fatalities involving big trucks and attempted to explain away the numbers as data-entry errors.[38] Later, when President Trump dealt with this issue head-on with his executive order to enforce English language proficiency requirements, the ATA issued a weak-sauce thank-you to the president for solving a problem that six weeks prior they had claimed did not exist.[39]

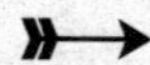

The outsourcing of American manufacturing jobs began in the 1970s, slowly and steadily increased over the next twenty years, and then really accelerated in the 1990s after Bill Clinton signed the North American Free Trade Agreement (NAFTA). At the time, this was seen as a boon to cross-border truckers, as the increased economic activity throughout the continent required trucking to sustain it, and you won't find too many Mexican or Canadian truckers complaining about NAFTA, now renegotiated and called the United States–Mexico–Canada Agreement (USMCA) under President Trump. Many truckers felt at the time, and maybe some do to this day, that free trade is a net positive for the economy, and I am not here to disagree or argue with that position. What many of them did not see back when NAFTA was passed, or when any of the other deals were executed that sent manufacturing to China, Vietnam, and elsewhere, was that eventually the voracious greed of certain actors within our marketplace would come for them, too. "You can't outsource truckers" is a true enough statement, but this truth has been circumvented by *insourcing* truckers instead, the result being that American and Canadian truckers are now assaulted with wage arbitrage against the whole world. Not only has the insourcing of labor to replace North American truckers cost us our wages; it has also increased truck-involved crash rates on our highways. No one has yet done the hard investigative work of connecting all these dots, though various colleagues and researchers I have quoted in the book are doing so with what publicly available data they can get their hands on. Just as states like California have refused to play ball with Trump's reenforcement of the ELP regulation for truckers, many agencies simply do not categorize crash data based on the immigration status, language skills, or validity of the licenses issued to the drivers involved.[40]

On June 27, 2025, Transportation Secretary Sean Duffy appeared on the *What the Truck?* program, hosted then by trucking-industry commentator Timothy Dooner, where he made some announcements meant to address this problem. Duffy acknowledged that he was hearing truckers' complaints, had taken on the research about non-domiciled CDLs from Shannon Everett and his team at American Truckers United, and was going to investigate.[41] Having already begun reenforcing the language requirements abandoned in 2016, and having shown that they understand the critical safety and market factors at play, Duffy and the Trump Administration have given even the most cynical among us reason to believe that they mean business in cleaning up our industry and turning off the spigot of cheap insourced labor. But will it be enough—or is it too late?

8

Truckzilla—Invasion of the RoboTrucks

How would you describe the difference between modern war and modern industry—between, say, bombing and strip mining, or between chemical warfare and chemical manufacturing? The difference seems to be only that in war the victimization of humans is directly intentional and in industry it is "accepted" as a "trade-off."

—Wendell Berry, "Word and Flesh"

The Mid-America Trucking Show, or MATS to regulars, is the biggest trucker and trucking-industry party in the United States, if not the world, and is held at the Kentucky Exposition Center in Louisville. Over three days every year, usually at the end of March, upwards of fifty-five thousand people participate in the show. Most of them are truckers or otherwise work in our world. The outdoor part of the show is where one finds many gorgeous rigs on display as part of the PKY Truck Beauty Championship. These trucks, shiny and bedecked with chrome and custom paint jobs, are a testament to the rugged individualism of their owners. Inside, displays of older trucks from organizations such as the American Truck Historical Society speak to that same venerable, individualistic culture, to a time when drivers' lives were less regulated and surveilled by state-mandated electronic intrusions, a time when engines were not subject to the castration caused by the climate alarmism animating the regulators of today. It's a venue in which you wouldn't expect to hear from one of the companies seeking to replace the American trucker altogether, but Aurora Innovation, one of the leading tech companies building driverless truck systems, decided to attend MATS in 2024 and discuss its robots anyway.

One of the meeting rooms in the East Hall of the Kentucky Expo Center is set aside for various lectures and programs that MATS calls the "Pro Talks Seminar Series." These presentations are typically given by regulatory-agency speakers, company officials, and consultants selling products or services to trucking fleets large and small, as well as other experts and truckers discussing various issues of the day. Aurora sponsored a presentation called "Navigating the Future: The Transformative Impact of Autonomous Trucking." The speaker sent by Aurora was a former trucker named Bryan Jones. Now a "Safety Driver Manager" for the company, perhaps Mr. Jones had decided to transition himself out of the driver's seat early, thereby guaranteeing himself a job in the driverless future that Aurora envisions for America's highways.

One would think that a presentation from a company like Aurora would elicit great interest from the MATS crowd; after all, Aurora, like others in the market, is explicitly seeking to render many of the attendees at MATS unemployed. Alas, by my count there were barely seventy people in attendance, and Jones managed to bore about half of them away before he finished.

Maybe more truckers would have appeared if Aurora had shown up after pulling off what many truckers have convinced themselves is impossible: a driverless, fully automated rig going down the American interstate.

On May 1, 2025, Aurora put out a press release announcing that in the previous month, its driverless trucks had gone "driver out" along Interstate 45 in Texas, running the high-volume corridor from Dallas–Fort Worth to Houston.[1] "Driver out" is the industry term for fully autonomous operation—the truck driving itself with zero human input or control. The announcement cemented Aurora's position as the first company to achieve this milestone in the development of robotic trucks. A few months later, Aurora announced that it had conducted the first nighttime driverless operations on the interstate, also in Texas.[2] (Another operator, Kodiak Robotics, is already operating driverless trucks on the less traveled private oil-lease roads in the desert country above the Permian Basin.)

How Aurora arrived at this milestone deserves a lot more examination and critique than it has received in the media, so let us return to their man Jones at the truck show. In his opening statement, Jones highlighted that one of the intents of Aurora's technology was to "not replace truck drivers, but add to the workforce." We have been hearing some version of this claim from autonomous-truck-system manufacturers for a long time, and it has always been at best an obfuscation, and at worst an utter falsehood.

In a 2023 interview with the popular podcast *On with Kara Swisher*, Aurora CEO Chris Urmson attempted to launder this lie about not replacing truck drivers with an appeal to safetyism.[3] Urmson cited the supposed shortage of truck drivers as a reason his technology is necessary, a claim that is also plastered all over Aurora's investment prospectus. He told Swisher that forty-thousand people die on American highways every year and that—somehow—his untested technology would solve this problem.

Raquel Urtasun, CEO of Toronto-headquartered Waabi and a professor of computer science at the University of Toronto, has also cited the bogus shortage of truck drivers and the dangers of the job as a reason to replace us entirely.[4] The American Trucking Association's decades-long mythmaking project about a supposed shortage of truckers has been very useful propaganda for autonomous-truck-system companies like Waabi, which is partnering with Uber Freight in the project of making truckers extinct. Waabi and Uber—whose original, though maybe not explicitly stated, intention was to replace the taxi driver—are a match made in robot heaven.[5]

Autonomous-vehicle pimps usually claim that they don't want to replace truckers but rather to "add to the workforce" or to make truckers' jobs "better." Yet if we examine what Aurora has been telling its investors for a few years, it becomes clear that this is disinformation. The basic logic makes no sense. The whole point of robot trucks is to have robots drive them, which raises the basic question, "What of the human driver?" The message of these companies to the public is misleading. It is meant to make it appear that they give a shit about the millions of people they seek to render unemployed.

But they are not allowed to lie to investors. Aurora's July 2024 investment prospectus describes the "jobs" they have to offer the truckers they seek to unemploy. One is "remote support specialist," which is a rather interesting title for what the actual job entails, which is a cross between being a drone pilot and being a babysitter. The remote support specialist, in Aurora's telling, will be like a remote safety driver, someone who is supposed to monitor the driverless truck from afar and intervene if a problem arises. This all seems benign; why wouldn't a trucker want to have a cushy job in an air-conditioned office, sitting at a bank of screens instead of in heavy traffic or rotten weather out on the highway?

There are more than a few problems with this arrangement, however. For example, as "the Aurora Driver's performance continues to improve," the company asserts, "we expect to reduce remote assistance costs." This claim, in bolded text, sits next to a graph showing that as the cost per mile of the Aurora Driver system decreases, the number of trucks that the remote support specialist will be expected to babysit increases to one hundred.

And what exactly is the remote support specialist going to be doing? In Aurora's telling, the specialist's job will be analogous to that of a drone operator, but instead of flying drones kamikaze-like into soldiers on the battlefields of Ukraine, or raining hellfire missiles on weddings in East Africa, the operators would be keeping Aurora's trucks on the straight and narrow, preventing them from going off the road or rear-ending other vehicles in stopped traffic and killing everyone inside them.[6]

Aurora's explicitness about having only one backup remote safety driver per one hundred trucks on the road shows that it is seeking to eliminate truckers altogether and keep the number of remote operators as low as possible. What kind of arrangement will a "remote support specialist" find himself in at Aurora? If the system on one of these trucks spergs out, or something happens so fast on the road the truck can't possibly stop or slow down in time, will the specialist be on the hook for any liability, as a driver in the seat is supposed to be now?

Another consideration is that drone operators in the U.S. military suffer from a substantial amount of post-traumatic stress disorder (PTSD), which is unsurprising, given the repeated exposure to front-row video footage of the murder and mayhem they are tasked to orchestrate from afar. Drone operation appears to have the same turnover problem that trucking does. What does it say about Aurora's claim about "adding to the workforce" for truckers when the number of jobs they want to give us is clearly meant to be significantly reduced—and will in all likelihood have a serious turnover problem?[7]

Furthermore, is it much of a stretch to imagine that remote support specialists for Aurora, or any other autonomous-truck manufacturer, given the task of monitoring one hundred rigs at a time, will be unable to respond quickly enough when a problem on the road arises? What happens if, God forbid, an Aurora truck's system fails and crashes into a stalled minivan? At one hundred trucks per operator, it seems that the poor bastard who takes on that role is inevitably going to bear witness to something bad, and unlike a drone operator, he or she won't easily be able to dehumanize the people involved as "bad guys."

As usual, the congressional tools of industry are adding insult to injury. Republican Representative Vince Fong of the 20th district of California introduced a wonderfully worded Orwellian piece of legislation in July 2025. Titled the AMERICA DRIVES Act, or "Autonomous Mobility Ensuring Regulation, Innovation, Commerce, and Advancement Driving Reliability in Vehicle Efficiency and Safety Act," the bill seeks to bar the states from keeping autonomous trucks off the nation's roads. "IN GENERAL.—A commercial motor vehicle equipped with a Level 4 or Level 5 ADS may be operated in interstate commerce without—(1) a human driver on board such vehicle; or, (2) a remote human driver."[8]

In essence, we can infer that Aurora and other players in the driverless-truck market wish to go full steam ahead in removing the human driver from the truck, and if possible they don't even want what little safety oversight might be afforded by a "remote support specialist" trying to juggle the monitoring of one hundred trucks.

Assuming that some new, novel, untested technology unleashed at scale on the populace is going to work on a pinky-swear from its manufacturers sounds awfully familiar, doesn't it? Nowhere in Representative Fong's bill does it mention anything about liability, mitigation, oversight, what happens in the event of a collision . . . nothing. Get the truckers out and let the robots loose.

What Fong does mention, though, on his own website, is the same damn lie that the manufacturers repeat ad nauseam: the driver shortage. It doesn't sound like you are replacing any workers or taking food off the table of millions of families if you just pretend they don't exist or are hard to come by. Fong (or a staffer) writes, "The current driver shortage is anticipated to double from 80,000 drivers in 2021 to over 160,000 by 2030."[9]

Another interesting bit of rhetorical salesmanship on Representative Fong's website is this whopper: "While Europe and China are rapidly integrating autonomous trucks into their supply chains, America is asleep at the wheel, hamstrung by a confusing patchwork of state regulations that threaten public safety, innovation, and economic growth."[10] This is called federalism, Representative Fong.

Meanwhile, at the *Washington Examiner*, Stephen Moore, a former Trump economic adviser, after claiming that our freight system is "overworked and under-resourced, which slows down deliveries and drives up prices," states that "autonomous trucking—yes, self-driving big rigs—is the solution to this challenge. But this sector has been hamstrung by senseless and outdated regulations, resulting in China-based companies taking the lead in developing autonomous vehicles. And here's the truth we can't afford to ignore: If we let China win on this matter, we won't just be buying their trucks. We'll be buying our supply chain from them, too."[11]

After seeing many of our manufacturing jobs sent to China over the past few decades, the American worker is told once again that we must sacrifice even more—so that China won't beat us. Haven't they already? Why would we compare the development of robot trucks in a somewhat free country like America to their development in a communist corporatocracy like China? What people like Fong and Moore don't seem to understand is that most working people in America do not *give a single shit* if China gets robotic trucks before us, and if you know anything about the truck market in the United States, you know that there are zero—count 'em, *zero*—Chinese-make or -model big rigs on the road in the United States. It seems politically unlikely that any president is going to allow fly-by-wire robotic big rigs that were made in another country on our roads.

Over and above the economic considerations, and the fact that domestic truck manufacturers have their own political pull, we must also consider security. Are American government officials so stupid that they would hand over the operation of our critical trucking supply chains to Chinese companies? Maybe they are, but I doubt it. By their very nature, autonomous trucks are plugged into the same networks upon which so many hackers and hostile actors run free, and let's just say that it has been demonstrated that large vehicles can make quite an impact when crashed into large crowds of people. Autonomous trucks are also, in a way, a more distributed version of the pipelines and electrical grids that deliver our energy; do we need another Colonial Pipeline shutdown, except this time affecting the entire country? I'm not the only person to consider these possibilities. An entire industry has sprung up around building digital security for the robots, lest hackers turn our interstates into a scene from *The Road Warrior*, where the hackers have replaced the leather-clad ferals of the Australian Outback. The market for this security is expected to be worth nearly $5 billion a year.[12]

The autonomous-truck manufacturers are grasping at an awful lot of buzzwords in place of the proverbial straws and making assumptions about how Americans will welcome sharing the road with big rigs that have no drivers in them. Maybe that's why they push legislation like Representative Fong's—because the autonomous-vehicle manufacturers understand just how wildly unpopular their products are, and what they mean for other motorists.

A particularly cogent critic of the autonomous-vehicle manufacturers is Dr. Missy Cummings, one of the Navy's first female fighter pilots. Dr. Cummings, who flew F/A-18 Hornets and later became an aeronautics engineer, has been studying the development of autonomous-vehicle technology very, very closely. She is currently a professor and researcher at George Mason University, where she directs the Mason Autonomy and Robotics Center.

Dr. Cummings is having none of this worry about China. *Forbes* magazine asked her whether she worried about China pulling ahead of the U.S. in automation and AI. She responded: "I'm actually not worried about that at all. . . . I think the thing that I do worry about is the 'Space Race' to get autonomous cars on the road. We're all using shortcuts for a lot of critical elements. The number one problem is people don't know the limitations of this technology. And authoritarian regimes usually foster an environment that discourages asking questions, which is dangerous."[13]

In a paper published in 2024, Cummings and co-researcher Ben Bauchwitz looked into "research gaps" in the systems that help autonomous cars navigate our streets, as well as problems derived from "simulated" testing, which the autonomous-truck manufacturers rely upon in making the claim that they have tested their systems. What Cummings and Bauchwitz found should slam the brakes on ridiculous legislation like that put forward by Representative Fong.[14] Their findings indicate that many autonomous systems are profoundly incapable of "reasoning under uncertainty" and get spooked by "hallucinations," which cause them to "phantom brake" for no reason, vastly increasing their rate of being rear-ended by cars following behind them. Phantom braking is already a problem with the front-collision-avoidance systems now mandated on human-operated rigs and is the cause of numerous jack-knife situations, placing many an innocent driver in the ditch with his semi, all because the system was spooked by . . . well, a phantom. The researchers also found that the systems used by Cruze, Waymo, and Zoox, three of the dominant robot-taxi platforms, have much higher incident rates per vehicle miles traveled than human drivers.

Car enthusiast magazine *Jalopnik* has reported on these incident rates as well. In 2023, comparing National Highway Traffic Safety Administration data to number of miles traveled, *Jalopnik* found that driverless-vehicle systems have a pretty high hurdle to clear in order to claim that they are, in fact, safer than human drivers: "A self-driving car can't be 99-percent perfect, it can't be 99.9-percent or even 99.999-percent safe. Human drivers, on average, avoid crashes 99.999819 percent of the time. *To beat that, autonomous vehicles will have to hit nearly six nines of reliability*" (italics mine).[15]

The concerns of Cummings and Bauchwitz are echoed by at least one trucker who is a safety backup and testing driver for one of these system manufacturers. For obvious reasons, this person and the company he or she works for will remain anonymous. The trucker told me via email:

> I joined the autonomous vehicle (AV) industry for a variety of reasons, but the most significant were the stability and predictability the job offered. Unlike many other roles in the transportation sector, the position allowed me to be home every day, with a manageable and consistent schedule. The pay and benefits were also unmatched in the industry at the time. On top of this, the idea of "testing frontier technology" was appealing, even though I couldn't shake the apprehension of what this technology could mean for the industry.

The job qualifications seemed daunting, asking for over seven years of driving experience and a deep understanding of how a tractor-trailer works. After speaking with a recruiter, though, it sounded like a perfect fit, and I felt confident stepping into the role. But it wasn't long before I began noticing things that didn't sit right with me, especially around safety concerns. I was asked to run a test—one that was critical to the advancement of the software. The problem? The software was unvetted, and despite the industry norm of running such tests on closed courses, these tests were now taking place on public roads—week after week.

[Eventually] the company relaxed the qualification of having a strong understanding of tractor-trailers. As a result, many of the new drivers had less than five years in the industry and, in some cases, had automatic restrictions on their licenses.

This shift in hiring practices raised a major concern: How can someone who doesn't even understand the air-brake system or how to optimize engine braking provide meaningful feedback on how the truck's software is performing? This is the very feedback engineers relied on to improve the systems.

And it wasn't just the drivers. Many engineers, and even some decision-makers, had zero experience in the trucking industry. In fact, for a lot of engineers, this was their second or third stint in autonomous vehicles, having worked previously on passenger-car AV programs. This was problematic, as I had to spend time explaining basic trucking principles to high-level engineers who seemed unfamiliar with the driving dynamics of an eighty-thousand-pound articulated vehicle. Engineers were ignorant [of] the driving culture and general courtesies of the road. Some engineers were dismissive of feedback, showing an arrogant and pompous attitude.

Another problem I encountered was the company's approach to development. As they pushed to meet their goals for launching, they began testing "pull-over areas" where the truck would stop if an issue occurred. Testing these areas was a long, tedious process that involved sending the truck deliberately into a situation that would trigger the "pull-over" command. In some cases, the truck had to pull off onto a frontage road, but if there was no shoulder, the truck would simply stop in the lane. This put both the truck and other motorists at serious risk, as traffic would often approach from behind without warning.

During one test, we warned against pulling off into a particular area because a large pothole had formed from all the trucks stopping in the same spot. Despite our concerns, management insisted we proceed, resulting in superficial damage to the trucks and, in some cases, injuries to operators due to the jarring impact of the truck falling into the pothole at a mere ten mph.

As the demands on drivers continued to rise, so did the risks. Drivers were asked to continue tests despite poor performance, and bathroom breaks were restricted while the trucks were operating autonomously. This led to growing frustration and unease among the drivers, who felt increasingly like scapegoats in the company's larger experiment. From the outside, the company's social media presence painted a picture of success and safety. Yet, behind closed doors, drivers felt undervalued, and the maintenance program for these trucks was shockingly inadequate. Trucks sometimes went out with significant issues, such as air leaks, flat tires, and broken lights—issues that would have been caught by an experienced driver checking the equipment before heading out.

One of the biggest problems I see in the AV industry is the self-certification process. There is very little government oversight, and the industry is essentially policing itself. This allows companies to test on public roads with little to no regulation, turning everyday drivers into test subjects for these unvetted technologies. It's a dangerous situation, and one that needs to be addressed. The motoring public aren't seen as individuals with families to protect; they're seen as actors in the experiment.

This "self-certification process" has rendered the policing of truck drivers' hours of service via electronic logging devices a laughingstock, as hundreds of ELD providers both on the market and on the sly advertise their offshore "back-end support" to trucking companies. This means they can fudge the numbers and let drivers work ungodly and dangerous amounts of time. It appears that in the race for first-mover advantage we are seeing the same problem with autonomous vehicles. Our anonymous testing driver continues:

Claims that LiDAR [Light Detection and Ranging] systems can see five hundred-plus meters can be misleading. While this may be achievable under optimal conditions, factors such as ambient lighting, road elevation, curves, and occlusion by large vehicles (e.g., trucks) can significantly impact perception quality.

Although LiDAR range has improved over time, it's still common during everyday testing for objects to be detected at shorter ranges than expected—especially road debris, which varies in size and shape.

As advanced as the technology is, it remains reactive compared to a well-trained, proactive human driver. Most experienced drivers are trained in the Smith System driving principles, which include "Get the big picture," "Leave yourself an out," and "Aim high in steering." These principles support safe and anticipatory decision-making. In contrast, autonomous vehicles rely on complex sensor data and calculations, resulting in decision-making that is often reactive and less timely than that of a human. This can lead to last-minute lane changes that disrupt traffic flow and frustrate other motorists.

Another issue with sensor-based systems is the occurrence of false positives—detecting objects that are not physically present. This can cause unpredictable behaviors, such as sudden braking or erratic lane changes, as the vehicle reacts to perceived obstacles. Such actions can frustrate nearby drivers and raise safety concerns.

Additionally, collecting sufficient data on the various configurations of tractor-trailers is labor-intensive. To optimize performance through machine learning, every variable must be considered—such as the kingpin-to-rear-axle ratio, axle weights, trailer type, and trailer length. This is crucial because not all trailers are uniform. Design variations can affect sensor perception. For example, intermodal containers have corrugated (wavy) sides, which have led to false positive detections along the trailer's sides. These false readings stem from the trailer's lack of smooth, flat surfaces. Similarly, trailers with side doors have also been found to trigger similar issues.

Our testing driver's remarks about the difference between a well-trained and highly skilled human driver and this machine being coaxed out of the ether resonate heavily with me, and will no doubt resonate with many lifelong truckers who read this. Some of us have the secret sauce: I've been driving professionally for nearly three decades and have yet to be involved in a collision or hurt anyone while out on the road, and I am not the only driver with that kind of record. Like my colleagues, I have learned from observation of traffic patterns what to expect and what to avoid, how to gauge the behavior of cars approaching from the rear, who looks like a drunk, what contractor has a ladder or some other item loose on his pickup, and what carload of teenagers needs more space and attention. After referencing the philosopher Michael Polanyi and his term *tacit knowledge* for what my fellow truckers and I have deeply embedded inside us, Karen Levy points to situations where AVs will have a hard time without it:

> Machines are increasingly better at learning the rules—but have a hard time when rules should not be followed, or how to balance among competing demands in safety-critical situations. . . . Indeed, some accidents have been caused by AVs hewing too closely to the rules. . . . Driving requires fluidity, attention to local custom, and communication with surrounding drivers and pedestrians—tacit knowledge that may be impossible for robots to fully grasp, but which is essential for the social co-ordination of driving amidst human beings.

Levy goes on to quote Missy Cummings, who puts it nicely: autonomous cars "don't understand social graces."[16]

Billions upon billions of dollars are being spent trying to teach a machine something I already know and have absorbed into my bones; that's a hefty price tag to obtain tacit knowledge. Is it possible for me or similarly successful drivers to teach robots what that secret sauce is? As it turns out, companies are asking for the recipe, but in a very disingenuous and extractive manner.

Paulette Nobles is a former driver at Hirschbach Transportation, a partner carrier with Aurora, and a company at the center of surveillance and automation efforts. She tells me: "Hirschbach came out . . . and finally admitted to the drivers that they have a working relationship with Aurora . . . that they have had for years. . . . They've been keeping it hush hush for quite awhile." Like me, Nobles is cynical enough to see through the marketing and flowery language employed to hide what is really going on:

> They're all excited about it [the partnership with Aurora]. . . . It's going to make trucking better. . . . They gotta spin it to make it appear so it's going to make drivers' lives easier, which is nonsense.

> We've always had driver-facing cameras, then in September of 2024, we got "AI" technology in our cameras. . . . It will tell you if you're distracted, or sleepy, or if you're not wearing a seatbelt. Our seatbelts are orange, so if you're wearing one of those hi-viz safety orange shirts it will tell you you aren't wearing a seatbelt because it doesn't see it. I've talked to other women here at Hirschbach and if they're well endowed in the chest it tells them they're not wearing seatbelts.
>
> If we've got this going on, there's a reason, and it's not to make us feel safer, it's to [have the AI] self-correct us. . . . I was speaking with an AI specialist who told me that odds are there are people watching us, probably in India, as they are programming AI to start looking at stuff.
>
> The thing is, we also have the dashcams incorporated into our camera, so every mile we drive, the view of the traffic around us, and the decisions that we make, is also being used to program the autonomous truck [systems]. . . . We do know that they are sharing the data with Aurora.[17]

In short, the artificiality of artificial intelligence requires it to be taught, and at Hirschbach truckers like Nobles were being used to instruct their replacements.

Aurora is not the only system developer that has experienced serious safety issues in the rush to get its product to market. In 2022, a truck being tested by TuSimple crashed against a median along Interstate 10 in Arizona.[18] TuSimple, a company that has since hived off its technology and employees into other entities, is now reportedly making video games in China, where it was caught illegally sending proprietary technology and data. Though TuSimple tried to blame this activity on a minor error, a lawsuit against TuSimple by John Vindland, an engineer the company fired, appears to reinforce the notion that the autonomous-truck-system companies are racing each other to be first on the market, and to hell with public safety.[19]

The lawsuit alleges that Vindman, working as a "Functional Safety Engineering Lead," was told to bypass certain processes by a C-Level executive and that the company canned him for refusing to sign off on "unmet safety standards." TuSimple denies any wrongdoing, of course, and the case has yet to go to court.[20] It is worth noting that TuSimple settled another lawsuit out of court, for a cool $189 million, after shareholders accused TuSimple of attempting to defraud them.[21]

Do these companies sound like the kind of entities we should be trusting to ensure that American motorists are safe around their robotic big rigs? I find it pretty insulting that hucksters like TuSimple think they can just ignore the hundreds of thousands of American truckers who have perfect or near perfect driving records.[22]

Matthew Crawford, in his book *Why We Drive: Toward a Philosophy of the Open Road*, tackles numerous questions related to the act of driving, regarding the motorcycle or automobile as "prosthetics" by which we navigate the world and exercise skill and agency. His book is replete with deep and probing questions that are not being asked about the driverless future that awaits us all, whether on four or eighteen wheels. In one passage, Crawford discusses what is really going on with these "nudges" meant to convince drivers like Paulette Nobles of the futility of having confidence and pride in their own developed skills—and thus to convince us all of the "inevitability" of driverless systems. "Given how much of our daily lives are nudged and steered into channels engineered by tech firms, one can no longer sensibly adopt a conceptual demarcation between 'the private sector' and 'government,'" writes Crawford. "In this moment of ambiguity about the driverless future, various interests have recognized a brief window of vast opportunity—if they can advance a profitable interpretation of cars, roads, cities, and mobility itself that will come to seem the only reasonable one."[23]

Despite evidence showing that (most) human drivers actually aren't all that bad (unvetted insourced truckers and those put through a very short CDL-mill course excepted) and that the safety claims of autonomous-vehicle systems companies should be approached with significant skepticism, what is the selling feature here? The autonomous-car manufacturers have a pretty major hill to climb, for an awful lot of people actually enjoy driving and are not going to pay a premium for a more expensive car for the dubious privilege of having that car drive them around.

"Driverless cars are going to happen, we are told, because it has been decided—by something called 'the future,'" writes Crawford. "It has become clear that the effort to develop driverless cars is not a response to consumer demand, but a top-down project that has to be sold to the public."[24]

The economics of trucks, however, are quite different. Truck drivers, unlike most of those behind the wheels of cars, are being paid for their driving efforts. Not as well as they should be, but still. In addition, many of the consumers are not the truck drivers themselves, but the companies that employ them and purchase the trucks—dodgy lease-operator scams notwithstanding. On that note, perhaps one of the few beneficial consequences to the driverless truck is the end of the lease-operator system. What driver is going to sign an agreement in which he is (falsely) led to believe he is purchasing a truck that he cannot even drive?

The sum total of American truck drivers' salaries is believed to be $200 billion a year. That is the loot all these autonomous-systems companies are hoping to grab for themselves. Aurora makes a point of describing the cost savings involved with its "DaaS," or "Driver as a Service" model, which is to say the subscription service Aurora's customer must pay to use the Aurora Driver system. Here's more salt for truckers' wounds—they are set to be replaced by robots, and the balance of the cost savings will be directed to the companies that orchestrated their replacement.

In an estimate given to potential customers of the Aurora Driver subscription-based service, we are told that the average human driver and any benefits he or she may accrue cost roughly ninety-seven cents per mile of the total per-mile rate cost structure of most trucking companies. Aurora claims, "We believe we have the opportunity to reduce customers' driver costs by 25–40%."[25]

This is an admission that there will not be a total removal of driver costs. But the Aurora Driver subscription service redirects a significant portion of the American trucker's salary to Aurora's executives and investors. Those trucking companies which purchase a truck operated by an Aurora automated system will actually be entering an arrangement with Aurora for the life of that truck, similar to arrangements where those who spend ungodly amounts of money on smartphones are basically chained to Apple or Samsung, dependent at first on regular software upgrades, and ultimately forced to purchase, at regular intervals, new phones.

Truck drivers are going to be replaced by the same arrangement, and those trucking companies which replace their human employees with these new systems are making a deal with a devil who can turn the truck off from afar if payments for the subscription are missed. Then what? Aurora and its investors profit while millions of unemployed truckers and their families suffer.

To consider the question of "Then what?" we return to Karen Levy. In a chapter of *Data Driven* titled "RoboTruckers," she reflects on what will happen to truckers in the interregnum between now and when the RoboTrucks take over the highways. "To be sure, technology-driven unemployment is a real threat, but robotic trucks are very unlikely to decimate the trucking profession in one sudden phase transition. The path to fully autonomous trucking is likely to be a gradual slope, not a steep cliff—a trajectory shaped not only by technical road-blocks . . . but by human, social, legal, and cultural factors, which economic forecasts about AI and job loss commonly bracket from consideration."[26]

A key point Levy makes about the legal aspect of this matter concerns inter-national relations. Though Congressman Fong's legislation seeks to harmo-nize via hammer the fifty states' varying regulatory approaches to autonomous trucks, what of Canada or Mexico? Will they get on the autonomous-truck band-wagon with the same gusto as politicians in the U.S., who are easily swayed by the avalanche of tech propaganda, or will they approach the situation with more caution? Each country comes with its own unique considerations: Canada would (one hopes) want these systems to be able to deal with the harshness of Canadian winters and the resulting road conditions, which make driving a risky proposition for half of the year. In Mexico, where the cartels seem to have more control over the country than the government, will companies feel comfortable letting their trucks loose without even a driver to act as some kind of security over the truck? Though some thieves have no compunction about committing violence upon their victims, a certain type of actor will have even less if he knows there is no driver in the truck. Why not let the bullets fly? It's not like they're going to hurt anyone.

Speaking of bullets and other types of vandalism, has anyone considered the "Irish Diplomacy" autonomous trucks risk being subject to within the United States? Unemploying large numbers of people with no plan about what to offer them is going to make a certain percentage at the very least *annoyed*; why wouldn't they throw caltrops on the highway in front of a robot truck, or use these unmanned trucks for target practice at night on a lonely stretch of highway in the middle of nowhere? There would be a certain cathartic release in a well-placed shot taking out some critical component of the truck, be it the LiDAR system or radiator. Think of it as Odyssean truckers fighting back against the Cyclops Trucks of the state and its corrupt tech managerial regime. Hell, these rebels would be folk heroes to many of their fellow Americans. I certainly wouldn't get in the way of my fellow Good Old Boys sharpening their marksmanship skills on equipment belonging to corporations that would snatch bacon from the mouths of our families.

Elements of the highest leadership in the land have been giving us mixed messages about what to expect regarding their attitudes about autonomous trucks. In a recent interview with *New York Times* columnist and *Interesting Times* podcast host Ross Douthat, Vice President JD Vance acknowledged concerns for those engaged in the economy of "atoms who are left behind in favor of the economy of bits," or software. Responding to a question from Douthat about China, tariffs, and differences in industrial policy across administrations, the vice president replied, "You see traditional Republican [policy] but we're talking about no tax on overtime, no tax on tips. These are things that give domestic consumers more money and if you combine giving domestic consumers more money with making it easier and cheaper to produce in America, and more expensive to produce overseas, then that is, in our view, at least, a form of industrial policy. . . . There are other things we are doing. . . . *The biggest industrial policy that we already have is a regulatory regime which is incredibly rewarding to software, to the world of bits, as Peter Thiel and Tyler Cowen might say, and is incredibly punitive to the world of atoms. We would like to reverse that or at least equalize it*" (italics mine).[27] Seems like Vance is expressing some concern for me and other working stiffs, right? Bummer he apparently doesn't know that most truckers are barred from mandatory overtime pay.

Douthat later asks Vance about the new Pope, Leo XIV, who took his papal name in part to associate himself with Leo XIII's encyclical *Rerum Novarum*, which spoke of the plight of labor in the face of the nineteenth-century industrial revolution. "You have been a point person for this administration on AI issues," said Douthat, "and I'm curious. . . . There are people who think, essentially, that we are getting a profound economic revolution driven by AI while you guys are in office. . . . First, how likely do you think that is? . . . How much do you worry about the potential downsides of AI, the cultural scale, the way human beings respond to a sense of their own obsolescence?"

Vance answered, "On the obsolescence point, I think the history of tech and innovation is that while it does cause job disruptions, it more often facilitates human productivity as opposed to replacing human workers. The example I always give is of the bank teller; in the 1970s there were stark predictions of . . . hundreds of thousands of bank tellers going out of a job. . . . What actually happened is we have more bank tellers today than we did when the ATM was created, but they're doing slightly different work, more productive."

Douthat then said, "Just to be clear, that is a prediction of, by the standards of the predictions people are making, a relatively slow pace of change, I think, right?"

Vance responded, "Well, I think it's a relatively slow pace of change, but I think on the economic side, the main concern I have with AI, it's not the obsolescence, it's not people losing their jobs en masse. *You hear about truck drivers, for example. I think what might actually happen is truck drivers are able to work more efficient hours, they'll be able to get a little more sleep, but they're doing much more of the last mile of delivery than staring at a highway for thirteen hours a day, so they're both safer, they're able to get higher wages*" (italics mine).

If this sounds familiar, that's because it is. This is the pitch of companies like Aurora, who have no idea what it's like to be a trucker, what creates trucking culture, what makes the job attractive, why truckers *like to be on the road*, or why maybe the job is not just about "staring at a highway for thirteen hours a day."

With all due respect to the vice president, he's being hoodwinked by ad copy from people trying to sell a load of crap to those who don't know any better.

Aurora might not be there yet, but Gatik AI, another player in the autonomous-truck market, is coming for the "last mile," even though the last mile is held out by people like Vance as truckers' last chance to remain behind the wheel. Gatik AI has already put its smaller, last-mile delivery trucks to work for the Canadian grocery-store giant Loblaws,[28] and in March 2025 the firm announced a major production deal with Isuzu to produce these smaller trucks at scale.[29]

As for the higher wages Vice President Vance predicted, I highly doubt we will see them. The replacement job that Aurora and the gang have in mind for long-haul truckers, beyond the marginal remote support specialist, is that of yard jockey, which involves hooking up RoboTrucks to trailers in yards and getting them ready to go. There will be far fewer of these positions than Vance imagines. If you ask long-haul truckers who have been in the business a long time to list the reasons why they signed up to be truckers, hanging out in one location all day hooking and unhooking trailers will not be on the list. Almost everyone who gets into trucking will tell you that part of the reason was to get away from being watched or micromanaged in an office, factory, or job site. The autonomous-vehicle industry gives away how little it understands its targets by insinuating that being in a yard or office all day is a trucker's dream job.

I don't expect the vice president to hang out at truck stops, talking to old road dogs like me, but I do expect him not to try and sell me someone else's bullshit, and that is exactly what he is doing in this interview with Douthat.

A phenomenon identified in many material-economy blue-collar jobs is the reality of who actually replaces workers thought to be made extinct by automation. More often than not, before the robots get our jobs, insourced labor does. This pattern is repeating in trucking, and to his credit, Vice President Vance acknowledged as much in a July 2025 tweet where he got most of the story correct: "All of the fear about AI causing mass unemployment serves to distract from the very real threat of continued job loss through dumb trade and immigration policies. President Trump's approach corrects this broken dependence on globalization: strike better trade deals, promote American exports, fix our immigration system, and invest in making workers more productive."[30]

I would submit to Vice President Vance and President Trump that if they want to make truckers more productive, putting them out to pasture is not the answer. They need to understand that truckers' seeming lack of productivity is mostly a problem created by our customers holding us up, arcane hours-of-service regulations enforced by demoralizing and unnecessary surveillance technology, and a system that keeps churning out the good drivers and flooding the zone with immigrants and domestic new guys who are not trained well and whom the system is explicitly set up to spit out. These are human, policy, economic, and organizational problems that robot drivers do not fix—unless, that is, the likes of Aurora and their lobbyists somehow find a way to make sure their robots don't sit at docks all day, a feat the vast majority of trucking companies and their supposed representative associations have been unable to pull off for decades.

Pulling drivers out of trucks is not only going to affect truckers and their families. How many truck stops that serve drivers everything that humans need out on the road, from food to showers to laundry services, are going to go out of business? What about the accountants and other back-end human-resources staff at trucking companies?

This concern was brought up in a somewhat infamous interview by Joe Rogan with Democratic presidential contender Andrew Yang in 2019. As far as I'm aware, Yang is the biggest-name member of the ruling class to express any concern for these workers, spread all across the country and often in small towns that are already short on employment opportunities. Mr. Yang describes the approach of artificial intelligence and automation as the "Fourth Industrial Revolution," which he claims will look nothing like previous industrial revolutions.[31] Buggy makers will not easily transition to making cars. Nearly everything will be automated, including many knowledge economy jobs, and much of what can't be has already been outsourced overseas.

Yang may have been the earliest to point this out, but from the opposite side of America's political spectrum Tucker Carlson also has concerns about the fate of America's truckers. In an interview conducted the same year as Yang's appearance on Rogan, Carlson told the Daily Wire's Ben Shapiro, "If I were president . . . we're not letting driverless trucks on the road, period. . . . Driving for a living is the single most common job for high school-educated men. . . . I don't want to put ten million men out of work because you're going to kill ten million families. . . . The social cost of eliminating those jobs in a five-year or ten-year span is not sustainable."[32]

Carlson may have been a little off on the number of truckers, but when you include all those truck-stop employees and other workers who service human truck drivers, perhaps ten million is close to the mark. Many in the political commentariat have been bleating about the rise of populism across the West since Brexit or the Yellow Vests or the election of President Trump in 2016. I wonder if these same commentators know what's coming politically when millions of truckers, support-services staff, and their families start seeing major deprivation.

It's one thing for the autonomous companies to receive skepticism from the likes of me or my fellow drivers, or from political operators like Yang and commentators like Carlson, but what about all those investors in Aurora? Surely someone besides my lonely self must be casting a critical eye on Aurora's claims?

One such firm is Bleecker Street Research, which released quite an interesting report on Aurora as an investment opportunity in May 2025. Obviously, the

Bleecker Streeters are coming at this from a financial angle, rather than worrying about truckers' jobs or highway safety, but their criticisms are worth considering. The Bleecker Street Research report states:

- Aurora is a pre-revenue autonomous trucking company recently worth $12 billion.
- Aurora recently completed its "driver-out" milestone, completing a commercial freight route between Dallas and Houston fully autonomously.
- While Aurora has called this a "commercialization event," it really exhibited how far behind the company is on a viable business model, and how unlikely it is that Aurora can scale the way it currently plans to.
- Our research revealed that PACCAR, a key Aurora partner and supplier that made the Peterbilt truck that Aurora modified, was apparently not on board with the company removing the safety driver.
- A PACCAR representative said, "We will not agree to commercialize anything that is not proven to be super safe. *We're not there yet*" (italics mine).
- Aurora claims that it will be able to scale to 10,000+ revenue generating autonomous trucks by the end of 2027, but a senior executive at its other OEM partner, Volvo, told us mass producing trucks in 2027 is out of the question: 2030 is more likely.
- Meanwhile, we believe Aurora will need $2–3 billion just to contemplate reaching commercial scale, well north of the ~$750 million Aurora claims to require now.[33]

Not exactly a done deal, eh?

Aurora knows how to do PR really well, however. Shrewdly gauging the zeitgeist, it has made the bold claim that its trucks will be better for the environment than those operated by humans. It's a smart marketing move, given that trucks and the people who drive them have been demonized for decades for belching black smoke from their diesel engines—even though we have been subject to twenty years of emission-control mandates that have removed all that soot. And never mind the fact that until our nationwide electrical grid and generating capacity are increased by several orders of magnitude, Aurora's trucks will run on diesel, too. Which will come first, the electric trucks or the electric drivers?

In making this claim about reduced emissions, Aurora cites the very things that are already the bane of truckers' existence: hours-of-service regulations and traffic—two things that are mostly out of our control, though these problems could be dealt with if truckers had more control over their own scheduling. But again, this is something a previous tech imposition worked to take away from us.[34]

What to do and to say about all this? The robot trucks are here, at least in the very early, bleeding-edge stage. Further development and implementation will have to take many other factors into consideration besides the technology itself. For instance, will various state regulators allow these trucks on their highways if voters do not approve? The Teamsters and other groups are already trying to pass state-level bills to require a human safety driver in these trucks at all times, which obviates the whole point of the enterprise. While I sort of get where the Teamsters are coming from with respect to safety, will it really be safe? Driving can already be something of a boring activity, at least for some people; will a safety driver be able to stay awake with even fewer tasks to interest him?

In Isaac Asimov's short story "The Evitable Conflict," which treats the issue of machines taking over human tasks, a character observes that "the kind of person who would be happy to ride back and forth without doing anything for nine years would be precisely the person least capable of coping with an emergency in the tenth."[35]

Buttressing this point, Karen Levy cites a number of studies that show—surprise, surprise—that the less a driver is involved with operating any vehicle, the more he begins to experience "skill atrophy" and "cognitive slowdown." We also know from a NHTSA study that in the event of an emergency, a driver babysitting an autonomous truck can take up to a full seventeen seconds to regain control of the vehicle.[36] Seventeen seconds is a long time at highway speed; who wants to be responsible for a robot if it takes that long to intervene? Might as well just drive yourself.

The reliability promised by the autonomous-systems developers may finally be duked out in court. I am told by a lifelong trucking-insurance-industry pro that ambulance-chasing trial lawyers are waiting for an opportunity to represent clients who have been involved in a collision with one of these vehicles, given the amount of money backing the companies building them. Who will be at fault? Whose insurance will pay the doubtless very large settlement or award? The autonomous-system company? The truck manufacturer? The trucking company? Imagine being the safety driver here, if one were required: all eyes would be on you.

I never imagined that I'd be rooting for the ambulance chasers, but these are strange times indeed.

Though it appears that the autonomous industry still has a number of hurdles to negotiate before it takes over certain parts of trucking, much less all of it, the industry is well financed and determined to strike it rich. With the likes of Congressman Fong working hard to make sure other elected representatives are barred from legislating any oversight on how these trucks are deployed, and the media seemingly in thrall to every new and shiny piece of technology regardless of consequence, society is being primed for RoboTrucks—regardless of any objections lodged by truckers or the citizenry at large.

Again, what to do?

In an interview with me, Matthew Crawford made a suggestion that echoes across time and back to those who were replaced before us: "I think we need to rehabilitate the term 'Luddite' as someone with a clear-sighted grasp of the political economy that stands behind automation and has enough spirit to make a claim on his own behalf for his livelihood and way of life."

The Luddites have been incorrectly remembered by history as knuckle draggers who were against technology as a whole and whose crusade during the first Industrial Revolution, of the early nineteenth century in the north of England, was mere terrorism along the lines of modern ne'er-do-wells like Ted Kaczynski. Of course, history is written by the victors. The truth is that the Luddites were not just smashing looms without reason.

In his book *Rebels Against the Future: The Luddites and Their War on the Industrial Revolution; Lessons for the Computer Age*, tech skeptic and Cornell-trained social critic Kirkpatrick Sale took a deep dive into the lives of those textile workers who were being supplanted by the advent of steam technology and found that they were not merely fighting for their jobs. Rather, "the workers' grievance was not just about the machinery . . . but what that machinery stood for: the palpable, daily evidence of their having to succumb to forces beyond their control, beyond their power even to influence much, that were taking away their livelihoods and transforming their lives."[37] The Luddites practiced a trade requiring a certain level of skill and craftsmanship and had developed a culture over many decades that became the foundation of rich communities—communities then erased by steam-driven factories.

Truckers, having shared a craft and work culture developed over many decades, are approaching a similar tipping point. Even if the autonomous trucks only come for the "middle-mile" jobs at first, and even if that takes a few more years to happen, such a development will unemploy hundreds of thousands of drivers, who will then fan out into those parts of the trucking industry where automation, for whatever reason, cannot yet be implemented. Those drivers will unintentionally exert downward wage pressure, and given the enormous influence of the general freight market on everyone else's wage or rate floor, we are likely to face another wage spiral in trucking like that seen in the years after deregulation. As older drivers take this as a signal to exit, the craft of trucking, and more especially its distinctive culture, will be further eroded.

Let's say that in some medium- to long-term timeline, after the autonomous companies work out the kinks in their system, many truckers are made extinct and rendered obsolete. Should the industry or the government make plans to give truckers a golden parachute for all the hard work they have done to keep society moving? Should truckers be offered taxpayer-subsidized retraining or reeducation programs? Seems only fair, given the decades of government handouts that brought so many people into trucking in the first place. Should we make Kodiak and Aurora and Plus AI pay for it all? They will, after all, be the beneficiaries of truckers' extinction, and they will continue to make profits through their subscription services long after we are gone.

Or maybe—just maybe—they will find themselves spending a ton of money repairing trucks that have been subject to a twenty-first-century version of the Luddites' smashing of the looms.

9

The Truck Stops of Babel

All-night country music keeps 'em going
And Will and Sonny keep on moving on
A good hot cup of coffee is waiting up ahead
And the rhythm of the highway hums along

—Merle Haggard and The Strangers, "Movin' On"

L eonard, let him take the bear!"
Such was the command of my mother to my father when I was five years old, and thus began my earliest memory of going trucking with my Old Man. He was working for an outfit on the north side of Toronto called Concord Transportation and had stopped at our townhouse in Beamsville, Ontario, where we had recently moved in a search for cheaper digs. The townhouse complex in Beamsville was home to a number of truckers, many of them friends of my Dad—Mark "Mouse" Williams, Hank VanDerScheer, Al Deveaux, Bill Bentley—and there was a guy around the corner who worked for a Maritimes-based outfit who always parked on the street as well. It was a good spot to live: cheap, and right off

A trucking family: Mom and my little sister Rebecca pose with the Old Man's R Model, Stoney Creek, Ontario, 1982.

the Queen Elizabeth Highway between the Greater Toronto Area and the two main border crossings into the United States along the Niagara River. Many a trucker lived in Beamsville and many still do to this day.

Dad had just stopped in to have dinner. He was planning to carry his load to the States, sleep somewhere along the way to bypass the morning traffic at the Peace Bridge in to Buffalo, and unload on time in Cleveland so as to get a back-load the same day. There was a school holiday or "professional development" day for the teachers at my school, so there was no reason for me to show up for my first-grade class. Let's go trucking with Dad. Cool!

While my father was eating and considering the matter of taking me with him, I went upstairs to retrieve my teddy bear to bring along for the trip. When Dad saw me holding it in the entrance to the kitchen, he exclaimed, "Big boys don't need teddy bears to go trucking!" My Mother won that argument. The bear and I hopped into the Freightliner my Dad had parked in front of our townhouse, and away we went to Cleveland, hooked onto a flatbed outfitted with a rack and tarp kit, which is like a modern version of an old covered wagon, except we were loaded with steel instead of settlers.

At some point in the course of the evening the Old Man cleared customs and made part of the trip along Interstate 90 between Buffalo and Erie before climbing in the bunk with me and going to sleep himself. I remember waking up to the truck running down the road and hopping into the passenger seat (with my teddy bear), taking in the scenery along the Interstate. Dad had out his collection of country music tapes (remember those?) and was cycling between George Jones, Hank Williams Jr., C. W. McCall, and Waylon Jennings. The only interruption to the music and Dad's talking was the crackle of other truckers on the CB radio. Not long after I woke up, my Old Man recognized another trucker going in the opposite direction. I don't remember the exact verbiage, but the two of them made plans to meet for breakfast at a truck stop Dad had already passed. He simply got off at the next exit, pulled a U-turn, and headed back to meet his colleague. This was how camaraderie was maintained in those days, and to hell with schedules imposed on the highway loner.

For a five-year old kid in 1984 who didn't get out much, it was all simply amazing. My Dad had reached through that CB radio and talked to another man of similar stature, and we went into a truck stop where nice ladies who looked like my Mom brought me pancakes while my Dad and his friend drank coffee and talked shop. If there was such a thing as little boy heaven, I was right in the middle of it.

We made it to Cleveland later that day, and I remember the Old Man getting into some kind of shouting match with the crane operators over unloading the steel. We were there for a while, but eventually the steel was unloaded and my Dad received backload orders to go to a town in Western Pennsylvania called Zelienople, where there was some kind of refractory plant that made firebrick for lining the blast furnaces at steel mills. I'll never forget that plant; the shipping guy who drove the forklift offered me donuts. Pancakes and donuts all in the same day, and I got to hang out with Dad in his rig! The reader will understand why this memory is burned into my mind and vividly recalled forty-two years later.

About a decade after these first-grade adventures with my Old Man, I took part-time jobs at a local truck stop, The Fifth Wheel in Grimsby, Ontario. I mopped floors in the restaurant, cleaned the truckers' showers in the basement, and worked out at the fuel pumps, where I believe I was one of the last of the "diesel jockeys" who would fuel up a trucker's ride for him before that job became extinct. Who wants to pay for someone to pump fuel? That cuts into the margins! Let the customer do it himself.

Popping hoods, checking oil, and climbing up to wash the windows of these guys who were just like my Dad was a good way to kill time in the afternoons and keep me out of trouble after school. I also learned about the varied cultural inclinations of some of the truckers who had rolled into the Fifth Wheel from far away. The Southerners who hauled Florida orange juice to Toronto were a hoot. Seeing one of them chew tobacco and spit it into a coffee can between the seats when I hopped up on the steps is another memory I won't soon forget, though at the time I wished I could have. We also had a lot of Frenchmen fuel up, and like my experience loading steel on the afternoon shift with the Paddock boys at Stelco, my job at the Fifth Wheel exposed me to Québécois culture in a way that my French teachers at school could never have done.

At one point there was a strip joint next door to the Fifth Wheel called The Hunt Club. Though it was slightly before my time, the way some truckers discussed the place, it must have been a happening location. That was before smartphones and hookup apps eliminated the in-person and collective nature of admiring the fairer sex at a bar, not to mention the opportunity to interact with a member thereof without the intermediation of tech companies.

After I got into trucking I often found myself at the Ten Acre Truckstop in Belleville, Ontario, a two-hour drive east of Toronto along Highway 401, and at one time one of the busiest truck stops in Canada. I remember the first time I pulled into the Ten Acre. I was on my way back to Hamilton and was going to meet my buddy Wig to switch trailers, turn around with another load, and head back east to Québec. While I was waiting for Wig I had time to go inside and get a shower and something to eat. Then another scene was burned into my young mind.

The Ten Acre was named for its massive parking lot. It could accommodate what seemed like hundreds of rigs, especially if you passed by on a cold winter night and saw all the running lights left on by the truckers inside getting a feed. The Ten Acre had a lot of pull-through parking places that were perfect for a Super B-Train, or "Super B" if you're a trucker from out west. Super Bs are a lot easier to park by driving in a straight line rolling forward than by backing up, and thus the Ten Acre, with its massive parking lot, seemed perfectly designed for the Frenchmen hauling lumber or steel on flatbed B-trains. And Frenchmen were definitely the most numerous among the clientele of that truck stop.

Walking into the dining room that first time was almost a psychedelic experience. The Frenchmen, loud and garrulous, sat around huge round tables that could seat eight to ten at a time. Barrel-chested, often sporting huge "duster" mustaches like my Dad's, and telling stories in their own tongue, they cut an imposing scene for a young Anglophone like me. The waitresses lapped it up—most of them spoke French, because of course, why wouldn't they? Sex sold at those big round tables. Tight jeans or leather pants and tops to match: I bet those girls made a fortune in tips from us truckers. The only dudes who worked at the Ten Acre were in the kitchen or out at the fuel island. The scene was the same another couple hundred miles east at the end of the 401, where it becomes Autoroute 20. Real's was the big truck stop on the Ontario side of the border with Québec and I was advised by an older trucker to call in: "The food is alright and the scenery ain't bad either."

As I progressed in my career and went farther afield, to the north and west of Canada, south into the United States, or throughout the lands Down Under, I had the distinct pleasure of catching the last days of a distinctive truck-stop culture. Truck stops comprised a combination of what sociologists call second and third places. The first "place" is home, the second is work, and the third is where people gather—bars, churches, or anywhere else—for convivial human connection. The particular kind of third place formed by truck stops was imbued with a type of working-class aesthetic that shares something in common with military mess halls and perhaps a more masculine approach to the classic American diner. They had their local flavor, too. You heard almost nothing but French at a place like Real's, and you felt like you were pretty far out in the woods at the old Tower Hill truck stop in Ignace, Ontario. No wonder you probably never heard of it.

Truck stops have always played an important role in the industry, and not merely as a place to park, get something to eat, and then go to bed, though that strictly utilitarian vibe is sadly becoming the norm today. Many of the larger stops, especially in the United States, offer a shop facility for mechanical repairs, a tire bay, laundry, and showers; some even have barber shops. The largest truck stop in the world, the Iowa 80 Truckstop in Walcott, Iowa, is a massive complex akin to a shopping mall. It features a huge chrome and accessories shop, a chiropractor, a movie theater, and, next door, a trucking museum. The Iowa 80 guys have locations across the Midwest and hold an annual "Truckers Jamboree"—more or less a truck show—in their multi-acre parking lot. The Iowa 80 Truckstop has never been closed since first opening its doors in 1964.

There's another massive truck-stop complex in Oregon that has been around since 1958. Jubitz, as it is called, sits just south of the Columbia River and right off Interstate 5. It was a pioneer in providing services to truckers. Founder Monroe "Moe" Jubitz—a southpaw pitcher for Yale University in the late 1930s who was recruited by the Yankees and Red Sox—was an early adopter of road-side billboards. He also pioneered a useful concept that is less annoying than billboards but has been abandoned by many businesses today: actually listening to his customers.[1]

Hearkening back to the days of honky-tonks and the working man's need for a beer at the end of a long day, Jubitz still has a bar on site called the Ponderosa Lounge where you can often find concerts by country bands. Having a bar on site for truckers might sound "dangerous" in that you don't want truckers to hit the road drunk, but if you are at the truck stop at all it usually means you're going to bed; I would invite the utilitarians and puritans to supply their own grocery stores if they believe otherwise.

I've also heard whispers of something referred to as the "Jubitz Girls," but that may have been before my time behind the wheel. Most of the corporate chain truck stops I've ever been to don't have a bar, much less anything in the way of attractive females—not even of the sort I used to see at Real's or the Ten Acre. Speaking of the Ten Acre, it has since been sold and the restaurant turned into one of these stale and gray corporate slop joints, the International House of Pancakes, whose signature menu item is as deficient in nutrition and taste as the restaurant is of character. I wonder if the Frenchmen still stop there.

My own life has been influenced greatly by an old honky-tonk that was located conveniently next door to a truck stop. It's gone now, like so many of the people and relationships it spawned over the years.

Country Bob's was a lively and happening joint located next to the old Travel Port truck stop along US Route 11 on the south side of Binghamton, New York. It closed not long after the proprietor, a Tennessean named Robert "Bob" Story, was killed in an accident on September 11, 2001, when one of the steer tires on the dump truck he was driving let go. Bob's was a legend in the Northeastern United States. Binghamton sits at the intersection of a couple of important routes: Interstate 81 runs south into Pennsylvania and then through Appalachia, and north to the Thousand Islands, where it crosses into Canada. New York Route 17, now being upgraded to Interstate 86, comes in from the west, carrying traffic from Western New York, along with an awful lot of traffic from Canada via the border crossings at Buffalo and Lewiston, New York. Most truck traffic going from the Toronto area to New York City or New Jersey avoids paying the high tolls on the New York State Thruway by taking Route 17 instead.

Back in the day, drivers from the "Golden Horseshoe" area of Ontario—the main manufacturing base of Canada, which wraps around the western edge of Lake Ontario, or what is now called the GTA, or Greater Toronto Area—would run (or try to run) three trips a week back and forth to the Greater New York City and New Jersey area. More often than not this involved delays necessitating overnighting it directly to Jersey and then unloading and reloading before heading back home. Many a driver was pretty cooked by the time he got to "Bingo" on the way back and would call into the Travel Port to park. Then he would head next door to Bob's for a feed—and in the case of some drivers, more than a few beers. Back before Qualcomms and cell phones, when communication was a bit more difficult, Bob's served as a relay station for messages. Regulars could leave important communications for other drivers to pick up there, be it about business, loads, drivers who needed assistance, or perhaps notes of a personal nature.

Country Bob's was also well known by Binghamton locals. Bob Story was a performing musician and hosted bands at his bar, which also served dinners, had pool tables, and offered the 1980s-era fixture of a mechanical bull. Between the somewhat exotic Canadian truckers, various bands, and the other travelers and weirdos who hung out at Bob's, it was an attractive spot for the people who live in the hills and valleys of northern Appalachia that surround Binghamton. One of those who hung out at Bob's was a young lady named Robin. She eventually became Dad's second wife and the mother of my little brother Ben and second sister Logan. My first visit to Country Bob's wasn't with Dad, unfortunately, but rather in the car with Mom. Realizing her marriage was in peril, she had tried to chase Dad down by driving all the way to Binghamton from our home in Canada with my nine-year-old sister Rebecca and me in tow. Mom, having found Dad's rig behind the Travel Port parked and locked, with Dad already gone and hanging out with Robin somewhere, scribbled a last-ditch message to him in lipstick on the driver's-side window. Alas, her efforts were doomed, as was the relationship.

Dad in front of one of
Uncle Bruce's logging trucks,
Armstrong, Ontario, 1988.

Bob's surely ended and started a number of relationships; hell, if it weren't for Bob's I might not have had two of my three siblings. In any case, these days several deplorable developments have destroyed the truck stop's status as a valuable "third place" where working men and women, often far away from home and putting in twice as many hours as the average worker, can congregate.

Since Bob Story died in 2001, we have seen digital technology step in to mediate many human interactions. Truckers are not immune to this trend, no matter how old school many of us may claim to be. One of my colleagues, someone I consider an old-school trucker, has studied trucking as a culture, among his many other intellectual pursuits. I love listening to owner-operator Chris Thomas of Morehead, Kentucky, talk, so let's hear him at length:

When I first started trucking, Travel Centers of America was a relatively new chain operating where many old truckers referred to as the "old Union 76" truck stop. Pilot had recently acquired the failed Williams Travel Centers. Petro and Flying J were still independently owned chains. The Iron Skillet and Country Market buffets often lavished truckers with Friday night prime rib specials. Love's was an up-and-coming operator with a much smaller footprint than they currently have. Wilco-Hess was still operating along the Atlantic Coast. Iowa 80 was much smaller than it is today. And many small independent truck stops operated under the NATSO banner or AmBest coalition.

My own neck of the woods was still home to a popular truck stop that fed many truckers for nearly forty years, Smokey Valley Truck Stop in Olive Hill, Kentucky. Ms. Noble in Corinth, Kentucky, was only in her late seventies and operating Noble's Truck Stop, [which] she had started along with her husband in the 1950s at another location before moving out by the Interstate. The old Monteagle truck stop was filled with the old outlaw type of truckers, who never got arrested, but always got the loads there. All of these are now gone or owned by other operators. . . .

I've enjoyed my life on the road, and I've enjoyed many stayovers at these stops, hearing many tales and stories from old hands at the trucker's counter. And although the "Truckers Only" signs are pretty much gone, you can occasionally catch some of the feel of the old days while having supper at the large round table at Dysart's in Hermon, Maine, or hear a few yarns at the counter of the Little Nashville Truck Stop in Illinois. I rarely passed Cochran's Travel Center in Ringgold, Georgia, when it was open; the smoked chicken wings were out of this world. I was in the Doswell Truck Stop in Virginia having breakfast with a Celadon owner-operator when he learned they were shutting the doors. In Trucker's World countless truckers were drinking a little too much in the little pub in the back while on a reset in Ohio. Little America, Wyoming, is still there servicing some of the toughest truckers out there. If you drive I-80 regularly in the winter, don't let anyone tell you it's easy work. I had a home away from home and made many friends during my years of staying night after night at Buch's Truck Stop in Steubenville, Ohio, working a long-term project.

New players too have come along. The Compass Travel Plaza in Demotte, Indiana, has been a great place to stop in for a break. And a few have tried and already sold out to chains, like the real nice one on the east side of Mankato, Minnesota, that's now a TA stop. These operators have an opportunity to provide great service and quality over some of the existing corporate-run chains, but it isn't easy. Truckers today are budget conscious more so than ever before, and margins are tight for these costly operations.

Truck stops are representative of the driving population, which is ever changing. Over time we've lost many of the sitdowns of smaller operators, replaced for the fast-paced by come-and-go stops like QT, KwikTrip, 7-Eleven, Raceway, and the list goes on. Large chains have been able to remain in business through their access to capital and economy of scale. Paid parking is becoming more and more prevalent than it was twenty years ago, although it's always existed in busy metro areas where parking was scarce. Trucking habits have changed, in part due to the nature of humanity. Just like business will chase low prices, humans do too. So they opt for in-cab meals supplied by groceries from large chain stores, and the modern convenience of technology has replaced the need for getting out of the truck for socialization and entertainment. Many small operators are struggling to stay in the game, and I'd imagine just as we are seeing the failure of carriers from the COVID surge in trucking, we'll see some truck-stop operators fail in the future. Nothing lasts forever it seems.

Chris highlights an interesting question about what's become of the social aspect of truck stops. Has the culprit been consolidation, the loss of honky-tonks like Country Bob's to "fast truck stops" that have fewer parking spots and only serve fast food, or is it the technology that connects us to home or Facebook or Tinder (or Grindr) and takes our attention away from our fellow drivers in the lot, or perhaps that other lone traveler sipping coffee at the counter of one of the few places still open late? Yes, even the Open All Night nature of many truck stops has been interrupted, between electronic logging devices rigidly enforcing the schedules of many truckers and COVID killing off late-night hours for nearly every type of public-facing business.

The ELD mandate has fundamentally changed truck stops, and the working lives of truckers who patronize them, for the worse. Many of the newcomers who were swept into the industry were not raised in trucking, or North American culture in general, and do not understand the etiquette and standards of behavior—the codes and unwritten rules that govern truckers' interactions at the truck stop. Combined with the inescapable Eye of Sauron the ELD represents, this makes for regular unpleasant experiences for professional drivers.

One of the more frequent and maddening of these is the practice of inconsiderate ignoramuses taking their mandated thirty-minute break on the fuel islands where drivers fuel up their rigs. These guys pull up, start fueling, and then set their ELD to the "off-duty" line, which means they must stay there, even if fueling a big truck only takes about ten minutes. Given that many truck stops have long lines of trucks waiting to fuel up during certain times of day, this is massively inconsiderate and has been the subject of numerous social media videos. Unfortunately, truck-stop operators haven't done much in the way of policing this practice, other than to put up signs asking these drivers, some of whom can't read English anyway, to fuel and move ASAP. Perhaps they need to hire bouncers.

While some of the recent arrivals are leaving their trucks in the middle of the fuel island for their half-hour break, they head into the washrooms, where another culture clash takes place, much to the consternation of the locals. In most restrooms, the idea is that you do your business, wash your hands in the sink, and carry on. Any further washing is expected to take place in the showers, which are available for a small fee at most chain and larger truck stops. Most truckers use frequent-fueler loyalty cards and get their showers for free.

This is not the case for those truckers whose cultures dictate that they must always be washing their feet. Instead of paying for a shower, many of these guys, utterly oblivious to the new culture in which they have chosen to live, wash their feet in public sinks. One could argue about the cleanliness of this practice and whether it is a health hazard or not, but other people who use these same facilities *really, really, REALLY* don't like it. Another major problem, at least with some of our friends from India, whose prime minister only a decade ago admonished his population to use the hundred and ten million public toilets the Indian government had just built, is that certain of their bathroom practices are legitimately a biological hazard.[2]

In parts of India where toilet paper—indeed, any plumbing at all—is a luxury item unavailable to the masses, many people do their business wherever they can, be it in a field or an alley, and they use disposable water bottles in combination with their hands to clean up the mess. Unfortunately, some of these practices continue in North America, even with the ready availability of toilet paper and a flush toilet.

In a recent viral video, a trucker named Wolfgang Wendland explains why this is a problem for everyone else expected to use public facilities:

I am so tired of walking into a men's room at a truck stop, and sitting down in a stall and having somebody beside me. . . . It sounds like they're sticking their hand in the toilet bowl. . . . They'll actually flush the toilet, stick their hand in it, if they don't have a bottle of water readily available, and they'll do this right here with the water to rinse themselves off, if you know what I mean. But if they have a bottle of water, that's when it gets really nasty and vile. They'll pour the bottle of water out and they'll do this with their hand right here. . . . You can just imagine. . . . That's how they clean themselves because for religious purposes I guess they're not allowed to use toilet paper. The problem with that is that water splashes everywhere. . . . It goes over top of the stall, on the toilet, on the ground, the handle, the door itself. It's an actual biohazard, and those same guys will get out and go to the sink and instead of washing their hands—no, they don't do that—they wash their feet in the sink.

I am appalled that we have gotten to a point where this is considered common practice. . . . About three or four weeks ago I was at a Flying J, and there was me, a little boy, his daddy, and a guy washing his feet in the sink . . . and the little boy said, "Daddy, why is that guy washing his feet in the sink?" And he says, "Oh son, those are just some nasty truck drivers, that's just what they do. I know it's filthy, that's why we don't like stopping at truck stops." . . . Maybe that little boy would have never wanted to become a truck driver, but I promise you one thing, if he ever thought about becoming a truck driver, that thought has now left his mind completely. . . . This is a whole different level, this is not about religious freedom, this is a biohazard. . . . I genuinely think the only thing nastier than a truck-stop parking lot is a truck-stop bathroom.[3]

When I drove logging trucks, or was hauling road trains in Outback Australia, options were extremely limited for facilities. I always carried my own toilet paper and a shovel and would walk out in the woods or the desert, far away from the road and out of sight, to do my business—admittedly caveman style and not to everyone's taste. That said, and to be perfectly honest, I'd prefer that to the average truck-stop toilet in 2026.

I will admit that truck-stop parking lots have not always been the cleanest places, even before the industry was flooded with insourced labor. Tales of "piss jugs" have become memes, lampooned in TV shows like *Trailer Park Boys*. But the washing of feet in sinks, and other situations described by Wendland, are the result of immigration policies that have forced working-class Americans not only to compete with Third World wage expectations but also to witness and tolerate cultural practices that are, well, not ours. Nor are they healthy.

You will never hear about any of that in the media, however. Instead, journalists and commentators have regaled their readers for a few years now with tales of the rising phenomenon of the *dhaba*, a term from India that means "roadside restaurant." With the increasing presence of Punjabi truckers in North America, it only makes sense that entrepreneurial enterprises would step up to feed them dishes from their own culture. That's perfectly fine. Who would complain about that? What rubs many a local trucker the wrong way, however, is the death of the small roadside American truck stop that serves home-cooked meals. These have slowly gone the way of the dodo, replaced by really terrible fast-food joints.[4]

Friend and fellow Road Warrior Wes Harman has this to say about recent developments in truck-stop culture:

On the heels of the rise of app culture came the Canadian experiment with importing foreign labor to take trucking jobs for a fraction of the compensation enjoyed/expected by native Canadian drivers. In less than a decade the native-born Canadian trucker has become a thing of the past as Indian Sikhs supplanted them from the industry.

As the Canadian experience began to be duplicated in the USA, the trends noted by Canadian truckers began to appear here too, and for the same reason (augmented by a massive influx of East African immigrants). The immigrant driver simply has no investment in the country. He is here to make money to send back to his home country, so adopting local norms or learning the language aren't prioritized . . . and are in fact considered unimportant as they do not contribute to his ability to make his remittance money. As a result, bathroom floors become littered every morning with discarded water bottles and toilet tissue resulting from Muslim drivers performing their morning pre-prayer ablutions (*wudu*). Parking lots become littered with trash, urine jugs, and bags of feces despite a profusion of trash cans close at hand. None of this is to say the pre-labor-dumping American or Canadian trucker was the most fastidious and exacting of citizens where littering was concerned, but old-timers will attest it is much worse now.

Another example of the negative effect of immigrant drivers can be summed up by recent developments at The Woodshed truck stop in Big Cabin, Oklahoma, along I-44. The Woodshed was an institution among truckers. A big lot, plenty of fuel lanes, and a quality twenty-four-hour diner. In 2024, a dhaba opened in an adjacent building. As a result the stop began attracting a huge transient population of immigrant drivers who would park in their haphazard fashion and walk next door to the Indian restaurant for dinner. As native-born drivers were supplanted, the cafe reduced its hours and eventually closed for business. Meanwhile the dhaba is thriving. It's not only native-born drivers whose livelihoods are disrupted by the ongoing influx of immigrant drivers. It's blameless American establishments having their profit centers destroyed. Big Cabin isn't a large town; a cook or waitress isn't going to be able to just go out and replace a well-paying job immediately.

A related underdiscussed problem with truck stops is the low-speed and high-cost collisions that take place in the parking lots. People who were handed their CDL via basement-tier truck-driving schools, or maybe through the bribery scams that plague state DMVs across the country, are often not trained to navigate tight parking spots competently, especially those that require a driver to back in.

My friend Mike Lombard, who was an owner-operator with Warren Transport for some time, experienced this firsthand:

I was parked at the Love's in Clive, Iowa, just outside of Des Moines, back in May of 2023. I had just finished exercising outside of the truck and was debating whether to shower or eat first, and luckily I made the decision to eat. I was sitting in the bunk with the curtains open just enough to let a little sun glare in when all of a sudden the truck started moving and I heard a crunching sound.

I came out of the truck and I was steaming, absolutely blew my lid. I owned this truck, took pride in it, it's how I earned an income. What set me off was the gentleman who backed into me. As he came back to investigate he kind of shrugged as if to say "whoopsie" and he didn't speak English.

I had to carry on with the load, all the way up to Thunder Bay, Ontario, even though the front corner of my truck was smashed to pieces; it was still drivable, but I had no front left headlight or signals, which is a DOT violation.

I brought the truck home to a body shop in Texas on May 22, and by the time they could get parts and get it out the door it was June 30, and cost fourteen grand. It took until November to recoup that and my lost wages from the insurance company. In the back and forth with incident reports and other paperwork to the insurance companies, I came to find out the guy was from Bosnia.

Over and above the *Mad Max*–like environment in the parking lot, imagine what it's like to work at a truck stop in 2026, where a number of your customers no longer even speak your language, where you have to wear a chemical suit to clean the bathrooms, and where, because of the regimentation forced on truckers by the ELD, the restaurants are a ghost town during the day. So much for the tips one could expect as a waitress when guys like my Dad would stop whenever they felt like it—and when they actually had a few bucks to spare.

The declining number of food options and increasing number of biohazards brought about by corporate greed are not the only challenges truckers face at one of the few institutions where they can park for the night; the parking itself may or may not even be available. The United States and Canada have a serious shortage of publicly available truck parking. Many truck stops therefore fill up much earlier than they did before the ELD mandate, leaving many truckers with few options to find a parking spot, especially if they arrive later in the evenings. A 2019 survey by the American Transportation Research Institute found that 98 percent of drivers regularly experience difficulty finding safe parking, which is not surprising given that there is only one available parking spot, be it at a truck stop or public rest area, for every eleven trucks on the road.[5]

Now that most OTR truckers are racing the clock to try and find a place to park when their time runs out, the preexisting truck-parking shortage has spawned a weird, new, and increasingly successful business, a sort of AirBnB app for truckers to find parking in places with available pavement.

Evan Shelley is the founder and CEO of a company called the Truck Parking Club that connects property owners who would like to make a little extra money on their excess parking space with truckers looking for a place to park.

Truck Parking Club is rapidly expanding, and though many truckers balk at the thought of being asked to pay for parking, this paid-parking option has many advantages.

The problem, Shelley tells me, "has been exacerbated by the buildout of infrastructure [and] decades of not being thoughtful about where to put rest areas. On the truck-stop side we've gotten to a place where there is one space for every eleven trucks and fifty-six minutes on average [for a driver] to find parking. What was maybe a small problem twenty or thirty years ago has become quite a big problem today."

Evan Shelley and his business partners made the connection between this problem and the untapped resource of spare parking at trucking companies, truck-service centers, storage facilities, towing companies, and all sorts of businesses that might not be truck stops but have large enough lots to make extra income by serving as temporary parking. Their app has proven quite popular, and what Shelley refers to as his "property partners," or locations offering parking space to truckers, number over thirty-three hundred at this writing. Shelley aims to have ten thousand parking providers on his app in the near future, which as a solution to the truck-parking shortage is exponentially faster than waiting for the government to build more rest areas or for truck stops to expand their own parking. On that note about government rest areas, Shelley says that the average cost to the taxpayer per each public truck-parking space is between $150,000 and $500,000. Stimulus spending? A jobs program for all sorts of government desk jockeys not involved in actually paving the parking spots? All of the above, probably. (Shelley, for the record, supports all government efforts toward solving the problem, as it is so massive that his company will still make money, even if those half-a-million-dollar parking spaces were built at speeds way beyond the usual sluggish pace of government.)

As for truck stops, Shelley notes that they used to make their return on investment in a parking lot fairly quickly, but due to changes in the industry truck stops are having a much more difficult time making a profit. Thanks largely to the flatlining of truck drivers' wages and to inflation, drivers are spending a lot less money at truck stops than they used to. Even though truckers aren't really the customers at truck-stop pumps—the carriers they drive for are buying all that fuel—truck stops are feeling the squeeze, and many are moving to paid parking.

"Truck stops don't want to have to charge for parking," says Evan Shelley.

"In a perfect world, you're not charging for parking. People are fueling at your store, parking at your store, going in your store and spending money in your store . . . but now we are in a world where that's not happening. Truck stops are becoming real-estate companies whether they like it or not. Understandably, from the driver's perspective, drivers are like, no, these truck stops can't do this to us. Independent truck stops have less of a choice than anyone thinks. They're not printing money. It's a pull from a lot of different directions. Truck stops do go out of business."[6]

Though many truckers bristle at the thought of having to pay out of pocket for yet one more expense while their wages are constantly under attack, there are advantages to paying for parking in locations that are not truck stops. Many of Truck Parking Club's locations have access to only basic services such as a washroom and perhaps not much more, but the service addresses a phenomenon that Evan Shelley refers to as "parking anxiety." Over and above the problem of finding a spot, and the near hour it takes some drivers to find one, many drivers are extremely wary of the inexperienced people who have been swept into the industry and the risk those folks present to the integrity of the mirrors, fenders, and hoods of their trucks. There is also the level of ambient noise at a truck stop, which causes some drivers sleeping problems. One of the main pieces of feedback Shelley gets about Truck Parking Club is the better sleep that drivers get due to the lack of noise at most of its locations.

Though some of Truck Parking Club's member locations are bare bones, others have a wide variety of amenities. Some locations are seeing an opportunity to return to the old days, offering the customers who are sent their way a taste of what it was like before.

Booker's Dude Ranch is one such location. A working horse ranch in the small East Texas town of Henderson, Booker's offers services to customers: it rents out event space for everything from weddings to conferences to truck shows, it has an RV park on site, and it seems to have been a perfect fit for Truck Parking Club. It is managed by brother and sister Michael and Chasaty Rainer, who hail from a trucking family. (Michael still drives his own Peterbilt, while Chasaty is a nurse.) Booker's bucks the trend of impersonal fast truck stops. Its owners understand many of the wider issues in the industry and the adversity truckers face daily. Chasaty refers to the Dude Ranch as a "homestop" where customers are not "just a trucker, you're like family for us."[7]

To the Rainers, that's not just a hokey or cynical marketing slogan. When drivers arrive at Booker's, Chasaty tells me, "We're going to check on your truck. We got people right next door, they can come and fix anything. If you're feeling unwell, I'm a nurse, we can take care of you. We do holiday dinners for drivers. We have musicians coming through. We can teach you how to ride a horse if you want."

Michael, having spent his whole life on the road, is wise to the many problems out there. He sees the Dude Ranch as a place to give his fellow truckers peace of mind: "When drivers park their trucks [at some truck stops] they have to worry about stolen straps and tools, even lug nut covers, or not being able to find a parking spot." He has heard many stories like Lombard's. "The truck getting damaged, take a fender off, take a bumper off. . . . Out here they don't have to worry about any of that."

Michael is well aware of the turnover problem in the industry and of the poor training provided by the CDL mills: "We do have a valet parking service because we do have a lot of new drivers come through, and I insist on parking their trucks for them. I don't know the nicest way to put it but some of the new drivers—not all—are very inexperienced."

Chasaty takes a holistic approach to her customers. She very much gets the "human element" that is often missing for drivers out on the road: "Sometimes the road can be real hard on your psyche, and you just need a minute of peace and not hearing anything or doing anything and we are real big on not just your personal health but your mental health out here, because it's a hard job, it's a stressful job. The emotional toll it takes on your physical body. . . . We want to make sure you are well as a person altogether, not just get you a little sleep, but be well."

Michael adds, "If you're missing home, been out on the road a long time, this is the spot to stop."

Though operations like Booker's Dude Ranch are small, out of the way, and definitely in the minority, and the nascent services of Truck Parking Club are still relatively unknown, they are filling a major hole in the market. Government policies at every level have failed the working trucker; entrepreneurs, those on the small scale and those aspiring to be large, provide a glimmer of hope for those who, like me, fear that the American trucker is driving ever further into a bleak and black night.

10

Punishment by Castration

—**Long Haul Paul Marhoefer, "My 359"**

In 2008, a TV-show phenomenon swept the nation and the world. *Ice Road Truckers* was a work-porn reality series, of a piece with another red-hot show, *Deadliest Catch*, also set in the Far North. Whereas *Deadliest Catch* was about crab fishermen working off Alaska's Aleutian Island chain, the theme of *Ice Road Truckers* was Canadian truckers hauling supplies to diamond mines in the Northwest Territories across a route mostly built on frozen lakes. How one

Ice Road trucker:
On Portage 48 of the
Tibbit to Contwoyto
Winter Road,
Northwest Territories,
Canada,
February 2009.

could make sexy and interesting a bunch of truckers crawling along at seventeen miles an hour across vast expanses of lake ice, truckers who spent sixteen hours behind the wheel from Yellowknife to the diamond mines they serviced, is a secret known only to TV producers. But somehow they did it. My time behind the wheel over four seasons on that very same Ice Road was marked by much different methods of warding off boredom than those depicted on the show.

Filmed during the 2007 season on the Tibbitt to Contwoyto Winter Road, *Ice Road Truckers* was, at the time, the highest-rated program ever broadcast by the History Channel. Though the show turned into a competitive personality drama not unlike, say, *Survivor*, it did highlight some of the realities of operating in the extreme conditions of the Canadian subarctic. Working in temperatures that regularly dip below −40 (which is where Celsius and Fahrenheit meet), conditions that even the most grizzled northerner will admit are "goddamned cold," requires operational and mechanical adaptations not seen further south, in the places folks in Yellowknife refer to as "civilization."

At the same time *Ice Road Truckers'* first season aired, civilization, as represented by the United States Environmental Protection Agency, was implementing legislation that would bring into focus the collision between the idealism that drives regulation—in this case an attempt to mitigate climate change—and those conditions of material reality which can flummox even the most experienced engineers.

In 2007 truck-engine manufacturers had to start complying with a suite of emission-control regulations meant to reduce particulate matter, or "soot," along with NOx (nitrogen oxides). These regulations resulted in the introduction of mandated technology on truck engines. As with most new technologies, they came with bugs to be worked out and consequences that would take time to realize. Saving the atmosphere is no easy task for those mandated to implement the necessary engineering—and more importantly, for those expected to pay.

The Far North of Canada presents grueling conditions for testing new technologies and discovering the adaptations and practices that will make them work. These are often only learned over many years of experience. In the years following the imposition of these emission-control mandates, the difference between new and unknown technology on the one hand and the older, established ways of doing business in this unique environment on the other was brought into very sharp relief.

The winter of 2009 was an interesting year on the Ice. It was my fourth season up there, and my third since the first season of *Ice Road Truckers* had been filmed. The series had recently been released in Canada. The decision-makers in the consortium that built and managed the Tibbitt to Contwoyto Winter Road were not exactly happy with how their operation was portrayed. The producers were denied permission to film a second series on that road and had to move along to another location. Scenes from other winter roads were misleadingly depicted as happening on the Tibbitt to Contwoyto Winter Road, and the perception of danger, along with the dramatic conflict the producers stirred up between the featured drivers, who were made out to be racing each other to complete loads, did not sit well with the consortium. Nor did it sit well with the safety nerds, who used the show as an excuse to crack down on the otherwise safe operators who regularly ran the Ice.

That winter of 2009 also brought significant challenges to my previous employers at RTL Robinson Enterprises, a Yellowknife-based, family-owned company that had decades of experience running the Ice. In the past, WestCan Bulk Transport, a company out of Edmonton, had usually supplied trucks and drivers to RTL. In 2009, however, WestCan brought north a number of brand-new trucks equipped with the latest in emission-control technology. West-Can had recently been acquired by a fund called TriWest Capital Partners, an investment vehicle that in this case had purchased a company it perhaps didn't have the necessary experience to run. The new owners and managers at this income fund had signed off on sending north twenty new Mack Pinnacles, a model equipped with an emission-control system that was clearly designed to work in California and not the Canadian Far North. WestCan has since been acquired by the Keenan Advantage Group of Ohio and rebranded—along with other trucking companies gobbled up in the decades-long trend of consolidation—into KAG Canada.

Typically, RTL had used its own assortment of much older equipment: trucks that would run the Ice in the winter and be used for road-construction projects in the summer. Experienced drivers had sought out the Western Stars used by RTL since the early 1980s. These trucks had old mechanically driven Caterpillar engines and were unencumbered by computer-controlled systems. They tolerated the cold and were easy enough to jerry-rig if there was a problem hundreds of miles north of Yellowknife. Due to a disagreement, I had left RTL in spring 2008 and returned to the Ice in 2009 in the employ of a farmer and owner-operator named Jim Lengyel, one of the longest-serving truckers on the Ice. I hauled fuel from Yellowknife to the Diavik Diamond Mine in one of Jim's old Peterbilts, a 1993 model 379 equipped with a 3406B Caterpillar engine and a fifteen-speed "around the gate" transmission. Jim had also sent a driver named Shawn up north, driving a similar vintage Kenworth, and the two of us were Ice Road buddies that season.

"Ice Road buddies" are pairs of drivers who are simpatico in how they run and who get along well enough to endure nearly two months of punishing schedules. As all trucks going north on the Ice are required to be parts of convoys, the minimum number of trucks being two, it pays to have a buddy who runs the same way you operate. You want to go up with someone who is a known and trustworthy quantity.

Shawn and I had known each other from previous seasons. We got along great, so we made a pretty good pair. We never got separated or had any problems, and Shawn was happy to sleep a little longer in Yellowknife whenever we rolled into town and this particular lady I knew there wanted me to come and visit. On the night we arrived, Christie even came out to visit my truck, parked next to the Petro Pass cardlock (an automated fueling station) across the street from the co-op grocery store.

The VHF radio crackled when Christie got in my truck. I heard Shawn's voice. "Didn't take you long, did it?" I turned the volume down and focused on my visitor.

We were there to haul fuel to the Diavik Diamond Mine, one of a small handful of diamond mines that had sprung up in the open tundra not far from the Arctic Circle. All the mines there ran on diesel: the haul trucks and other heavy equipment, the electrical generation, on-site pickup trucks, explosives, all of it. Each mine had a substantial tank farm that could store a year's worth of fuel— fuel that could only be reasonably delivered in the winter along that Ice Road. Otherwise, it had to be flown up in a C-130 Hercules transport aircraft outfitted with liquid bladders at astronomical expense. There was a short window in the winter when those Ice Roads were usable; the season would last between six and ten weeks, depending on weather and the amount of supplies ordered for the year.

Given the narrow window of opportunity, the mines and the trucking companies that supplied them would get a special waiver from the normal hours-of-service regulations governing the time a trucker was allowed to work. Under this waiver, drivers were permitted to work fifteen hours a day, seven days a week, for the duration of the Ice Road season while supplying the mines. It's hard work, and it takes a certain kind of person to do it. Many of the guys who ran the Ice would come back every year. The camaraderie engendered between Ice Road truckers is often spoken about wistfully and with longing by everyone who has done it. It transcends whatever particular company you worked for up north, or whatever mine you hauled to.

Though I was running with Shawn to Diavik for my man Jim under a different company than RTL, RTL had trucks running there as well, driven by many of my friends from previous seasons. We ran together in convoys, yapping on the VHF radio, and the companies we each worked for made not much difference in how we got along. We all helped each other out and shared experiences with our equipment.

My friends at RTL/WestCan that year had some fairly major problems with the new Macks they had been assigned. That became a concern for everyone. The emission-control systems on those trucks wouldn't work properly in the cold, and if the computers that ran the engine detected that the exhaust going out the pipe wasn't as clean as the government had determined necessary, they would shut the trucks down. That kind of thing is a huge pain in the ass on pavement in more temperate climates, never mind when you're driving across a frozen lake pulling a Super B-train tanker unit hauling 50,000 liters of diesel fuel. The lake ice is meant to be rolled across, not parked on. A frozen-up truck stalled on the ice presents a major hazard to everyone; it endangers the proper functioning of the entire system and the delivery of necessary supplies to the mines.

I was told by my colleagues at RTL that in the course of one night, half a dozen of these new Macks had frozen up. When Larry Wheaton, operations manager for RTL, came into the office and was relayed the news, he employed language not suitable for the ears of children. Frozen trucks were a huge problem. They had to be rescued and hauled back to Yellowknife to be returned to life, taking up many hours and miles for other truckers to retrieve them, and replacement trucks had to be found to put back under the trailers now sitting on frozen lakes. There was also the human element, with drivers annoyed and not making money while waiting for trucks to be fixed or replaced. It added up to many headaches and significant cost for everyone involved.

Eventually the engineers at Mack came up with a solution to the shutdowns imposed on their trucks by computer code written to appease the Gods of The Sky (and the EPA) rather than the stern code of the north. This involved the drivers running in a lower gear and at a higher RPM so as to keep the engine operating at a higher temperature. This kept the emission-control system happy; it required the higher temperature in order to burn off the soot and NOx that are the mortal enemies of the climate-change crowd.

The only problem with running at a higher RPM was that it burned a lot more fuel than running in a more appropriate gearing. A lot more. In a single round trip between Yellowknife and the Diavik Diamond Mine, the old, mechanically driven 3406B Caterpillar in my 1993 Peterbilt, pulling the exact same load as those new Macks, would burn between 580 and 620 liters of fuel. What about those Macks running at a higher RPM in a lower gear so as not to freeze and stop working? They were burning between 800 and 1,100 liters for the exact same trip.

The whole enterprise, presented to your average environmentalist, is bizarre to begin with: using hundreds of trucks to haul millions of liters of diesel fuel to subarctic mines, fuel burned for electrical generation and heavy equipment digging for diamonds, is not exactly good for the atmosphere; perhaps considerations of fuel mileage are marginal. However, when we are talking about hundreds of loads per season, where an additional 200 to 500 liters per trip are burned, it does add up, and it makes one wonder if the imposed emission-control systems were worth it.

Some may argue that the Ice Roads are a unique exception, that emission-control mandates cannot be dismissed just because one model of truck experienced such profound problems during one Ice Road season. But this situation is just a particularly egregious example of a much larger trend in which the benefits of various tech mandates, when properly examined and placed in context, come into question, at least by those who are forced to pay for the equipment and deal with the problems when it fails.

The Owner-Operator Independent Drivers Association, the oldest and most well-known organization representing truckers' interests in DC, published a white paper in 2014 criticizing the EPA for what OOIDA called the EPA's "myopic cost benefit analysis" concerning emission-control technologies.[1]

Due to EPA mandates, engine manufacturers had to substantially reengineer their products, and these efforts did not produce the durability and reliability their previous offerings had come to be known for. In fact, after many years of Caterpillar attempting to reengineer its highly successful 3406E C-15 platform with the ACERT system, it succeeded only in making that system unreliable and more costly. So Caterpillar essentially gave up producing on-highway diesel engines for the North American market, despite decades of producing some of the finest diesel engines known to man. It's a shame what the government did to Caterpillar's engines; many truckers, including some friends of mine in Alberta, referred to the ACERT as a "boat anchor."

OOIDA's white paper contains damning statistics regarding the additional costs and headaches burdening the operators doing business with these new and castrated engines. For example, engine manufacturers "would need to spend $385 million on Research and Development over five years," in addition to "$7 million annually for a team to carry out engine research." The "new emission-control devices would add $7,000 to the price of the truck"—while reducing fuel efficiency. Finally, the report found that the EPA had grossly underestimated the pain its regulations would impose. "Looking at the cost estimates of EPA along with the actual increase in cost of the new cleaner engines, the report finds that the actual cost was more than $21,000 while the EPA estimate was $5,000."[2]

Later in life, when I moved to the United States and began trucking for companies in 2016, the EPA headaches continued. The guys I worked for in Syracuse had bought a lemon of a Kenworth T-660. Its emission-control system was constantly failing. Never mind that the T-660 is an uglier-than-sin aerodynamic abortion that appears, like so many other new vehicles, to have "lozenge-shaped" as a primary design principle. In the eighteen months the Syracuse guys owned this particular truck, between parts, labor, downtime, towing, and all the costs associated with repairing just the emission-control system, they estimated a loss of $65,000. They probably only paid about $180,000 for the truck brand new, so adding an additional third to the price tag within a year and a half was completely unsustainable. And this is before we consider the headaches and lost wages for the guy driving that truck; thank God it wasn't me.

When I moved along to another company to haul propane for a couple of years, the pattern repeated. I drove a 2019 Freightliner equipped with a Cummins engine that had been castrated by one of these selective catalytic reduction systems; it went to the local Freightliner guys south of Binghamton three times in the two years I drove it just to have problems with the emissions system addressed. The service manager informed me that 75 percent of his business consisted of servicing emissions systems alone. Seventy-five percent!

After I parted ways with the propane company and went back to logging, the 2017 Peterbilt 579 I drove, equipped with a PACCAR MX-13, was stricken with the same issues; it was constantly going back to the Peterbilt dealer in Owego, New York, to have the damn emissions system fixed or parts replaced. A wiring harness specific to the DEF tank controls (DEF is diesel exhaust fluid, the water and urea mixture that selective catalytic reduction systems use in the alchemy required to purify emissions) had to be replaced at a cost of six grand; once again, the service managers had some stories for me. Before I had been hired, that truck had sat there for six months while they tried to diagnose problems with the emissions system. Imagine asking a carpenter not to use his saw for six months because of some damned government-mandated extraneous and unnecessary system attached to the saw. Sorry, carpenters, maybe I spoke too soon, because it appears that the safety neurotics are working on just that. NPR reports that the "federal Consumer Product Safety Commission (CPSC) appears poised to mandate a SawStop-type safety brake on all new table saws sold in the United States."[3]

One wonders if the cost of the high-tech sensors involved in SawStop technology and the initial extra several hundred dollars are only the beginning. But . . . back to our trucks.

A piece of capital equipment that is out of commission for six months does not make for a successful business, and when you multiply that by millions of trucks across the economy of North America, the costs become mind-boggling. My associate Marty Paddock had this to say about emission-control system mandates: "We cannot afford to be the cleanest greenest society in the world. It is not economically viable, and we will not survive it. A measured, well-thought-out and [well-]planned response with realistic goals within an achievable timeframe, again exercising common sense and accountability, is the only thing that will work."

The cost of these mandates in terms of both sale and repair deserves calculation by some brave economist who is willing to confront the new civic religion and upset the faithful with a massive dose of reality.

And what of drivers? Trucking, traditionally, has very narrow profit margins, so the pot of money from which drivers' wages and benefits are derived is restricted to begin with. Companies forced to spend incredible and unsustainable amounts of their small margins appeasing the EPA are left with even less to hand out to drivers, who, over and above reduced opportunities for pay increases, are also left to deal with trucks that go into "limp mode" while trying to safely navigate the interstate. Limp mode is what happens when the computer that manages engine performance, programmed to meet EPA regulations, "derates" the power availability on an engine and stops working properly. You ever see an eighteen-wheeler creeping down the interstate doing five miles an hour with its four-way flashers on and wonder why that guy is driving so slow, causing a hazard for himself and every other motorist on the road? That's limp mode. Sometimes the systems don't even let you limp. You just die right on the road, which then necessitates a very expensive tow-truck rescue, or swapping out the tractor, which requires another driver, with all of the time, expense, and downtime involved.

Many in the industry have attempted to avoid these mandates using various methods and strategies; some involve keeping older and exempt equipment on the road, and others require deleting the emission-control systems from newer trucks entirely. Both strategies carry risks, but given the extraordinary cost of compliance, the risk is worth taking for some. And the government has taken note.

Deleting emission-control systems is a fairly straightforward undertaking, though it can void the warranty on an engine. In fact, this is standard operating procedure for used trucks that leave North America and are sold on the second-hand market. Places like Costa Rica or Nigeria, where many used American trucks are eventually sold, lack just about all the emissions-control systems and expertise necessary to keep those systems running. They do not have access to DEF or the distribution networks or the funds to pay for it, and they definitely can't afford six-thousand-dollar wiring harnesses and other high-value parts such as sensors and filters. Mechanics trained in the arts of diagnosing Pandora's Clean Air Boxes are also hard to come by.

The truth is, most Americans, especially owner-operators and lease operators, can't afford this shit either, and many have made the choice to take the risk of deleting these systems, which is illegal and punishable by heavy fines from the Angry Gods of the EPA. And boy are they angry if you delete.

There have been numerous high-profile cases where the EPA has made examples of diesel service shops that delete or otherwise turn off emission-control systems. One shop and several of its employees in Michigan were assessed $1.8 million in fines, and their actions were referred to as a "conspiracy" by prosecutors, as if they were plotting some gigantic crime rather than just helping people evade the government and its costly mandates.[4]

Another shop, this one in North Carolina, was assessed $3 million in fines and an additional $7 million in civil penalties for similar "crimes."[5] (One wonders if the EPA, given the chance, would do the same to the Mexican truckers who cross into the United States every day with secondhand American trucks that have had their tubes untied.) And it's not just shops being fined; small trucking companies are also in the dock. A six-truck operation from Oregon was fined $100,000 for turning off the emission controls on its trucks. Incredibly, a Wyoming man spent seven months in federal prison for deleting emission controls in diesel trucks.[6] (He was pardoned by President Trump in November 2025.)[7]

Funny how it is always the working man who must bear the costs imposed by punitive mandates, a swatted stick rather than a carrot for the diesel-powered donkey. We have the technology to measure miles-per-gallon fuel efficiency and calculate the cost per ton-mile traveled; maybe the government ought to issue a fuel-tax rebate to truckers who use technologies of their choice and proven driving methods to reduce fuel consumption, or some combination of both. It used to be commonly understood in the industry that the most critical factor in fuel savings is the guy behind the wheel and his operational skill. But most of the industry seems hell-bent on eliminating those guys and having technology take over.

There are non-draconian steps we could take to achieve some of the stated goals of the regulators. For instance, truckers burn a lot of extra fuel idling their trucks in winter and summer for the climate inside of their cabs; perhaps compelling distribution centers and other facilities to get them loaded and unloaded in a faster and more time-efficient fashion would result in sizable reductions in fuel emissions. Perhaps we could upgrade our infrastructure to allow for longer and higher-capacity rigs like they have in Canada, Australia, and most of the rest of the world. That would give us more bang for the buck and be much more fuel efficient, but it would require cooperation between the federal and state governments, as well as a higher-quality level of operator, which this industry appears allergic to producing and paying correctly anymore.

Nah, carrots make no sense to regulators with a stick fetish, and more importantly, carrots don't make any extra money for the government.

Many truckers, not eager to be trapped in the cat-and-mouse game being played by the government and truck and engine manufacturers, have chosen to keep using older equipment that is exempt from the emission-control mandates and, depending on its age, exempt even from the electronic logging device mandate.

Trucks in the United States equipped with engines built before the emission mandates came into effect are still allowed to operate; how nice of the government to not completely rob a man of his tools—at least for now! Many operators are doing everything they can to keep them on the road. I have met a number of family-owned small fleet operators who hew to this strategy. One chap I met at the Mid-America Trucking Show in Louisville in 2024 filled me in on how and why he keeps older equipment central to his operations: "We have tried to run the newer trucks but the cost of buying them new these days is astronomical, and then there is the emissions systems, which can break a guy if you end up with a lemon. It's just too much. We keep a number of trucks between 1997 and 2002 models, and when they get miled out we strip them down to the frame and rebuild them: engine, wiring, anything it needs, new paint, the works. Yeah, it costs us over a hundred grand, but a new truck spec'd the way we need it would be pushing three hundred or more, and then we lose on all the downtime they spend at the shop."

There was at one time a cottage industry in America of building what were called "glider kits." You'd buy a new truck from a manufacturer like Peterbilt or Kenworth, but without any of the drivetrain. The engine, transmission, or differentials would be supplied from an older truck, most likely rebuilt or otherwise refurbished, and installed on the new "glider" in a shop specializing in such work. This cottage industry had its heyday in the first twenty years of this new millennium, when truckers who didn't care to be burned by new trucks with compliant engines could keep their older motors.

One of the biggest and best-known glider-kit manufacturers, Fitzgerald Gliders, with locations in Alabama, Virginia, Kentucky, and Tennessee, gave up on building gliders for their customers in 2021. At first the government put a cap on each glider manufacturer, limiting them to selling three hundred units a year. Then in 2021 new Clean Air Act regulations specified that the emissions standards of any truck had to match the model year of the truck's manufacture, not just the engine.[8] This basically killed the glider-kit industry and further reduced the choice of trucks available to owner-operators and small fleet owners, who were typically the biggest buyer of gliders. The second Trump Administration came out guns blazing against this type of regulatory regime, especially concerning the power of the California Air Resources Board (CARB) to set rules for the rest of the country, because the CARB habitually imposes regulations that favor electric-vehicle manufacturers at great cost to everyone else.

Jeremy Wolfe explains in a FleetOwner article: "CARB only sets emissions standards for California and participating states but is still an influential regulator of commercial vehicles. Its influence is due in part to the state's economic size: California had the fifth-largest GDP in the world in 2023. With California's size, plus that of the several other adopting states, CARB regulations have a tremendous impact on interstate carrier and OEM [original equipment manufacturer] operations." Says David Heller, vice president of government affairs for the Truckload Carriers Association, "There's a tremendous global presence based on California alone that creates, basically, a de facto national administration."[9]

Wolfe continues, "For trucking, the major CARB regulations in the crosshairs are Advanced Clean Trucks, Advanced Clean Fleets, and the Heavy-Duty Omnibus. ACT and ACF mandate the sale/adoption of zero-emission trucks, and Omnibus sets strict emissions requirements. Like GHG3 [the EPA's "Greenhouse Gas Emissions Standards for Heavy-Duty Vehicles—Phase 3"], the CARB regulations limit the availability of—and help raise the cost of—new trucks."[10]

These regulatory changes are future facing, however, and it remains to be seen if Trump's deregulatory approach will do anything to reverse the 2021 legislation that killed the glider kit and has forced a number of trucking operators to purchase expensive and ugly equipment they probably wouldn't have otherwise.

Ugly? Yes, ugly.

Before the government started mandating cleaner-burning diesel engines, many trucking companies were voluntarily looking for ways to reduce costs. Fuel is the one area where you do have some limited control over how much you spend. Thus, in the 1980s, aerodynamic design features became an option on new truck models. Most famously, Kenworth introduced the T-600 model in 1985. The T-600 was the first truck offered on the American market designed from the ground up with fuel-efficient operations in mind and aerodynamics as a primary design consideration. Compared to traditional "square hood" designs, and driven correctly, the "Anteater," as the T-600 quickly came to be nicknamed by nearly everyone in trucking, did get better fuel mileage, and it did so without any government mandate.

Alas, the Anteater started a voluntary trend that eventually became mandated, as the hysteria around climate change caused the EPA and other arms of government to seek any way possible to force people to reduce their carbon footprint. And so it went with mandating aerodynamic designs for all vehicles, which is why when you go down the road today, nearly all cars and trucks look the same, their personalities replaced with a beige and demoralizing sameness. Look at the trucks on the road. All other things being equal, what untrained eye can tell a Western Star from a Freightliner from a Volvo these days? They all effectively look the same and contribute to the ugliness that pollutes the collective aesthetics of our roadways.

One problem with aerodynamic design mandates is that aerodynamics are not the only factor at play with fuel efficiency. They can be rendered utterly meaningless depending on the load being pulled by the truck and the terrain in which it operates. Speed is also a factor, as aerodynamics become far more important the faster you go, and trucks aren't really supposed to be moving that fast. Driving fast is the number one way to kill fuel economy, which is why during the OPEC crisis of the early 1970s the feds mandated a nationwide fifty-five-mph speed limit. The reasons truckers are often incentivized to drive fast when they shouldn't are connected to various policy failures and economic incentives that defy logic or reality; they are discussed throughout the rest of this book.

Why would anyone care about aerodynamic designs or styling? Some people view trucking as merely a utilitarian and necessary evil and would never consider the appearance of a truck to have any importance. Those people are usually not truckers. Trucking is not part of their identity, as it is especially for those whose life in trucking is married to a particular kind of load, such as hauling logs or livestock. For such truckers, their drag coefficients mean the truck could be twenty-feet high and full of square angles and it wouldn't make a damn bit of difference to their fuel economy; logs are heavy and have numerous edges that catch wind the whole way back, and livestock trailers have thousands of large holes that make pulling them down the road akin to driving with an open parachute. Why should operators hauling these types of loads, or oversized and heavy equipment, be forced to purchase ugly aerodynamic trucks? What happened to freedom of choice? Fuel-efficiency regulations are devised with the standard semi configuration in mind: a tractor pulling a tandem axle box or van trailer. All others are ignored by the hammer of state.

On the matter of trucks as an extension of identity, my good friend and life-long trucker Long Haul Paul Marhoefer had this to say about the life-altering effect of a truck he started driving during an especially low period:

It was the winter of 2005. My marriage to my lovely wife Denise was slowly dying in the throes of a twenty-four-year low. On April 9, 2001, I had been in a multi-trauma accident which had left our family in straitened circumstances. It left me so addled by PTSD that we plunged into a four-year estrangement. I guess I was simply too hard to be around for a while.

So I took to living on the road, joining the ranks of the unhoused, no longer a functioning husband on any level except the paycheck I continued to sign over to her, a co-parent only, and staring down the barrel of an eventual dissolution. I was living in that trucker limbo where it was all over except the paperwork. Or so at least it seemed.

Word came of a job opening. It was a friend of a friend. We'll just call the proprietor of the company Blackbeard because he was kind of a pirate. The job description went something like this: "The truck you'll be driving is a maroon 379 with about eighty chicken lights. Oh yeah, the fenders are black. You'll be working as an independent contractor. We'll be paying you on a 1099."

It was one of the most beautiful trucks I'd ever seen, let alone driven. In the wake of the accident, everything in my life had gone wrong. My house was in foreclosure, my car had been repossessed, I owed back taxes to the IRS and my wife didn't love me anymore. I had a job with no benefits, no workman's comp, no tax withholding; yet behind the wheel of that truck, I didn't have a care in the world. Women would pass me and hold their phone numbers up in the windows. Female truckers would engage me on the CB and begin disrobing while driving. I'm being absolutely honest here. How could something so superficial as the truck one drives confer such rock-star status? I wondered. Somehow, the truck had become an extension of my identity, the outward expression of some innate mojo or desirability they perceived. Or maybe I had become an extension of all the beauty and grace the truck held within her.

John McPhee, in his book *Uncommon Carriers*, took a ride in such a truck. The driver of that truck says he "understands what it's like to be a beautiful woman to have people glancing at you." Somehow that truck changed me. It banished my hangdog demeanor. I began to win back a certain confidence. I was no longer the guy who wrecked his truck and was the local hard luck case. I was somebody. The truck came with its own price, though. Days off were frowned upon when you worked for Blackbeard. I'd never worked for such a slave driver as that guy. On one of my half days off, on a rare visit to my former house, my estranged wife asked, "Where'd you get that truck?" Soon she wasn't my estranged wife anymore. We had a lot of making up to do. Working every day for Blackbeard didn't make sense anymore.

These days I drive a cookie-cutter fleet truck, a Freightliner Cascadia. No one ever holds their phone number up in the window, but that's okay. This August 22 will make forty-four years for Denise and me. We are in the process of restoring a 1970 Peterbilt and we're going to make it a retirement vehicle.

You might think I'm being a crank, or that Paul's story is exceptional, but go to any truck show across the USA or Canada and there are barely any aerodynamic trucks on display. There is just something about those designs that is vexatious to the spirited. Perhaps, like me, other truckers see embodied in such designs not only the systems of control that make our lives more difficult but also the political enemies who impose them. When one goes to the Mid-America Trucking Show, there are two main truck displays: outside, where the PKY Truck Beauty Competition takes place, and inside, where the American Truck Historical Society shows off its members' "old iron." There are almost no aerodynamic trucks to be found in either of those displays, and when such trucks do show up at MATS or some other truck show, it is typically to show off the drivetrain or other technical aspects found under the hood. To give manufacturers like Mack and Volvo (well, same company these days—Mack is owned by Volvo, which is owned by Renault) their due, they have been able to achieve great fuel efficiency with their trucks. But this efficiency has been achieved, mostly, with advances in engine technology or the employment of lift axles and low drive-gear ratios rather than aerodynamic design. The upfront cost of that technology and the add-ons that make the trucks super fuel efficient also makes them more expensive to purchase. This is America, and those who wish to invest in such technology and succeed while using it ought to be allowed to do so, just as those who wish to achieve success via other methods ought also to be allowed to go their own way. That's not how it works, though, even with ostensibly "green tech" truck companies.

Chace Barber is a lifelong trucker, hauler of logs, backyard engineer, tinkerer, traveler, and entrepreneur out of British Columbia. He and some associates and business partners have been working on an idea that has been banging around Chace's head for many years. They are building a hybrid diesel-electric truck that employs regenerative braking like you find on a Toyota Prius, largely to take advantage of the potential energy of logs traveling downhill. They combine that innovation with a backup diesel engine, rather like how a rail locomotive is powered by a diesel engine that drives the electric wheels on the rails. Thus far their system has been working great. Chase's company is called Edison Motors; one of its prototype models was christened Topsy after a misbehaving circus elephant that employees of Thomas Edison's electric company were asked to help electrocute in 1903.

With Chace Barber and his truck Topsy—
the hybrid that U.S. regulations effectively bar
from the Land of the Free.

Edison's hybrid platform has attracted a great deal of attention, as it offers many advantages over other electric truck offerings in range, utility, and towing capacity, all due to Chace's focus on heavy-haul applications. An Edison truck can be plugged into shore power to charge its batteries. If the batteries run low, you can fire up the backup diesel generator. As the smaller engine runs at a steady RPM at peak torque, it produces far lower emissions than a typical truck motor and only runs part of the time, much like the motor in a Toyota Prius or other hybrid. The fuel savings will be substantial, and Chace is offering retrofit kits for older trucks, which enable one to replace the axles and original motor, and then install batteries and the whole works on an existing vehicle. It all constitutes a major step forward if reducing greenhouse gas emissions is your goal. Plus, Edison's truck designs follow those of previous (and now extinct) British Columbia–based logging-truck manufacturers such as Pacific and Hayes. Edisons look like a truck, not a lozenge.

You would think that the climate alarmists at the EPA would be falling over themselves to get Edison Motors trucks onto the American market—and you would be utterly, hopelessly, sadly, very wrong.

When I asked Chace whether Edison would be making trucks for the American market, he told me no. Why? Because "it costs so many millions and millions of dollars to go through Federal Motor Vehicle Safety Systems certifications in the US, even though they are almost exactly the same as those we passed in Canada."

He went on to outline the regulations he must comply with, even though his product is meant for a niche market within trucking and already surpasses engine emissions regulations by its powertrain: "You've got to calculate drag coefficient, and you've got to do wind tunnel testing. There's a points system, and if you've got external air breathers you lose points. You have to sell so many aerodynamic highway freight trucks in order to sell one heavy haul truck. What a stupid system: you have to sell forty highway trucks for every logging or oil and gas truck. Why does the government have to dictate this? You can't use a Freightliner Cascadia in an off-highway mining application that's never going to see the pavement and is hauling four hundred thousand pounds."

Like so many other owner-operators, Chace Barber has tasted the frustrations of dealing with the junk trucks produced under the EPA's war against a certain type of working-class trucker:

I was logging so I always had the big high hoods and I did have problems with emissions. We bought one new-to-us used truck; it was only two years old. In the six months we had it, that thing spent three months in the shop with emissions codes and after month six, I'm lemon-lawing this, take this shit back, I'm not making another payment. We just ended up rebuilding a bunch of mechanical Cummins Big Cam 400s. Honestly, I was getting better fuel mileage with my Big Cams than guys were getting with their brand-new trucks. I'm saving money, getting better fuel mileage, they're easier to work on, better up time, so I just stuck with rebuilding the Big Cams.

To match the American government's regulatory stupidity, the Canadian government has now mandated such extreme fuel-efficiency numbers for trucks that Kenworth put out a bulletin in late 2024 telling its customers that it would be restricting the sale of manual transmissions to only 10 percent of the trucks it sells. Once again, instead of training professional drivers how to use a manual and giving them the skills to get optimal fuel performance in shifting, the government believes that new technology must be imposed on all.[11]

Trucking-industry reporter Rob Carpenter shows us with hard numbers something most old-school truckers have known for years—automatic transmissions allowed the industry to be flooded with mewling cabbages.

In 2005, when 95% of Class 8 trucks rolled with manual transmissions, America recorded approximately 4,500 fatal crashes involving large trucks. Fast-forward to 2021's peak of 5,788 fatalities, a 29% increase, and you'll find that manual transmissions had all but disappeared from new truck sales, replaced by automatics in 75–80% of the fleet.

This is the inevitable result of a two-decade assault on professional trucking standards, dressed up as "solving the driver shortage" but really about cramming unqualified bodies into seats at rock-bottom wages.

I've spent 30 years watching this industry, and what we're witnessing is a systematic dismantling of everything that once made truck driving a skilled profession. The automatic transmission revolution was just the beginning.

. . .

To master a 13-speed or 18-speed manual in a loaded 80,000-pound machine required timing, coordination, and mechanical understanding that separated the wheat from the chaff. You couldn't fake it. You either had the skills and dedication to learn proper shifting technique, or you washed out.

Today's automatic transmissions? Any chucklehead with a pulse can operate one, and that's precisely the point. Several weeks ago, we had a tanker hijacking in Los Angeles. Only possible because the truck had an automatic transmission. Anybody can drive one.

The transformation happened at breakneck speed. In 2005, automatic transmissions represented a mere 2–5% of Class 8 truck sales. By 2017, the split was 50-50. Today, you'd be hard-pressed to find a manual transmission in a new long-haul tractor.[12]

Kenworth, the beloved PACCAR brand that recently celebrated one hundred years of building trucks, has also decided to stop building its most successful models: the T800, which was one of the most popular and longest-lasting trucks in the Canadian market due to its durability and dependability; the legendary W900, whose lines are recognizable from a mile away and whose history dates back to 1961; and the C500, a heavy-duty specialty truck favored for construction and oil-field work and a regular fixture on the roads of Alberta and Texas.[13] In a world marked by enshittification and nothing working, the government bears a great deal of blame for killing perfectly functional equipment with long histories of success and forcing on the consumer and the economy much more expensive equipment that is prone to failure—all in the name of saving the atmosphere from those dirty truckers.

Brandon Daily is one of the mechanics who have worked on trucks and the modern emission-control systems that have cursed so many of them. Brandon, who lives in Western Pennsylvania, is a diesel mechanic like his father, Mike. At one time Brandon worked with his dad in the family business, which included a shop and mobile road service. No more. Brandon has moved on to working for a regional gas station chain, performing maintenance on equipment such as fuel pumps and the store's fridges and heating systems. He made this career shift after becoming frustrated with not only having to service the new trucks on the market, with their inferior quality and emission-control systems, but also with having to wrestle the guilt that comes from putting crappy replacement parts on crappy trucks.

Many others also realized how bad things had gotten during COVID, when limited availability of parts due to the worldwide supply-chain crunch impacted everyone. Perhaps this was part of the motivation behind the CHIPS Act, implemented under President Biden, which sought to "reshore" the production of semiconductors from China and other faraway locations. An awful lot of trucks that broke down during COVID *stayed* broken down for many months—not only from the intrinsic frailty of the systems mandated by the government but also because those systems heavily depend on chips and sensors and control boards manufactured in China and Taiwan. No wonder the market for used trucks is as high as it's ever been: an older truck with American-built parts that is not larded down with computers is not the liability that newer trucks have proven themselves to be.

Mike Daily, Brandon's father, observes, "Poor quality parts has really become an issue within the last eight to ten years. We didn't used to have the issues where we bought a part, put it on the truck, and two days later, two weeks later, we have to replace it again. We'd put things on, they lasted. That is not the case right now. We have a lot of issues with quality. A lot of it is the foreign stuff, Chinese-made stuff. The quality is just awful."

Brandon describes it as a calculation on the part of manufacturers looking to increase profitability and hide under layers of intermediaries and separation: "Because they're hiding behind a lot of nameless corporations, there is no one really to go to and grab their shirt collar. It's all nameless, it's all someone else's problem. They will give you a new part, but they won't refund you for your time wasted. There's almost no accountability."

Brandon relayed a story to me about how representatives from NAPA, the parts-store chain, showed up at his and his father's shop to talk up their parts and schmooze for sales. Previously, the same NAPA guys had admitted that after replacing the starter in their delivery truck three times with a NAPA-branded starter, and having it quit soon after, they had gone to a scrap yard to find an old OEM starter. Brandon was having none of it and told the representatives that they should go to confession instead.

If only America's truckers could tell the government and the corporations that are mandating and shortchanging them into extinction, "Go to confession!" Whether God himself could change their thinking is questionable. In any case, the damage being done to America's trucking industry, and by extension to the men and women who drive trucks, is nearly incalculable. How much value has been lost to the black hole of EPA mandates? How many small trucking companies, after all the other struggles they go through to stay afloat, finally pack it in after yet another of their trucks is bricked in a driveway because the Ghost in The Machine won't let it run for reasons that have nothing to do with its mechanical ability?

In Henry Hazlitt's classic 1946 text *Economics in One Lesson*, he describes "the seen and the unseen" with regard to the effects of regulations and government spending. The "art of economics," writes Hazlitt, "consists of looking not just at the immediate but at the longer effects of any act or policy; it consists in tracing the consequences of that policy not merely for one group but for all groups."[14]

No one in government over the past two decades appears to have considered the long-term effects on the trucking industry of the massive cost increases associated with mandating various technologies, including emission-control systems. And because climate change functions as an unquestionable and dogmatic faith system, no one has seriously approached the idea of researching or investigating how much regulatory policies have robbed one of the most economically attacked groups of workers in America: truckers.

Perhaps in the deregulatory environment of the second Trump Administration truckers will be relieved of some of these burdens. That seems our only realistic hope. Responsibility and accountability have been successfully diffused throughout so many levels of government and bureaucracy that the working man has no recourse when the government messes with his truck and his livelihood—even his identity. That's why we must keep the old trucks alive for as long as possible, and hope like hell the powers-that-be don't legislate them out of existence before we are replaced by robots.

11

Who Speaks for Truckers?

You got a lotta nerve to say you are my friend.

—Bob Dylan, "Positively 4th Street"

In 2007, when I was twenty-eight years old, I had a difficult decision to make. My mother suffered from myotonic dystrophy, a subvariant of muscular dystrophy, and she hadn't worked in years; she lived on a disability pension in a small income-adjusted co-op apartment building. She also suffered from clinical depression. Mom's sister Sandra, who lived in the same apartment, also had serious health issues and was severely disabled. My maternal grandparents had their own problems: my grandfather was in the very early stages of dementia, and my grandmother probably had one of the worst and longest-undiagnosed cases of manic depression the world has ever seen. This manifested itself in a completely unpredictable personality. At some point my grandmother had developed a beef with her landlord, and that beef spiraled out of control. My grandparents, retired pensioners, were about to be kicked out of their rental.

I was always on the road, spending a great deal of time in Western Canada instead of my hometown of Beamsville, Ontario, and it pained me that this side of my family was in this precarious position. By 2007, I had saved up a modest amount of money, and in order to buy some peace of mind and save myself from worrying about my insane grandmother being kicked out of yet another apartment, I decided to buy the family a house. I found a small home that was perfect: a one-floor bungalow, no stairs to navigate, and not far down the street from the co-op building where my aunt lived. I could put Mom and my grandparents in there together. They would be proximate to my aunt, I would be the landlord, and since there were three bedrooms I'd have a place to hang my hat whenever I came home. Soon I had moved Mom and her parents in.

I went up on the Ice for the last time in Winter 2009, and while I was up there my grandmother died of cancer. When I got back, my mother was extremely distraught and my grandfather's dementia was advancing. I needed to find local work instead of being gone all the time. Local work—or any work, for that matter—was pretty scarce at the time. We were in the middle of a full-blown recession, and almost nobody was hiring. Though I had enough in the kitty to keep us going for a couple of months, sooner or later I was going to have to find something. Options appeared limited. Then I thought of hauling fuel to gas stations, which is very much a local job: after all, most fuel is transported by pipeline from refineries over long distances to terminals, and then delivered locally by truck.

Sure enough, I lucked out and was hired by a company out of Toronto that had a yard further west in Oakville, about a thirty-five-minute drive from my place. Sweet! I trained for a couple of weeks with a lifelong fuel hauler named Mark Hayer, who showed me the procedures for delivering to gas stations, and soon enough I was put in a rotation, working alternating twelve-hour night and day shifts. Maybe the job wasn't optimal, and I certainly spent a lot of time in the Greater Toronto Area's infamously terrible traffic, but it was a job, and it kept me home every day to be of service to Mom and my grandfather.

One day, after I'd been working for a few months, I pulled up to the Shell Keele Terminal on the north side of Toronto for another load of gasoline. I noticed some people sitting outside the gate in lawn chairs, an unusual sight. I went into the terminal, loaded up, and exited the terminal. A security protocol nearly universal in the world of hauling fuel is that when your truck and trailer(s) clear the automatic gate, you stop and wait for it to close, so your truck blocks access for anyone who might want to drive in while the gate is open. While I was stopped and waiting for the gate to close, one of the folks sitting in a lawn chair approached my truck and asked if he could give me a pamphlet. The person in question was a member of the Teamsters, which was trying to organize the company I worked for. There was a union card with an envelope inside.

I had never met a Teamster nor considered joining the union. Despite all the press they get, the Teamsters only represent roughly 5 percent of truckers, and it's been that way for some time now. Why were they trying to organize the fuel haulers I worked for? I hadn't had any problems with them, at least not yet.

I never did find out who was trying to organize my workplace or why—maybe because I was based in a satellite office outside the city, or maybe because I was new and hadn't been privy nor paying attention to employees' issues, real or imagined. Should I sign the card? I didn't feel like I yet knew enough about the Teamsters or what would happen if they managed to organize the company.

Like most truckers, I understood the rough outline of the Teamsters' story: about Jimmy Hoffa being the Big Guy back in the 1950s and '60s and about how most truckers were unionized before deregulation. Spend enough time around truckers who imbibed an awful lot of late-night AM radio back in the 1980s and '90s and it becomes clear that most of the long-haul guys want nothing to do with the Teamsters, either for political and ideological reasons or because of their experiences with organized labor. When you consider that many truckers interact with facilities represented by other unions, and the unfortunate proclivity those places have for delaying truckers in the loading and unloading process, you understand why. Sometimes the antipathy is put down to the perception that union workers are lazy, but my take on such delays was that they probably had more to do with the rigid application of rules. Employees would drop everything at break time, even if you were almost finished loading or unloading and wanted to get going, and the steelworkers at Stelco whom I used to deal with often seemed to have no consideration for the lineup of trucks waiting to get loaded. Wasting people's time is a universally loathed sign of disrespect.

When I asked around, most of the other drivers at the fuel company were ambivalent rather than hostile toward the Teamsters. The main reservation appeared to be that the Teamsters would likely bring in pay by the hour versus the weird incentive system we had, which consisted of a low base hourly rate topped by a per-load rate. If your load rates added up to more than the base hourly rate, you were ahead. For most of us that was the case, so if you really hustled and had luck with traffic you could make decent enough coin.

I was feeling the pinch of paying for a house and looking after Mom and my grandpa, so questions about money were fairly important. When I worked on weekends and hustled, I did pretty well—would the Teamsters' pay system interrupt that? Would some new seniority system prevent me from volunteering for extra shifts? At one point I was working every Sunday covering a truck whose shift drivers were men of faith and didn't want to work on the Lord's Day. The company was happy, I was happy, and they paid me extra for it. Would the Teamsters' bureaucracy interfere with this arrangement? I had plenty to consider.

Though the Teamsters failed in their organizing drive, I've often wondered what would have happened if they had succeeded. Events later in life led me to believe that I might not have enjoyed working under their representation, regardless of the pay arrangements.

In early 2022, when the Canadian truckers' Freedom Convoy took the country and the world by storm, institutional labor organizations and unions lined up to denounce the Convoy almost as soon as it arrived in Ottawa. Trudeau and his government were quick to label the truckers as "extremists," "racists," "white supremacists," and the other thought-terminating clichés modern progressives typically employ to vilify their political enemies. The Convoy was made up predominantly of truckers, and you would have thought that the Teamsters might view it as a recruiting opportunity. They could express solidarity with workers in the same industry during a very trying time in which the ruling class was completely out of control. Teamster leadership in Canada, however, fell in line with the government.

"The so-called 'freedom convoy' and the despicable display of hate led by the political Right and shamefully encouraged by elected conservative politicians does not reflect the values of Teamsters Canada, nor the vast majority of our members, and in fact has served to delegitimize the real concerns of most truck drivers today," said Teamsters Canada President François Laporte. Laporte also accused the protesters of "intimidating" Teamster members who worked in Ottawa, or otherwise preventing them from going to work: "We firmly believe in the right to protest government policies and voice a wide array of opinions, but what is happening in Ottawa has done more harm to Teamsters members, be they truck drivers who were trying to deliver their loads, or hotel, restaurant and healthcare workers who were intimidated, abused or prevented from accessing their workplaces, by several protesters."[1]

Bummer that nobody ever heard the truth, as the inquest into the Convoy, the Public Order Emergency Commission, which convened in October 2022, was mostly ignored by the media when the facts it uncovered utterly gutted the fear the media had whipped up against the peaceful Convoy protesters. The Convoy was accused of lighting an apartment building on fire, closing businesses, and robbing a soup kitchen—all untrue, just like Laporte's fatuous accusations. It's also funny how all these years later, the one guy who waved a Nazi flag for a couple of minutes in a clearly staged photo-op has never been found, putting the lie to the Royal Canadian Mounted Police's (RCMP) old motto "The Mounties always get their man." Not when he's one of your own!

The collaborators with tyranny aren't only at the top. Even at the level of shop stewards, Teamsters were fretting about members supporting the Convoy instead of meekly going along with union leaders in slagging it: "I'm a shop steward in a Teamsters shop and it pains me to tell you that many of our members are more likely to be in the convoy than demonstrate against it. Somehow the left lost labour a while back."[2]

Speaking of the Left, not only are an unfortunate number of people on that side of the political highway clueless about the history of trucking. They are also clueless about Jimmy Hoffa, the man who built the Teamsters into the largest labor union in American history during his leadership between 1957 and 1971. Though Hoffa's legend is tarnished by his association with organized crime, he accomplished a great deal for the working class in America, and there are important and timely lessons to be learned from the man.

Historian Thaddeus Russell's *Out of the Jungle: Jimmy Hoffa and the Remaking of the American Working Class* goes beyond the usual caricature of Hoffa as a mobbed-up savage. Russell posits the thesis that one of Hoffa's keys to success was a "market-based" approach to organizing. By winning the best contracts and offering members better deals than other unions, Hoffa was able to expand the membership and power of the Teamsters. (He also sometimes busted the heads of his competitors, of course.)

Contra the distance between most union leaders and their members, Hoffa was famous for having a literal open-door policy: "While other major union leaders in the postwar period became increasingly involved with the affairs of government and even further removed from the daily operations of their organizations, Hoffa maintained an unusual intimacy with both his union and its members," writes Russell. "Visitors to the Detroit Teamster headquarters were often astonished to find that Hoffa's office opened directly into the hallway, with no reception area shielding him from the rank and file. No appointments were made. Rather, he extended an open invitation to come with their problems, and as a consequence the corridors of the Teamsters building were frequently filled with men waiting to see him."[3]

Hoffa, unlike many labor leaders, was not a leftist ideologue, even though he cut his teeth in labor organizing under the tutelage of Farrell Dobbs, a Trotskyist who eventually became a leading figure in the Socialist Workers Party. Hoffa had an antagonistic attitude toward ideologically motivated unions like the AFL-CIO. He preferred to focus on his Teamsters' practical concerns. For a while, he also had an oppositional attitude toward politics, at times claiming to be both "a Democrat and Republican," though eventually he forged something of a "permanent alliance" with the Republicans. This choice made him a political target of the Democrats for the rest of his career.[4]

At the height of the Teamsters power, they are estimated to have represented 70 percent of the truckers in America. As we have seen, today that number is only 5 percent. During much of their era of decline the Teamsters were led by Hoffa's son, James P. Hoffa, who had worked for the Old Man's union his entire life. Junior became president in 1998 and led the Teamsters until 2022. His tenure was mixed. On the good side, he fought to keep Mexican trucks out of the American market, understanding fully that they would eventually be exploited by shippers to make domestic deliveries in violation of cabotage laws, which stipulate that only American trucks may pick up and deliver loads within the United States. Lo and behold, since Mexican carriers have been allowed north of the border zone and throughout the rest of the country, cabotage has become a major problem.

On the bad side, Junior fought any flexibility in the hours-of-service regulations that governed long-haul truckers, even though the vast majority of his membership were not long-haul, OTR truckers. How I manage my own day as a professional with decades of safe operational experience is none of Hoffa Jr.'s business, nor anyone else's.

I extended a request to the Teamsters for an interview with their current leader, Sean O'Brien, for this book. Mr. O'Brien and I have published essays in the same outlets: *Commonplace*, the website of American Compass, a labor think tank; *Compact*, a quasi-populist politics and culture online magazine; and *Newsweek*. I even wrote a positive piece about O'Brien's appearance at the 2024 Republican National Convention for *The American Conservative*. Given our overlapping circles, and that we share similar concerns for truckers, I hoped to get a chance to speak with him. The Teamsters' media people in DC responded to an interview request and said they would find someone other than O'Brien, who is, in fairness, a busy guy. Eventually they stopped answering my emails, and no interviewee was sent my way.

I would like to think O'Brien hearkens back to the days of the elder Jimmy Hoffa, who, like O'Brien, had a tough-guy persona and swore like a sailor. O'Brien even once came to fisticuffs with Senator Markwayne Mullin (R-OK), which echoes Hoffa's penchant for using violence when necessary (Senator Mullin and O'Brien eventually talked out their differences).

The modern labor movement has a problem in the divergence of interests between its members and its leadership. Most union leaders today come from what Barbara Ehrenreich referred to as the "Professional Managerial Class." They are university trained and credentialed and more often than not have never sweated a day in their lives—not to earn their keep, anyway. They also have fixations on those cultural issues which obsess the progressive political class and often offend regular working people. O'Brien stands as an exception to this rule, having a long career and family pedigree in the Massachusetts trucking industry; O'Brien himself drove a truck for a large crane company. No wonder that professionalized and ideologically driven unions castigated O'Brien for accepting an invitation from President Trump to speak at the 2024 Republican National Convention. O'Brien doesn't think like they do. He disputes the view that "if you are a Democrat you shouldn't be talking to the Republicans. I'm like, that's bullshit. How are we going to get stuff done in this country? . . . If you're looking to truly collaborate, and make things happen, you've got to talk to people that you normally wouldn't."

In an interview O'Brien gave to Tucker Carlson, he described how deregulation resulted in the loss of four hundred thousand Teamster truck-driving jobs, but he also spoke of his rebuilding efforts since becoming general president in early 2022, which include setting his sights on Amazon.[5] O'Brien highlighted the low pay and working conditions in Amazon warehouses, which lead to the kind of rampant employee turnover we see in certain parts of the trucking industry. He also discussed Amazon's use of scummy carriers in recent testimony to the U.S. Senate Subcommittee on Surface Transportation, Freight, Pipelines, and Safety. In that testimony O'Brien noted that "a 2022 *Wall Street Journal* investigation found that trucking companies hauling freight for Amazon have been involved in crashes that killed more than 75 people since 2015."[6] If O'Brien had included a separate investigation by CBS released late in 2024 and then added up all crash-related fatalities these contractors have been involved with between the CBS report and his testimony in July 2025, he would have been talking about at least 150 people, if not more.[7] How did Amazon manage to double the number of people its contractors have played a role in killing in such a short time?

On the other hand, O'Brien has not criticized President Biden's Trucking Action Plan, which, if you will recall, worked with certain states to issue non-domiciled CDLs to migrants with little in the way of vetting or training.[8] O'Brien must understand labor markets and how wage floors work, as well as the dangers posed to his members as they tango with unsafe carriers and drivers on the highway. One would think the Teamsters would be engaging in a full-court press in opposition to this mass scab-labor operation. Yet O'Brien has offered only a muted response to the problem of insourced truckers; the only place I can find him mentioning that issue at all is at Fox News. "I think it's extremely frightening, to be honest with you. You had a lot of trucking companies that were actively recruiting in foreign countries to bring people over here on those work visas . . . and train them and put them on the roads— where they're not from this country, they don't know this language."[9]

This is the message that needs to be put on the loudspeaker and cranked up to eleven.

In O'Brien's discussion with Tucker Carlson, he mentions that his priorities are improving material conditions and pay for his members. But even though the Teamsters can negotiate for their members, the wage floor for all truckers is set by those willing to work the cheapest, and abusing insourced labor is the cheapest way to go. O'Brien's failure to emphasize that point, possibly in order to maintain his bona fides with the Democrats, is only going to lead many nonunion truckers to think that he isn't serious about representing their concerns. So why would they ever sign up to be Teamsters? Jimmy Hoffa would have immediately seized on truckers' concerns about being forced to compete with unvetted and poorly trained insourced labor.

Our friends on the left often cite the work of United Farm Workers cofounder Cesar Chávez for his role in fighting for better wages and working conditions for farm workers in the Southwestern United States. But Chávez had a keen understanding of economics. He knew quite well that the wages of the workers he advocated for would be undercut by illegal labor. Therefore, he was a staunch critic of illegal immigration and the companies that took advantage of it.[10]

Sean O'Brien is well aware of the moves being made to automate truckers' jobs away in the near to medium-term future, but he needs to act much more boldly—before the robots get here—to ensure that migrants do not replace American truckers first.

Many other organizations besides the Teamsters claim to speak for truckers, and some that don't speak for truckers are perceived as doing so by the media and the general public. Example A is the American Trucking Associations, the corporate lobby group whose actions I have discussed elsewhere in this book. The antithesis to the ATA is OOIDA, the Owner-Operator Independent Drivers Association, which has been advocating for the interests of small-business truckers since 1973, when OOIDA was formed in the shadow of the OPEC crisis. In 1991, OOIDA incorporated as a 501(c)(3) nonprofit corporation and limited itself to research, criticizing regulations that have a negative impact on truckers, and proffering alternatives that take into account the humanity of its members. It also operates its own media outlet, Land Line Media.

OOIDA has issued numerous white papers and solid research in the fight against bad regulations and poor policy decisions. More often than not, it finds itself in opposition to the ATA, which is usually on the side of the punitive administrators who draw meaning in their lives from interfering in ours. Whether fighting the imposition of ELDs and the proposed speed-limiter mandate (which would have removed driver agency in determining the speed at which one's truck operates; it was effectively killed in July 2025 by the FMCSA, thank God) or supporting the Guaranteeing Overtime for Truckers Act, OOIDA is consistently on the side of truckers, and the ATA is on the side of massive corporate fleets and those fleets' owners.

One of OOIDA's core principles is that all its officers and directors be, either now or previously, professional truckers. They are also all elected by OOIDA's members.[11] This reminds me of the management at Earl Paddock Transportation, the company where I started my career. Scott and Mac Paddock both drove for their Dad; my old dispatchers Hank VanDerScheer (rest in peace, Henry), Gene Champagne, and Rob "Wig" Wigington were all drivers; and their over-size-load planner and permit manager Jim Bailie was both a driver and an owner-operator. The ATA, like many labor unions, is "professionally" operated like the slick corporatist administrative state functionaries they are. There are no drivers to be found in the leadership.

Consider the biography of ATA President and CEO Chris Spear. Courtesy of the ATA website, we learn that Mr. Spear has been many things, including "Vice President of Government Affairs for Hyundai Motor Company, serving on the Alliance for Automotive Innovation Executive Committee; Senior Vice President of Legislative Affairs for the American Trucking Associations; Vice President of Emerging Markets for Honeywell International, based in Bracknell, United Kingdom; and, Vice President of Honeywell Global Government Relations in Washington, DC and Brussels, Belgium, managing corporate interests in the US, Europe, Middle East, Africa, Central Asia and Latin America."[12]

If that's not enough for you, consider that "Mr. Spear served in the US federal government as Deputy Representative for the Coalition Provisional Authority in Iraq. Prior, he was nominated by President George W. Bush and unanimously confirmed by the US Senate as Assistant Secretary of Labor for Policy. During his appointment, he was the President's Senior Advisor to the Iraqi Ministry of Labor; Commissioner on the President's Mental Health Commission; and, Executive Committee Member of the US Architectural and Transportation Barriers Compliance Board. Before his nomination, Mr. Spear worked as professional staff in the US Senate."[13]

A regular working-class hero, Mr. Spear.

In a chat I had with Lewie Pugh, the executive vice-president of OOIDA, he was quick to point out that OOIDA is "not a labor union. We can't call for strikes. For all the people that tell us, 'When are you going to call a strike?' we can't do that. It's against the law."

He explains, "The thing that makes me proudest of OOIDA and sets us apart was that it was founded by a group of truckers. Lots of bad things going on, we're going to go to DC and straighten it out. [We] went out to DC, talked to lawmakers, came home, thought [we'd] go back to trucking and the world would be a better place, but here we are fifty years later and we are still fighting some of the same fights."

There are a number of other trucker-advocacy organizations out there that are smaller in stature and roughly align either with the ATA or OOIDA. For instance, the Truckload Carriers Association is on the ATA side, and the National Association of Small Trucking Companies (NASTC), which acts more like a product and service membership club that obtains insurance and fuel discounts, is on the OOIDA side.

Most egregiously, a smaller and less well-known lobby group called the Trucking Alliance conceals its utter disdain for truck drivers behind the mask of safety. This veritable who's who of CEOs and presidents, which includes a number of legacy names in the business, supports intrusive legislation and regulations that imply a belief that their very own drivers are dangerous incompetents who can't be trusted and deserve no respect as professionals.

For instance, the Trucking Alliance proposes to close all exemptions to the ELD mandate, including exemptions for those who operate within a 150-mile radius of their home terminal and go home every night and for those with equipment older than model year 2000. I guess they didn't get the memo that the ELD mandate has not done anything to improve road safety, with truck collisions and driver citations for aggressive driving going up ever since it was implemented. They also want to expand the mandatory USDOT drug-testing regime from CDL truckers to anyone who drives any delivery vehicle for a living, and they want the testing expanded from a simple urinalysis to mandatory hair follicle testing. Yet the Alliance is strangely silent about the government handing out money to truck-driving schools so they can lure more chumps into the industry, the kind of people who already may have drug problems. No, it's best we punish everyone, including professionals with decades of experience, via insulting and needless invasions of their privacy.

More importantly, these cretins are trying to have it both ways with autonomous trucks. They want robotic autonomous-truck systems, but they still want human drivers kept in the trucks—which gives them someone to blame when the robots make a mistake. If you're a trucker reading this book, I recommend you go to the Trucking Alliance website, and if you find that your employer is one of these jokers, I suggest you quit. They have made it abundantly clear that they have no respect for you as a professional, and they are aiming to make you a liability babysitter for the robots they simply cannot wait to replace you with in the driver's seat.

Much better is a smaller outfit looking out for the little guy. The National Owner Operators Association (TNOOA) is fairly new on the block but has come out swinging, advocating a significant reform of the Motor Carrier Act of 1980 as well as demanding that the FMCSA enforce transparency regulations regarding freight brokers who act as middlemen between shippers and small trucking companies. Boasting thirty-five thousand members across the country, TNOOA, like NASTC, also offers purchasing discounts as well as assistance with numerous issues facing truckers, including problems foisted on them by less scrupulous companies. Though the name National Owner Operators Association implies just that—Owner Operators—the "Tuna Guys," as some of us have taken to calling them, have also made themselves available to employee drivers, with TNOOA leaders and members offering advice and rendering direct assistance. Whether it is helping truckers stranded when their companies go out of business and they can't buy fuel to get their trucks home, or helping truckers collect wages when a company tries to stiff them, or offering advice about what to do when a trucker is misclassified as an independent contractor instead of an employee, the Tuna Guys have done their best to try and help. Perhaps there is something to be said here about the advantage of being a small and nimble organization not hobbled by a bureaucracy with hundreds of thousands of members and dozens of full-time employees.

In short, when you hear from an organization with the word "trucking" in its name, do not assume that the organization in question has the best interests of truckers in mind. If such an organization is backed by massive trucking companies with thousands of trucks, like the ATA or its cousins up north, the Canadian Trucking Alliance, you can rest assured that the interests of the trucker, be he an employee driver or a one-truck owner-operator, are never going to be addressed.

A primary goal of these organizations is to influence government policy. But what of the policymakers themselves? Are there any truckers, current business owners, or perhaps former drivers, in government at all?

Georgia's 10th congressional district representative, Mike Collins, a Republican, has been in the trucking business for over three decades. He appears to be the only Congresscritter with any exposure to trucking whatsoever.

And what of the Federal Motor Carrier Safety Administration? Does it have any actual truckers on staff, or at least staffers with some on-the-ground experience in trucking?

A browse through LinkedIn shows us more than a few FMCSA employees, and nearly all of them list their previous careers as working at some other government agency in a management capacity or as enforcement officials; no former truckers are to be found. The FMCSA's own website shows us much the same: all of the principal personnel listed are career bureaucrats or lawyers, with not a trucker or anyone with any experience in the operational side of the industry among them.

The FMCSA has several advisory committees. One in particular, the Motor Carrier Safety Advisory Committee, has sixteen members: almost all of them are cops, union leaders, members of advocacy groups that are antagonistic to truckers, and corporate nerds from the ATA. Only one is a former trucker: Todd Spencer, the president of OOIDA. How a committee like this pretends that it can tell me a single thing about the safety of my job is completely ludicrous, and that it has the ear of regulators who are going to tell me how I do my job is an affront to democracy. Where are the truckers? I wonder how Todd feels about being a token.

President Trump's new head of the FMCSA is a former cop from Florida named Derek Barrs. Mr. Barrs's lengthy résumé shows that prior to his nomination and confirmation as administrator of the FMCSA, his experience with trucks was limited to roadside inspections; otherwise he seems to be quite the meeting-enjoyer. His most recent position was as associate vice president for HNTB Corporation, some kind of infrastructure advisory group whose contribution to society is hard to actually nail down, and he also "served" as a member of the American Trucking Associations Law Enforcement Advisory Board, the Florida Trucking Association, the Flagler Sheriff's Employee Assistance Trust Board of Directors, and the Flagler County School Board.

Though Mr. Barrs has an impressive résumé for a potential bureaucrat, he has a sum total of zero experience in trucking outside of telling drivers how to do their jobs by ticking boxes on forms or writing tickets. Has he ever spent weeks away from home being paid minimum wage for his efforts? Ever chained up a set of trains to get over a snowy mountain pass? Sat in unpaid detention for hours while missing countless family events?

Nope, none of that—though I'm sure he has attended many wrecks and knows full well the deficiencies of truck-driver training in America. Will he criticize his backers at the ATA for their decades-long campaign to throw new and poorly trained drivers out on the road? Seems doubtful—but we'll see. (Unfortunately, our friends at OOIDA backed Mr. Barrs's nomination—for what realpolitik reason I don't know.)

Administrator Barrs has also closely worked with the Commercial Vehicle Safety Alliance and was part of a working group looking into automated trucks back in 2019.[14] There is not much to get excited about in the report from this working group: it's just cops and bureaucrats obsessing over definitions and signaling to their masters how they are going to enforce the rules of the road on robots. The report says nothing about displacement of drivers, nothing about the interaction between RoboTrucks and human road users, nothing about the deeper implications of flipping a switch and rendering millions of people unemployed, and nothing about removing the human element from trucking.

I understand that the FMCSA has a particular mandate and can't regulate all the many problems facing trucking. That said, the head of the FMCSA, whose primary job is making sure that truckers are operating safely, ought to take a holistic view of the entire industry: what makes it tick, economics, training, retention, and how the most important people in the safety of trucking—truck drivers—are treated. Derek Barrs and other lifelong cops and bureaucrats, by their very careers and class positions and lack of firsthand, granular experience in trucking, are not the people to be setting policy for a job they will never understand.

How do we get the message through to bureaucrats and functionaries that what they have been doing doesn't work? When presented with evidence that the ELD mandate wasn't doing anything about road safety, former FMCSA acting head Robin Hutcheson told Land Line Media podcast that her administration had "no plans" to revisit the mandate.[15]

Ah, government.

Maybe it's time for a truck driver to head the FMCSA?

Lee Schmitt is an owner-operator from Wisconsin who has been in the trucking industry for nearly four full decades. Lee currently hauls oversize loads all over the country and often takes his wife Lisa with him in the truck. As long-time members of OOIDA, the Schmitts also have a substantial history in trucking advocacy. While working with a now-defunct group called CDL Drivers Unlimited, they organized a "Truckers Town Hall" during the Iowa Republican caucuses in the 2024 presidential election cycle. Held at the Iowa 80 Truckstop, this first-of-its-kind town hall exclusively for truckers saw Republican presidential candidate Vivek Ramaswamy address the audience and hear their concerns. Ramaswamy introduced his children to the truckers, and his kids got to check out the inside of truckers' cabs at the event.

After President Trump took the Republican nomination, Lee Schmitt threw his hat in the ring for leadership of the Federal Motor Carrier Safety Administration.

Lisa Schmitt tells me that "not once has any [FMCSA administrator] ever driven a truck. In the Motor Carrier Act of 1999 that establishes the FMCSA, it is required that the administrator have 'professional experience in motor carrier safety.' You can translate that lots of different ways: a guy who has been a safety officer at a carrier for five years, or someone who has already worked at FMCSA for five years. I suppose you could say that's 'motor carrier safety,' but we believe that driving out on the roads and living under the regulations and seeing how the regulations translate to real life on the road ought to be a requirement."

Lee and Lisa are from Secretary of Transportation Sean Duffy's district in Wisconsin and have a history of advising and working with him. It's not like they don't have any experience in seeing how the government sausage is made, and after so many years of the FMCSA failing to deliver on increased road safety, maybe someone like Lee—who has over thirty years of safe operating experience—is the right person for the job.

But Lee Schmitt didn't get the job—this time.

The time has come for a new approach to trucking safety, ideally led by a driver like Lee Schmitt. Trucking faces enormous challenges in 2026. The longer the same class of functionaries controls the narrative through corporate lobbying groups like the ATA or lost institutions like the Teamsters, the longer they will kick problems down the road—at the expense of truckers' livelihoods and the lives of American motorists.

12

Necessary Parasites

—Buzz Martin, "Used Log Truck"

As if truckers didn't have enough problems already, we also have to deal with entire industries that seem to be set up exclusively to soak us for every penny they can.

Which brings us to the subject of brokers.

It is mostly undiscussed in the wider media, and even in the business media, but freight or load brokers—3PLs, in corporate jargon, or "third-party logistics" providers—are a key component of the trucking industry. These businesses act as middlemen in connecting shippers with trucks to move their freight. This has grown into such a massive part of the trucking industry that many brokerages earn billions annually; the largest freight broker in America, CH Robinson, grossed over $15 billion in revenue in 2023, and the rest of the top ten were all north of $2 billion. Freight brokering is a huge business.[1]

That's a lot of cake for being a middleman. Freight brokering doesn't apply to most of the industry, however: many companies have direct relationships and contracts with carriers, and some manufacturers have their own fleets of trucks, referred to as private carriers. The part of the market outside of private and contract carriage is referred to as the "spot market," and the load volume and carriage rates seen there are often indicators of the health of the trucking industry as a whole and the rest of the economy, writ large.

Prior to the deregulation of the industry in 1980, freight brokering wasn't really possible. Brokering loads requires truckers to whom to sell those loads, and the market for truckers was more or less closed off, except for the exempt agricultural-products wildcats who occasionally pursued work in the regulated market. Once the industry was deregulated, brokerages began to pop up, and forty-plus years later they are lodged deep in the fundament of the industry, like a deer tick about to give you Lyme disease.

In 1985, after deregulation came to Canada, my Uncle Chris and Aunty Gina, along with their business partner Jeff Moore, saw an opportunity and started a small freight company. When my uncle retired and sold his shares, Jeff took the business, then called Lakeside Logistics, and sold it to a logistics operation out of Texas, which then sold it to Uber Freight. Which is to say, the small three-person operation my Uncle Chris started in 1985 became so successful that Uber Freight used it to move into the Canadian market.

Uncle Chris's first rule of business reflected his small-company and trucking roots: "I always told everyone working for me, 'Make sure you pay the truckers— and we have to be honest with customers about what we can actually deliver.'" Alas, in 2026 the ecosystem of load brokers in the North American trucking market has not only ballooned to unsustainable proportions; it has also attracted a whole lot of entrants who do not possess the same sensibilities as my uncle.

According to numbers from the Federal Motor Carrier Safety Administration, there are now nearly twenty-five thousand registered freight brokers operating in the U.S. trucking market.[2] While the industry falsely claims that we have a shortage of drivers, we *do* need a culling of brokers. There are so many middlemen, in fact, that they have their own trade organization, the Transportation Intermediaries Association.[3] What really sets brokering apart, however, is the evolution of its own particular work culture, a redneck–frat boy version of the *Wolf of Wall Street* that even has its own novel.

Confessions of a Freight Broker, by Cameron B. Ritter, is a satirical examination of this culture. The novel's protagonist is a young guy named Chris who is hired by a brokerage despite having no experience in trucking whatsoever; he has to learn along the way. One of the things Chris learns is that, for many in the business, the delivery of value to the shipper and the trucker isn't exactly front of mind. Ultimately, it is about money—more precisely, about how much money can be extracted from wannabe independent truckers who don't understand their own operating costs or have business strategies to keep them moving, long term.

Chris is taught by his employers and fellow brokers how to take advantage of both shippers and the wannabe independents. In one passage, Chris's associates squeeze an extra $600 out of a load merely by using different phone numbers when cold-calling a lumber-mill owner in Mississippi. On the first call, he quotes a very high rate, and then on the next call, pretending to be someone else, he quotes a lesser (but still extortionate) price, getting an additional $600 over what the load normally paid. Naturally, none of this profit is shared with the trucker who hauls the load.[4]

In a chapter titled "Workplace Diversity," Chris learns how the U.S. trucking industry has been penetrated by drivers of Eastern European extraction who do not always operate for legitimate companies or possess the proper work authorization. "I remembered a load Noah told me about last week," says Chris. "He booked one of these backhaul loads that netted him $500 in commission. He said it was some 'Vlad'— which is a term everyone used for Slavic truckers— Too many Ks and Vs and Ys (in their names) to pronounce, so we just called them all Vlad."[5]

Ritter's description of life in the world of moving loads—always full of problems and drama—rings true. As my friend Long Haul Paul Marhoefer put it in *Overdrive*, "The timing of *Confessions of a Freight Broker* could not be any more serendipitous," as legislation is being floated to investigate this particular sector of the trucking industry amid owner-operators' complaints about many brokers' predatory practices.[6]

An oft-heard term in this discussion is "broker transparency," or the lack thereof. Brokers hold most of the cards in shopping around for trucks, whereas truckers generally have no idea what the load originally paid or any of the details of "accessorial" charges. There is actually a regulation on the books stipulating that brokers must reveal this relevant information to carriers, but it has become widespread industry practice for brokers to make truckers waive the right to that information as part of the deal. This move effectively sidesteps the rule, Code of Federal Regulations 371.3, that requires that the records brokers keep include the following:

> The amount of compensation received by the broker for the brokerage service performed and the name of the payer;
>
> A description of any non-brokerage service performed in connection with each shipment or other activity, the amount of compensation received for the service, and the name of the payer; and
>
> The amount of any freight charges collected by the broker and the date of payment to the carrier.

In addition, and crucially, "each party to a brokered transaction has the right to review the record of the transaction required to be kept by these rules."[7]

A functioning economy depends upon the availability of price signals, so that all parties to a transaction can make informed decisions. Yet brokering as practiced in the American trucking industry is so intensely competitive that if everyone knew what the original offered price on a load was, it would create, as industry commentator Kevin Rutherford put it to me, a "race to the bottom," making the rate undercutting that already plagues the market even worse. A representative from The National Owner Operators Association who wishes to remain anonymous, given the threats and abuse TNOOA has taken for its advocacy, tells me, "There has been an explosion in brokers and agents. There is a requirement under FMCSA regulations that in order to be approved as a broker you must have a minimum of two years' experience in the industry, but nobody is enforcing it."

TNOOA is also concerned about the information that is not relayed to carriers when they waive their right to see transaction records. This data includes detention time, which is supposed to be credited to the carrier and can sometimes be the difference between making and losing money on a load.

Just as backdooring ELDs to adjust drivers' hours and let them work themselves to death is orchestrated from offices in Eastern Europe, many load brokerages and freight agents are located offshore, making it impossible to enforce regulations while they extract value from the American trucking industry. While having a middleman who has market knowledge and connections to loads can be useful and provide value to both shippers and the truckers looking for work, the extractive parasitism that has become endemic to the industry is making the operational side of trucking far more difficult. Operating a truck and paying for fuel, insurance, maintenance, and a decent driver is all very expensive, and having the ever-shrinking pie of revenue meant for the trucker shrunk even more by some load broker in Serbia who has no truck to pay for or maintain is squeezing American truckers even further.

Michael Belzer, the former trucker who is now an economics professor at Wayne State University, has been banging this drum for a while now. The name of his website is "Safe Rates" for a reason: it is impossible to operate trucks safely and pay a driver a decent wage, one reflecting his or her level of professional skill and competence, if whatever is left over after the brokers have taken their cut is below operating cost.

On the spot market, where many loads are brokered through intermediaries, the situation is grim. As *FreightWaves* puts it, there are "too many trucks, not enough freight."[8] While the trucking market is taking a good long time to correct itself from the flooding of the driver pool by Biden's 2021 Trucking Action Plan, it remains to be seen if the market for brokers will tighten up.

A longtime operator in the industry named Dale Prax, now a consultant who helps companies avoid "freight fraud," has floated a promising proposal.

Prax, a Marine veteran with more than thirty-three years of experience in trucking and freight brokering, is the founder of FreightValidate, through which he identifies and isolates bad actors on both the carrier and broker side of the trucking equation. Prax is highly sought for his services. "Freight fraud" is a broad term. It can include brokers taking money without ever finding a truck to move your load, brokers taking loads from other brokers and then selling the load (an illegal practice called double brokering), brokers not paying carriers, and carriers making off with the freight on their trucks and selling it on the black market, having never delivered it to the customer. This particular problem is massive; it is estimated to cost the wider economy something on the order of a billion dollars a year. A great deal of that is at the expense of truckers.[9]

Dale Prax's solution to freight fraud would put more money in the pockets of the people who do the work of moving America's economy: truckers.

He has proposed that freight brokers, 3PLs, and anyone involved in the intermediary ecosystem between truckers and the shippers whose freight they haul be required to have a TWIC (Transportation Worker Identity Credential) card. A number of people across our supply chains are already required to have a TWIC, including all port workers and the truckers who haul on and off those ports. TWICs were introduced as part of the Maritime Transportation Security Act of 2002, a response to 9/11.

Though many drivers—myself included—bristle at having to carry around yet one more piece of redundant government ID, and some of us have a principled objection to requiring it of others as well, either we do something like this or we do nothing about the parasitism of offshore brokers and other intermediaries. The market is clearly not working to clear out bad actors. I'd rather the market be closed off to opportunists and parasites. If a TWIC card requirement for brokers helps with that, so be it. Think of it as the cost of entry to joining a guild called Trucking in the USA.

Obtaining a TWIC card is no easy task. It involves a substantial criminal background check, an in-person interview, and a biometric data check.[10] Most relevant to Prax's proposal is that you must meet residency and status requirements to obtain a TWIC. In short, you gotta live in the United States to have one, with a few exceptions for Mexican and Canadian truckers, who have to go through the same background checks and in-person interviews.

The ability of the freight fraudsters, double brokers, organized cargo theft rings, and other miscreants to get away with what they do is often facilitated by their overseas location. There are brokers and freight agents all over the world operating in the United States trucking market, and, to quote President Trump, "They're not sending their best."

When one of these outfits takes payment for a load and then stiffs a carrier or orchestrates the theft of high-value cargo from a trailer that disappears, it is impossible to hold the bad guys accountable—because they do not live in the United States. Freight brokers must be registered with the U.S. Department of Transportation to operate, and if the USDOT mandated a TWIC card for the owners and staff of all freight brokerages, at least we would have some confidence that those entities are in the United States, and there would be some chance that they would be held accountable if they got up to any nonsense. Trucking is a business that deals in physical material reality, moving loads from point A to point B, and those directing that traffic could at least do us the favor of living in the country where that traffic moves, which would make it much less likely that they would get away with soaking the industry for $700 million or more a year. And if their own families were driving on our roads, maybe they'd be choosier about the carriers to whom they farm out loads.

When the October 2008 financial crisis shook the world, the trucking industry felt the economic earthquake almost immediately. Within a few short months of the crash, housing starts froze up, major oil-development projects ceased operations, the forestry business went into a tailspin, and numerous other industries that interface with trucking simply came to a halt. Work was hard to come by; 2009 was the only time in my life, until 2023, when finding a job in the trucking business became difficult to impossible.

I vividly recall driving by Ritchie Brothers Auctions' facilities, just south of Edmonton along Highway 2, and seeing their yards full to the brim with trucks, trailers, and acres and acres of heavy equipment: road construction, oil field, forestry—you name it, just thousands of vehicles and appurtenances as far as the eye could see. The volume of trucks and trailers was truly astounding: reefers, logging trailers, flatbeds, vans, and every conceivable type of freight-hauling equipment were parked in long rows. Word was that this was the biggest auction Ritchie Brothers, one of the largest auction companies on earth, had ever held in Canada, if not the world. There was no work to be had anywhere, and everyone was selling their gear.

Ritchie Brothers was not the only company packing fields with equipment that owners were desperately trying to sell. In 2009, as thousands of companies were going belly-up, the financing and credit companies that had made the loans for all this equipment were taking repossession across North America.

Harvey Beech is the founder and president of EOS Trucking, a fleet of three hundred trucks based in North Little Rock, Arkansas. Harvey is, like many of us, a son of a trucker, and his company is multigenerational: his daughter Allie, vice president of operations, represents the third generation. Harvey sat for an interview with me to relay how a similar, albeit smaller, financial storm has been brewing in the American trucking industry for a couple of years now, though the way it is playing out and the timing of a potential crash appear to be decidedly different than in 2008–9.

"In 2008 there were oceans of trucks, and when I say oceans, I mean fields full of repossessed trucks along Interstate 40 in North Carolina and Tennessee," Harvey recalls. "My drivers were telling me about seeing the same in Texas. They had to mow fields of pastures to park all the trucks that had been repossessed."

Harvey was still working for his father's company at that time, but he struck out on his own to start EOS in 2013. He explains what the financing of trucks looks like for a newish company like his: "Most midsized carriers have to take out commercial loans to buy equipment, until you work your way up to the size of a company like Heartland Express, and then you can just pay cash. We grew pretty rapidly between 2018 and 2022, and we did this by taking out those commercial loans, usually financed around three to five years. We financed everything for years and that served us well until recently. We've had to sell trucks with equity to continue throwing cash into this dumpster fire."

The "dumpster fire" Harvey refers to is the freight market, post-COVID demand spike, which has been described as a "freight recession" by everyone in the industry for three years running. With rates dirt cheap, and the freight market showing no signs of recovery, observers are scratching their heads as to why the overcapacity in the market has yet to shake itself out. Harvey Beech and many of his associates have some ideas based on the inverted actions of those who issue the financing for many of the trucks we still see on the road.

"Payment deferrals" are agreements according to which lenders allow stressed companies or customers a degree of leeway in making payments, often waiting a few extra months for payments to come in before making moves to recoup the loan, or in this case repossess the equipment being financed—the trucks. Many trucking companies have burned through their cash reserves, and according to Beech—as well as his insurance agent and fuel retailer—his competitors are not making payments to their other essential product and service providers, either.

In 2023, EOS Trucking, having battled through a solid year of freight recession, was attempting to structure its financing to weather the storm in anticipation of an upturn in the market in late 2023, during the typical Christmas rush, or in February 2024, when the post-Christmas lull in freight demand typically ends.

No such luck.

Harvey explains: "As everyone runs out of cash, there's a lot of things they will stop paying for, but one of the first things some carriers do is request deferral, which means you're not making your truck payments, and you are going upside-down every month that goes by. Eventually, the banks are supposed to repossess the trucks. [In February 2024] we're looking around. Where are all the repossessed trucks? They're not repossessing trucks, and my God, my cash reserves are gone because I've been making my payments."

Despite the hard times, Beech and many others in the industry did whatever they could to do right by their financing agreements. They have been standing by for two years waiting for competitors to lose their equipment, for the market to wash them out and restore balance to the system. But that is not happening, and it is not happening at scale.

"I sat down in a meeting with a peer group of fourteen other carriers," says Harvey. "Everybody was singing the same blues, just bleeding, bleeding, bleeding. In 2008, it was 90–120 days before the tow trucks would show up and repossess trucks. There has not been a turnaround here because the financial institutions have not executed properly. There are companies out there who have been on deferral for six months, a year, eighteen months. They are not repossessing the trucks."

Beech and his associates believe that lenders are trying to put off an inevitable minicrash of their own institutions, a repeat of 2008, but instead of a total collapse of the economy this would be merely a collapse of their own companies, which are now underwater on overvalued trucks that they financed in 2021 and that have depreciated over several years of age and operation and haven't been paid for. Beech's thesis is that the lenders who got greedy during the COVID demand spike gave out loans for trucks that were way overpriced in a short and hot market and find themselves today in a deep, deep hole: "They cannot repossess the trucks, because when they repossess those trucks that were overpriced to begin with and are now underwater, they have to record that loss. If they repossessed all this equipment they would collapse."

Beech and his associates detect a nefarious incentive behind the disparity between those who make their payments for as long as they can and those given seemingly unfair treatment via extended deferrals. Between the financial institutions failing to repossess trucks during this down cycle and shippers squeezing carriers with low rates, it is difficult for them to see anything but.

"I'm angry, okay?" he says. "I've had my cash reserves yanked from me, and it's a combination of government policy and these financial institutions and these truck makers. And we've never seen the shippers behave like this. They have reached into the trucking industry and taken all of the cash reserves they could possibly take in the form of paying everybody slave freight rates. Now they have reached through the trucking industry into the OEM's pockets. There's never been this widespread nonperformance on loans."

Another factor at play here is the type of entrant invited into the trucking market by President Biden's 2021 Trucking Action Plan: the small, foreign-owned and -operated companies described elsewhere in this book. An advantage many of these operators have over American-owned and -operated companies is that they don't use financing when purchasing trucks; financing is, for some, *haram*, "sin."

In the Muslim faith, the practice of lending money at interest is called *riba* and is considered a major sin. From the Islamic Circle of North America, a Muslim advocacy group: "The prohibition of riba in Islam stems from several fundamental principles. First and foremost is the concept of social and economical justice. Islam views the charging of interest as an exploitative practice that widens the gap between the rich and the poor. When a lender charges interest, they are guaranteed a return regardless of the borrower's circumstances or the success of their venture. This transfer of risk from the lender to the borrower is seen as unjust, particularly when it leads to a cycle of debt that can trap individuals and families in financial hardship."[11] This assessment of debt peonage will ring in the ears of many truckers who lost their shirts in lease-operator scams.

I spoke with a used-truck dealer who owns several locations in New Jersey about how budding truckers, new to America from Muslim countries, go about paying for their trucks. "Every one of these guys shows up with a cashier's check," he says. "I don't make any money on the financing, but they pay up front and it's good for cash flow. I have no idea where they get the money, but I suspect it's from their friends and family back home."

Perhaps sending wage remittances to those extended kin and community networks back home is part of the deal. While no one has any hard numbers on what percentage of remittances sent abroad are from insourced truckers, we can assume it's a decent chunk of change, given the vast total.

The last study in which we can find granular details on the total amount of remittances leaving the United States is from Pew Research, which documented a staggering total of $138 billion leaving the country in 2017.[12] That was nine years ago, before the flood of illegal migration into this country seen during the Biden Administration, and prior to the Biden task force's efforts to put hundreds of thousands of those people into the trucking industry. It seems likely that many of these truckers send their money home. But if operators like Harvey Beech continue to struggle, or go out of business completely, will they or anyone else care?

One of the major costs of operating a trucking company, or any business or household, is insurance. As the old saying goes, "Shit Happens," and for as long as we have been moving around and bumping into each other, we have attempted to pool our resources as backup in the event of a problem. Founded in 1689, Lloyd's of London, an insurance pooling syndicate, set the tone for transportation insurance by insuring the mighty sailing vessels that engaged in the early global trade that made the British Empire what it was. Lloyd's backs many underwriters around the world to this day.

You may have noticed that your own car or pickup-truck insurance rates have skyrocketed of late. Insurance doesn't operate like a normal product or service. The price isn't much influenced by such factors as monetary policy, interest rates, international tariffs, or the price of energy. No, the price of insurance is determined by much more human considerations, as well as government policy—much of it bad.

Where it concerns trucking, most insurance companies and their websites tell you the same things: insurance rates are going up due to the rising costs of everything from truck payments to parts, as well as due to rampant freight fraud and cargo theft. The overly complex nature of modern trucks is not only making the trucks more expensive; it has also sharply increased the cost of replacement parts and repair. This presents quite the irony: a front-collision avoidance system that does not prevent a frontal collision makes the repair bill that much higher, because you also have to fix the system that failed.

Lawsuits are another problem. Trucking companies and equipment manufacturers sometimes find themselves on the receiving end of "nuclear verdicts" in which juries award seven- or eight-figure sums to plaintiffs in injury cases involving truck crashes. We'll get to them later.

Insurance-industry people are strangely difficult to get on the record about what's going on in the trucking insurance market and why all the bad actors continue to be insured. I asked numerous agents, adjusters, and other industry professionals for interviews, and nearly all refused to go on the record. What is it that the insurance people don't want you to know? Is there some secret actuarial code that might give away who the real guilty parties are? Is it proprietary? I am but a layman in these matters, but I did find two trucking insurance industry pros, one of whom has been in the business for over three decades, to speak with me.

You might think to yourself, "I've got a great driving record, and even though everyone's rates are going up, I should get a discount for my many years of safe driving." As they say Down Under, "You're bloody dreamin', mate."

I spoke with Darren Yancy, an independent adjuster and transportation industry underwriter in Texas who has over thirty years in the business on all sides of the equation: selling insurance, adjusting claims, fighting with attorneys, and even running his own trucking company. Unlike many of his counterparts in the business, he was happy to discuss its inner workings, and he exuded both the charm and the hard-nosed realism that animate the Texan national character.

I put the question to Mr. Yancy: Why don't the insurers offer discounts relative to the amount of safe driving experience some people have, so as to make the system fair and load the costs onto those with unsafe records?

"Your logic is correct," he replied. "Unfortunately, there is not a mechanism currently in the marketplace that puts it together. The reality is that they're looking for a minimum number of years of experience behind the wheel, two or more, and a minimum number of years in the marketplace, going through three or more. You're not getting a break for your years of experience versus another guy. The problem we've got right now is the losses are so heavy that they're not interested in putting any discounts out there."

The industry is spreading out those substantial losses by increasing rates in areas beyond trucking.

Yancy went on to describe how drivers who have less than five years of experience have a 70 percent chance of "hitting something," which tracks with the Virginia Tech study showing that same cohort of drivers has a 40 percent higher chance of being involved in a serious collision than more experienced drivers. Yet those of us with a lifetime of safe experience, which is actually a decent percentage of drivers in the industry, get no significant discount, and lose out on a potential competitive advantage.

I asked the other insurance industry expert who agreed to speak with me, Jessica Howington of Idaho-based United Commercial Insurance, if consideration was given to immigration or language-proficiency status, given the high number of recent arrivals who have entered the trucking business in the past few years, and the fact that many are issued "non-domiciled" or "limited-term" CDLs before being turned loose on our highways—with zero truck-driving experience.

According to Howington, "Even the non-domiciled CDLs are required to have two years of U.S. experience on their motor-vehicle record for most of the best markets. There are some markets (Progressive, Geico, and Berkshire Hathaway) that allow less experience."

Just as the truck stops of this country are becoming Balkanized due to non-enforcement of immigration laws and the efforts of certain states to do everything possible to assist migrants over their own citizens, so are many retail insurers that interact with small- to medium-sized trucking companies run by people of the same ethnicity as the truckers buying the insurance. For instance, Punjabi trucking companies in the Central Valley of California are serviced by an ecosystem of Punjabi insurance companies (and attorneys) selling them their policies.[13] And good luck getting any numbers out of them as far as what their clients are actually paying or the deals they are making with insurers who seem oddly willing to take massive risks by insuring recent arrivals with no trucking experience.

Many of these smaller, migrant-run trucking companies have been caught buying policies that cover only a small number of trucks, even as few as one, and then applying that policy to many trucks, as if it were a fleet policy. Given lax inspections by law enforcement, this critical detail is often missed and does not become apparent until an investigation takes place after a serious collision.

Typically, if a roadside or weigh-station inspection reveals that the driver of a truck lacks proof of insurance, he has committed an out-of-service violation that results in the truck being parked until insurance coverage is obtained and the driver produces proof of that insurance. Penalties include fines and the possibility of the truck being towed away. Alas, we usually don't discover that a truck lacks legitimate insurance until it is too late—and often, trucking companies continue operating even after their policies have been canceled.

A Colorado crash in June 2022 wiped out the entire Godinez family after their vehicle was struck by a driver named Jesus Puebla, who didn't even have a CDL, never mind his trucking company having any insurance. (Its safety rating had tanked from pulling stunts like hiring drivers who had no CDL.)[14]

Big trucks in the United States are required by law to carry a minimum of $750,000 in liability insurance, a standard that has been with us since 1980. This coverage is woefully inadequate, especially given the damages typically awarded in collision litigation. Many carriers voluntarily carry more, and many shippers require more, but three-quarters of a million is the base government requirement. And that math ain't mathin.'

A tragic 2014 crash in Texas that killed seven-year-old Zachary Blake and rendered his twelve-year-old sister Brianna a quadriplegic led to a nuclear verdict when in 2018 a jury awarded the family of these children $90 million. Although the driver and the company he worked for, Werner Enterprises, were found to be 84 percent liable for the incident, the facts show the ruling to be something out of a Kafka novel.

Land Line Media explains:

On Dec. 14, 2014, the Blakes were traveling east on Interstate 20 in Texas in a pickup truck driven by Zaragoza "Trey" Salinas. Weather conditions began to worsen, coating the windshield of the truck they were traveling in with ice. While traveling 50–60 mph, a car ahead of them began to fishtail. Salinas also lost control and careened across a grass median, entering the westbound lanes.

At this time, Shiraz Ali was driving a truck for Werner going west on I-20. He was driving below the speed limit when the pickup truck began to spin. Also present in the Werner truck was Jeff Ackerman, a Werner driver-trainer. According to the appellate brief, Ali reacted within half a second, hitting the brakes.

Even the Blakes' expert witness conceded that Ali's reaction was "very quick" and "appropriate to the conditions."

During the trial, it was revealed that westbound I-20 was not slick like the eastbound lanes, due to heavier traffic melting the ice with friction and heat. Witnesses stated that even though they felt no one should have been driving on I-20 that day, they did not fault Ali for the crash.

In addition to Salinas making statements suggesting guilt and responsibility, a Texas Department of Public Safety trooper defended Ali's actions. Trooper Villareal, a 17-year veteran who investigated the accident, concluded "this is truly an accident," Ali "didn't do anything wrong," and there was nothing Ali "could have done to avoid the collision." A higher-ranking trooper who approved the report concurred.[15]

Fortunately, the insane ruling that awarded the family $90 million was overturned in July 2025 by the Texas Supreme Court. Even so, the case serves as an example of the power of juries, almost always composed of people who know absolutely nothing about the trucking industry or driving a truck at all, and who can be led by attorneys into granting gargantuan judgments. Nuclear verdicts are on the rise: in 2023 the United States trucking industry faced $165 million worth of them.[16]

A nuclear verdict, which is defined as any judgment in a case over $10 million, is the nightmare of every small-fleet trucking owner in the country.

Ed Ruhe is a principal at GLM Transport, a small trucking company out of Van Wert, Ohio, that specializes in hauling refrigerated goods. In a telephone interview he relayed to me how the thought of any of his trucks being involved in a fatal crash "keeps me awake at night."

"I don't ever want to hear about one of my trucks hitting a school bus," he said. "Never mind the nuclear verdict or losing my business, but if anyone got hurt or killed that would be the end of me."

Ruhe has made investments in technology that, from the outside, appear to be the due diligence of a safety-conscious trucking company owner who wants to do right by his drivers and the motoring public. His trucks are all new and he recycles them out after they hit three hundred thousand miles. They come equipped with the latest in expensive lane control and front-collision avoidance technologies, as well as forward and driver-facing cameras. Ruhe also employs a couple of health and safety nerds, who are the type of micromanagers that would grate heavily on the nerves of someone like me. He has no metrics by which to show that any of this has prevented a collision, nor does anyone else—but that is not the point. By having all the latest bedazzling high-tech equipment in the truck—which by its very placement insults the intelligence and professionalism of the guy behind the wheel—and by placing him under 24/7 surveillance, GLM and every other trucking company employing such technology are hedging against nuclear verdicts.

The perception created by employing this technology, whether it produces the increased safety it claims to or not, is enough to satisfy attorneys and juries that the companies have done their due diligence. Having a fleet of drivers with decades of experience or more? Nah, that doesn't matter. Tech has made those drivers' experience irrelevant, even if all the driver-facing camera does is tell you what happened and has zero powers to prevent an inexperienced driver from causing a collision.

Managing the perception of the trucking industry by juries is a key feature of trucking companies' operations, as those juries have the power to make or break you should any trucker be involved in an incident that results in a trial.

Jeremy Citron is an attorney with the Citron Law Group. His practice specializes in representing truckers in such cases. Citron tells me:

Juries are a phenomenal cross-section of people. They're from all different walks of life, and they have a discussion on reaching a verdict. It's largely a compromise discussion on dollars, but they're coming up with large numbers, in part, because we have just come through massive inflation for the past two or three years. Jurors understand that the cost of living for the average American is rising astronomically. That's one aspect of it. Another aspect is that people [on juries] are getting really sick of people not being accountable for their own actions. Juries are empowered to seek that accountability.

The reason that we only have dollars, and that we get shocked by the concept of a multi-multi-million-dollar verdict, is because the numbers are so large, but that is the only justice that lawyers are able to obtain for their clients. We are not able to go and get a restraining order against pain for the rest of our clients' lives; there is not a judge in the world who can do that. The only thing we can get is money for people as a result of what decisions they didn't make and what has happened to them.

Another attorney who specializes in truck-crash cases points to a small number of insurers who seem to have no problem insuring carriers who employ insourced labor with zero experience in the business. Grant Lawson is an award-winning attorney in Casper, Wyoming, and a managing partner with The Law Firm for Truck Safety. He described for me the games that certain insurers play when they are fully aware of the lack of professionalism of the carriers they insure. Many of them are familiar with the problems illustrated by the case of the Colorado crash in which the truck involved had no coverage at all.

Mr. Lawson tells me:

For a number of years I've had numerous cases where a motor carrier gets insurance at the minimum $750k of coverage, but they're playing a game where Insurer X will issue a policy to Carrier A, and when one of Carrier A's drivers goes out and gets in a crash, guess what: the insurer tells you that Carrier A didn't have that truck or driver listed on the policy, so you don't have any coverage.

There's a few class actions going on about this right now. It's got to a point where the insurers can game the system and they're issuing these policies but yet they're finding ways to not step in to provide a defense and leaving these companies and their drivers out to dry and saying they do not have a responsibility to cover.

So I get somebody who gets hurt badly, and I go in and sue the trucking company and go after the insurance they have, and the insurance company says "We're not defending, there's no coverage" because they can play the game, they don't really care. You can spend all the time and money, spend a year and a half down the line getting in front of a judge, at a minimum, to go and get a judgment and try and get the $750k. It's a great game for them. They don't have to spend any money, they don't have to step in, they may have to pay that out at some point in time, but you know what $750k can do in the markets for a year and half? It can make you a lot of money, so why would you pay that out when you can keep making interest on it?

The system is gamed so hard by a couple of real bad-actor insurance companies.

The American trucker is stuck between many rocks and many hard places. The value of what he is paid for his services is being parasitized by intermediaries, some helpful, but many operated from afar and only in business to take a cut of his work. He is also having a war waged against him by the very companies that finance and insure his operations. Imagine doing everything you can to make payments on your truck, through years of lean and hard times, only to have those same financial institutions simply waive the payments of competitors who haven't made the same sacrifices. What of these insurers who make no substantial delineation between new drivers, often insourced to America from the Third World or Eastern Europe, and American drivers with decades of experience? Where is the fairness in that? When these new and inexperienced drivers make obvious rookie mistakes that kill and maim innocent motorists, their negligence results in everyone else being punished by government regulation, often through insulting and demeaning surveillance technology unbefitting a free society. Why is the government allowing decent and professional operators to be punished like this? Why are American motorists expected to accept this risk to their families' lives on American roads?

I asked Grant Lawson what it's like to carry the burden of everything he knows from these cases: the daily interviews with family members going through loss, the permanent injuries, the loved ones gone forever.

"I don't leave my office at five o'clock, ever, let alone leave my office and leave everything at my desk," he said. "I carry these things on my shoulders at all waking moments of the day. And I defend truckers, too. Good truckers are at the same risk from bad truckers as other motorists, and they deserve the same representation when they are hurt by these other bad actors."

The mind boggles at the injustice of it all. And it often seems like no one is asking these questions or advocating for the necessary and life-saving reforms.

It is simply amazing, and a miracle of divine origin, that anything gets delivered to your local grocery store at all. How much longer will those shelves remain stocked?

13

The Truckers Strike Back

With glowing hearts we see thee rise,
The True North strong and free!
From far and wide,
O Canada, we stand on guard for thee.

—Canadian national anthem

On Sunday, January 23, 2022, hundreds of truckers in British Columbia assembled to depart for the Canadian capital of Ottawa, some twenty-eight hundred miles east, three-quarters of a continent away. Originally called the "Convoy for Freedom," this road trip in the dead of winter across a country known for snow and cold had for its noble purpose the delivery of a simple message: We have had enough of the COVID regime. It is time to stop punishing people and ruining their lives.

Other truckers had already demonstrated at the small town of Emerson, Manitoba, which sits on the border with Pembina, North Dakota, and is the busiest border crossing on the prairies. Although most of the world had been suffering under nearly two years of maddening and cruel COVID restrictions, what was happening in Canada was beyond the pale. Prime Minister Justin Trudeau had engaged in an official campaign of scapegoating anyone who disagreed with his handling of COVID, libeling those who opposed his measures as racists and misogynists—as if race or sex had anything to do with the problem at hand— and openly questioning whether dissenters should be tolerated at all.[1] Trudeau's government had essentially declared those who chose not to be vaccinated against COVID as second-class citizens, barring them from any participation in federally regulated life, including travel, all while granting exemptions for Temporary Foreign Workers to come take Canadians' jobs.[2]

In the second-largest country on Earth, banning people from entering airports or getting on airplanes is no small inconvenience. It was especially odious in that, as would be shown later, the Canadian government had no scientific basis for the restrictions it insisted on imposing on its citizens' lives.[3]

A man named Tony Olienick from Claresholm, Alberta, had seen enough and decided to take part in the budding nationwide protests. At first, Tony had wanted to join the Convoy that left from British Columbia and was fated to pick up large numbers of supporters and truckers as it made its way east. He was going to ride with a friend whose truck had a sleeper cab, but at the last minute that friend couldn't make it. So Tony joined a parallel Convoy heading to a protest planned for the tiny border town of Coutts, Alberta, where Alberta Highway 4 meets the northern terminus of U.S. Interstate 15 near Sweetgrass, Montana. Tony drove a Western Star dump truck owned by the small quarrying and excavation company Tony and his father had operated. Like almost everyone else in Canada, Tony had seen families ripped apart over vaccine mandates and other restrictions and seen small businesses lost forever due to the actions of the federal and provincial governments. He was aghast at how dissenters were being demonized by Prime Minister Trudeau.

It ought to be noted here that in 2019 the prime minister's government gave out $595 million in direct subsidies to Canada's major media companies, which were claiming they would go under without taxpayer assistance.[4] In the years since, that subsidy has been "topped up" with grants and add-ons,[5] effectively making the mainstream media in Canada a ward of the state to the tune of roughly a billion dollars—a bill that Trudeau has, through a shakedown of U.S. social-media companies, partially handed off to Americans.[6] This does not include monies for the state broadcaster, the CBC, whose annual budget is now on the order of $1.5 billion a year.[7] It is therefore not surprising that when COVID hit, Trudeau had near-total control of the mainstream narrative, including the ability to insult and defame his fellow citizens with impunity. He grasped this opportunity with gusto. Trudeau's media apparatus would smear Tony Olienick and many others for years to come.

Canadian truckers, like their counterparts in the United States, had been expected to keep working throughout the COVID lockdowns that effectively shuttered most of the rest of society. People still needed to eat, and essential items still had to be delivered, so the truckers continued to roll, with almost zero assistance or services from anyone. Restaurants, truck stops, and rest areas were closed in 2020 and often remained so well into 2022. In the depths of the COVID insanity, truckers were barred from using many rest areas. Ridiculously, Pennsylvania shut down all its interstate rest stops, including all the service plazas along the Pennsylvania Turnpike. *Truckers, please deliver the essential products that allow us to hide at home while you have nowhere to go to the bathroom nor to find sleep for the night.*

Many factories, warehouses, distribution centers, and other facilities that truckers interact with to load and unload the goods and raw materials that build our economy also treated truckers with irrational fear. Truckers were banned from using customers' washrooms, a practice that was already a problem before COVID. Many facilities wouldn't let truckers get out of their trucks at all, except to open or close the doors of their trailers. Despite signs reading "We Love Our Essential Workers!," truckers were feared and left to fend for themselves while working very long hours. Regular hours-of-service limitations were lifted under an emergency waiver for anyone hauling goods deemed to be "essential" to the economy, and the normal micromanagement of truckers' time was set aside so that truckers could work even harder than usual.[8]

Elements of the general public appreciated what the truckers were doing, but Justin Trudeau and the technocrats had ever more cruel and unusual punishments in store for them. In late 2021, the Trudeau and Biden administrations began discussions about mandating COVID vaccinations for all truckers crossing the border, even though truckers had been going back and forth without such a requirement since the beginning of the pandemic in March 2020. Neither administration took into consideration the solitary nature of truckers' work and how they were already treated like lepers everywhere they went. Neither cited any evidence that truckers were a vector for the spread of COVID. Neither even seemed to remember their commitment to the driver-shortage narrative. Even the Canadian Trucking Alliance, enthusiastic supporters of the COVID regime, estimated that twenty-two thousand Canadian truckers and sixteen thousand American truckers would leave the occupation as a result of vaccine mandates. Surely that should have been seen as a disaster to avoid at all costs.

Traditionally, about 80 percent of the freight crossing the U.S.–Canadian border is handled by Canadian trucks. There are several reasons for this, but the primary one is that it makes sense to take backloads into Canada on trucks that have already traveled south. Thus the mandate was going to affect Canadian truckers more than American, and, as advertised, the rules were pretty strict. Any Canadian driver who did not elect to take the juice would be required to quarantine for fourteen days after returning from the U.S.—an unpaid vacation that few truckers can afford. Many Canadian truckers, especially those who live close to the border, make two or three trips into the U.S. a week, or even a day, depending on distances between loading and unloading points.

Canadian truckers had already been facing another, little-discussed piece of adversity when crossing the border. They were dealing with Canadian Border Services Agency officials who took their jobs a little too seriously during COVID. Instead of querying truckers in the usual way about how long they had been gone or what load they were carrying, border agents had been empowered by the Public Health Agency of Canada to become triage nurses, asking truckers about their health, how long they had been out of the trucks, whom they had interacted with, and other probing questions delivered with all the grace one might expect from a petty tyrant with a badge.

One trucker who had had enough of the capricious treatment doled out to her by CBSA and other government officials was Brigitte Belton. Upon hearing about the upcoming vaccine mandates, Belton, who had been kicked off Facebook for questioning the government's handling of COVID, made a video on TikTok. It was this video that seeded the idea for the Freedom Convoy.

Belton's video met the mood and the moment. In the weeks between the government's announcement of the vaccine mandate and the Christmas holidays, truckers all across the country met to pursue Belton's original idea of a "slow roll" protest to let the government know they would not take the crushing of their work and economic fortunes lying down. The mandate was set to go into effect on January 15, 2022. Canada's government officials braced themselves for protests. But they had no idea how wildly popular the Freedom Convoy would become—and just how many truckers were going to show up in Ottawa and other locations across the country.

Canadians often pride themselves upon their modesty and kindness. But they also have a saying: "Canadians are nice, *until they are not.*"

The truckers of Canada who assembled the largest and most successful populist uprising in recent memory were ready to stop being nice—at least to their rulers.

On Saturday, January 29, 2022, thousands of trucks and other vehicles from across the country entered the city of Ottawa. I was there to welcome the Western Canada convoy with a group of friends on an overpass above Highway 417, about half an hour west of the city. The truckers were animated by righteous frustration, yet I saw thousands of people full of love for one another, smiles, outbursts of hugs, and national flags attached to hockey sticks. There was even a sense of relief: it was as if a nation exhaled and exulted, "Finally, the cavalry is here to save us from our captors." There are no words to adequately describe the feeling of everyone I interacted with on that overpass and also later when we went into Ottawa to join the party on Wellington Street.

People outside Canada could tell that the cause of the Freedom Convoy was just. When I went back to America after that weekend in Ottawa, as the Convoy settled in for what would be a three-week-long winter encampment, I was amazed to find my American neighbors cheering us on in solidarity. I delivered propane and hauled logs in the weeks after I came home, and I had never seen so many Canadian flags flying in the United States. It was unbelievable.

People I met while working or otherwise traveling, upon finding out that I was a native Canadian *and* a trucker, would exclaim, "Good for you guys; someone had to stand up to this nonsense," or "Man, I thought Canadians were pussies, but those truckers have made me change my mind about you guys." At the time, I had been living in America for six years, and almost no one had ever said anything about where I was from. For a hot minute, I was a minor celebrity simply for being from Canada.

Up north, however, things were not looking good for my colleagues in the protracted standoff between the truckers and a government whose officials refused to speak with them. In total, thirteen Convoys had arrived in Ottawa, and numerous protests were held at other sites across the country, most famously at Coutts, Alberta, and on the Ambassador Bridge, which connects the Canadian city of Windsor with Detroit and is the busiest of all border crossings between Canada and the U.S. Although everything was more or less peaceful—despite the outright lies and fabrications of the Canadian media about the truckers' behavior in Ottawa—the two border-protest sites gained the attention of very powerful people outside Canada whose interests were not at risk from the hockey games, bouncy castles, and techno parties taking place in the streets of Ottawa.

In Coutts, Tony Olienick had found an atmosphere similar to that which presided in Ottawa. People were peacefully assembling and saying no to the mandates that were ruining their lives. He met and spoke with Americans who had come to the Sweetgrass side of the border and to bask in solidarity and common cause with the protesting truckers. Tony also volunteered as a sort of security detail for the protest site. It should be noted that although the government and media were claiming that the protesters had shut down the border, the crossing itself remained open for all but three days during the three weeks of the Coutts protest. Other, nearby border crossings remained open the whole time and were available for trucks to use, although with more limited hours than the normal 24/7 customs services available at Coutts.

The perception that Coutts was closed, along with the growing protest at the Ambassador Bridge in Ontario, which forced most truck traffic to cross at the Bluewater Bridge between Sarnia and Port Huron, was useful for those who were antagonistic to the aims of the Convoy. Wild and unsubstantiated claims about the cost to the economy were thrown around, mostly based on guesstimates made by business associations. Were there delays at those other crossings from diverted traffic? Obviously, and they were sometimes substantial. Did the protests cause delays in shipments and disruptions to the fragile nature of just-in-time delivery schedules for automakers? Of course.[9] Yet not one of those who complained about the supposed costs of the Convoy ever compared these guesstimated costs to the costs to the entire world from the madness of the COVID regime, which lasted the better part of three years, not three weeks, and was solely the responsibility of government, not of citizens who wanted their lives back.

The whining of the automotive industry, one of the most powerful corporate interest groups in America, got the attention of the Biden Administration.[10] Brian Deese, director of the National Economic Council, got the ear of Trudeau's Deputy Prime Minister and Finance Minister Chrystia Freeland, who set up a call between Trudeau and Biden on February 11, 2022. It is believed that this phone call set the wheels in motion for the ultimate crackdown on the Convoy.

Biden's White House put out a statement about the call with Trudeau, and it is worth a read:

> Today President Biden spoke with Prime Minister Justin Trudeau of Canada to discuss the ongoing blockade of key bridges and crossings between the United States and Canada, including Detroit/Windsor, Sweetwater/Coutts, and Pembina/Emerson. *The two leaders agreed that the actions of the individuals who are obstructing travel and commerce between our two countries are having significant direct impacts on citizens' lives and livelihoods.* The President expressed his concern that U.S. companies and workers are experiencing serious effects, including slowdowns in production, shortened work hours, and plant closures. The Prime Minister promised quick action in enforcing the law, and the President thanked him for the steps he and other Canadian authorities are taking to restore the open passage of bridges to the United States.[11] (italics mine)

Significant direct impacts on citizens' lives and livelihoods. Oh, like the long nightmare of the COVID regime?

The Coutts border crossing was only ever fully closed for three days, and two other border crossings were available to use. There are no automotive plants in that part of the prairie on either side of the border, and the only road closure that took place anywhere near Coutts was of Alberta Provincial Highway 4 at Milk River, a few miles north of Coutts; it was closed by the RCMP, not the protesters. In any case, the protest at Coutts was about to become the centerpiece of Trudeau's rationale for the invocation of the Emergencies Act, whose outrageous violations of basic liberties included throwing an innocent trucker in jail, where he remains three-and-a-half years later at the time of this writing.

By this time, the Freedom Convoy protest sites were crawling with undercover officers, or UCOs, who poked around looking for any hint of illegal activity or actionable intelligence that could be used against the protesters. Meanwhile, the federal government was waging a media smear campaign later found to have been planned by the staff of Public Safety Minister Marco Mendicino.[12] This campaign failed to dent the widespread support the Convoy had in Canada and around the world: almost everyone except the most hopelessly naïve saw right through a staged Nazi flag photo and the usual tiresome accusations of white nationalism and racism. Anyone who went to a Freedom Convoy site to avail themselves of reality unmediated by state propaganda was surrounded by solidarity, happiness, and a genuine outpouring of love. Trudeau was losing the PR battle. He needed scapegoats. He searched for a pretext for invoking the Emergencies Act, something he had been considering since the early days of the protest but couldn't pull off because those damn truckers were so well behaved.[13] Allegations from UCOs at Coutts would give Trudeau everything he needed.

Tony Olienick is a very forward and passionate person, friendly to a fault, and at the time of his participation at Coutts he was single.[14] The RCMP knew that most of the protesters at the Freedom Convoy sites were dudes: about 95 percent of truck drivers are male on both sides of the border, despite the work of various women's groups and initiatives of all kinds to get women behind the wheel. So the RCMP sent a flock of hot young ladies as undercover officers to see what they could find out.[15] Tony walked right into their ruse, offering his opinions about everything under the sun. These ladies had inserted leading questions into discussions of a delivery to Coutts involving Tony, in which discussion he and Chris Carbert allegedly looked at each other and smiled at the suggestion guns might be involved in that delivery. The women passed this purported intel up the food chain of the RCMP command, citing a date and time for the delivery and naming the people believed to be involved. Instead of arresting Tony, Chris, and the supposed delivery people, Jaclyne Martin and Jerry Morin, the officers were told not to interfere. This was the first of numerous strange decisions on the part of the RCMP and the government. Instead, Tony's alleged remarks about taking part in a revolution and dying for the cause—none of which were recorded and for which the ladies produced no evidence—were used to obtain authorization to wiretap the phones of Tony and others. Those wiretaps illegally exceeded their time limits. Even so, no actionable communication was intercepted about any revolution or anyone dying for anything, and the delivery of "guns" that the undercover officers created out of thin air was proven at trial to consist of a change of clothes, a guitar, and an angle grinder. To this day, no recordings or evidence of anything the undercover officers alleged Tony Olienick to have said has ever been produced—we literally have to take the authorities' word for it.

In Ottawa, meanwhile, meetings of Trudeau's innermost circle, and the Incident Response Group it convened to handle the protests, were in full swing. After Trudeau's February 11 phone call with President Biden, in which the prime minister had advised the president that he "had a plan" to deal with the protesters, that plan came into focus. It involved the unfounded and unrecorded allegations of the undercover officers in Coutts. The results of their fishing expedition were used to justify a raid on the travel trailers and other accommodations used by the protesters, as well as on other properties in the area around Coutts. The warrants used to effect these raids are still the subject of controversy, which we will get to later.

Beginning on the evening of February 13 and continuing into the following day, thirteen people involved with the Coutts protest were arrested, and a number of items were seized from numerous locations.[16] These items, including the kinds of hunting rifles and shotguns commonly found in rural Alberta households, were then arranged for a propaganda photo. This photo was released to the world just as Trudeau and his team were announcing the invocation of the Emergencies Act, under which the prime minister took the draconian measure of freezing protesters' bank accounts, essentially taking their money and locking them out of the economy. The province of Ontario also froze all donations sent from Convoy supporters via the crowdfunding website GiveSendGo.

Trudeau's actions against the Convoy sent shockwaves around the world. But he had his staged photo of hunting rifles and shotguns, which he and his ministers could point to as justification for cracking down on the largest peaceful protest in Canadian history. The government also charged Tony Olienick, Chris Carbert, Jerry Morin, and a man named Chris Lysak with "conspiracy to murder police officers," even though all four men were arrested without incident and the following day everyone at Coutts left and went home peacefully.[17] The departure of protesters from Coutts was documented in a viral video of protesters and RCMP officers exchanging hugs and shaking hands, something that didn't square with the charges laid at the feet of the guys who would come to be known as the Coutts Four.

A few days later, heavily militarized police officers cracked down on protesters in Ottawa after arresting two of the most high-profile figures associated with the Convoy, Tamara Lich and Chris Barber. The only violence to ever take place during the Freedom Convoy's stay in Ottawa started then, with police firing tear-gas canisters at point-blank range into the crowd, smashing the windows of people's vehicles, belting protesters with the butts of rifles, arresting people and dropping them off in the middle of nowhere in the freezing cold, and trampling a Native woman with one of their horses. Hundreds of people were arrested and charged with numerous bogus crimes, including intimidation and the government's favorite charge of all, "mischief." In Canada, the charge of mischief is a property crime punishable by up to ten years in prison. Because of the wide and opaque definition of the charge, it is very easy to convict people of mischief, even if they have done nothing more than show up at a protest.

Chris "Big Red" Barber, who drove the famous bright red W900 Kenworth at the head of the Western Canada Convoy into Ottawa, is an independent trucker from Saskatchewan.[18] He and his son Jonathan run a small company with a handful of trucks that moves large, and sometimes very large, agricultural equipment for farmers on the Canadian prairies. They often travel to factories in the United States to pick up new machines and bring them back to Canada for their customers. Chris was among the organizers of the Western Canada Convoy. Once it settled in Ottawa, he took on a prominent role via TikTok in relaying messages to supporters, as well as helping with on-the-ground day-to-day needs and the organization of the truckers.

Chris sat down for an interview to tell me about his experience of going from a trucker struggling like everyone else to being—simultaneously—an Enemy of the State and a national hero:

A few of us decided to stand up, get some conversation going on social media. One of the other people involved reached out to me and said, "I'm going to lose my job on January 15th. I no longer have a way to make a living or make payments on the truck."

At that point I was already vaccinated. I knew the mandate was coming. Being a business owner who hauls agricultural equipment back and forth across the border, my customers rely on me and have relied on me for many years. If I didn't take it, I'd be handing my customers over to the big carriers who forced the vaccination on their drivers.

So we planned to stand up and do something and at least try and have a voice against the tyrannical Mr. Trudeau and his deputy, Freeland.

A week and a half later I met Tamara Lich for the first time, and we left with the Convoy from Redcliff, Alberta, on January 24th.

Tamara Lich and Chris Barber rode together across Canada to Ottawa, with Tamara assuming a fundraising role by running the GiveSendGo and GoFundMe campaigns for the Convoy and setting up a finance committee to oversee it all. The Freedom Convoy raised approximately $24 million CAD from these crowdsourcing sites, cryptocurrency donations, and other methods, but no one will ever know how much in total was donated because of the plentiful but uncounted in-person cash donations made to truckers. In her book *Thank You, Truckers! Canada's Heroes and Those Who Helped Them*, Canadian independent journalist Donna Laframboise, a former columnist for the *Toronto Star* and *National Post*, documented the stories of hundreds of truckers and their supporters. Almost every trucker who went to Ottawa recounted being given not just food and clothing and invites for accommodation or showers, but also envelopes of cash to help them stay in Ottawa.[19] This show of grassroots support was what worried government officials and their media lackeys the most, with one CBC reporter famously claiming that donations to the Convoy were being orchestrated by Russian President Vladimir Putin.[20]

Back in the real world, Stephanie Carvin, an international affairs professor at Carleton University, told the *Globe and Mail*, "The sheer number of donors suggests that organizers tapped into a community of 'true believers' both in Canada and beyond. This movement raised more money in a week than all the political parties in Canada did in the fourth quarter combined." Indeed, when we compare the $24 million CAD the Convoy raised over the course of a few weeks to the annual fundraising of the Liberal Party of Canada, which in 2022 totaled $14.9 million, it becomes clear why the Freedom Convoy was demonized.[21] If donations represent the will of the people, the Freedom Convoy was almost twice as popular as the governing party in Canada.

Before the final crackdown on the Ottawa portion of the Convoy, Lich and Barber were arrested.[22] Barber was soon released, but Lich, who had no criminal record and was all of five-foot-nothing, was kept in jail over two separate periods for forty-nine days in a symbolic persecution meant to send a signal to anyone who dared help lead a peaceful but effective protest, especially one that was wildly popular around the world—certainly more popular than Canada's Liberals.

Lich and Barber were hit with numerous charges, including counseling to commit mischief, mischief, disobeying a court order, intimidation—an entire package of spurious nonsense that was also applied against hundreds of other truckers and their supporters.[23] These included Guy Meister, whose Mack truck was parked at the corner of Sussex and Rideau streets in downtown Ottawa and who did nothing except stand around drinking coffee with his fellow Canadians. Meister had to return to Ottawa from his home in Nova Scotia—a round trip of about two thousand miles—some nineteen times for court appearances. Originally charged with obstructing police and "mischief," Guy was found not guilty of the obstruction charge but guilty of mischief in May 2025, though ultimately he got probation instead of suffering the punishment demanded by the Crown: six months in prison for the crime of drinking coffee next to his truck in the street.

The capricious and vindictive nature of the Trudeau Regime is likewise seen in the case of Harold Jonker, a trucker and local politician from the Niagara region of Ontario. Jonker, much of his family, and drivers from the trucking company he manages took part in the Ottawa Convoy and left without trouble when the protest was dispersed. Jonker was censured by local authorities for his participation in the protest, and fifteen months later, in May 2023, he was summoned to Ottawa to face a litany of charges stemming from his peaceful and uneventful Convoy presence. Why the delay of fifteen months? Well, perhaps beause in late 2022 Jonker was featured prominently in an independent documentary about the Convoy. Fortunately, Jonker was ultimately acquitted of all charges.

The trial of Chris Barber and Tamara Lich, which began in September 2023 and finally concluded over two years later, holds the record for the longest mischief trial in Canadian history.[24] Though the government has yet to provide details, the Barber-Lich trial is believed to have cost the taxpayer over $10 million in court costs and lawyering. But those bills are just the beginning: documents shown in Parliament in September 2025 revealed that the Canadian federal government had spent over $21 million in civil litigation, and paid lawyers another $3.6 million, in fighting challenges to Trudeau's invocation of the Emergencies Act—and there are federal agencies that have still not reported their expenditures in pursuing Canadian truckers to the ends of the earth.[25]

In April 2025, Lich and Barber were both found guilty of mischief, and Barber was found guilty of "counseling to disobey a court order."[26] Forty-five days of courtroom action spread out over a year-and-a-half trial, and then another half a year of sentencing deliberations, finally concluded on a rainy October Tuesday in Ottawa, in a sentencing hearing that started half an hour late and dragged on for three hours, itself symbolic of both the absurd length of this story and the Canadian state's dysfunction. After all this expense, after all the vilification in the media, after the hundreds of cases against unknown truckers and their supporters, Chris and Tamara were handed a conditional sentence of house arrest. Given the exceptions for work and the farmer-trucker lifestyle Chris Barber leads, the sentence is going to make very little impact on his life.

Barber and Lich estimate that they spent over forty grand each in travel costs over the duration of this pointless exercise, and donors picked up the $2.5 million in costs for defense counsel.[27] Though the government didn't get its pound of flesh in putting them away for hard time, "the process is the punishment," and that punishment serves as a stark example of the subtextual class war in North America in 2025. The West has a lot of problems at the moment, and punishing truckers for standing up for themselves indicates that those problems are not going to be solved by our current ruling class.

The Coutts Four have had a more tragic and infuriating story.

All were denied bail, even though three of them had no criminal record; Chris Carbert's record amounted to a minor drug possession charge when he was a very young man. None of them had a history of violence, nor any reason to be considered a flight risk. They were all more or less self-employed tradesmen and upstanding members of their communities.[28] Two different judges, however, denied them bail, based on the extremely inflammatory "conspiracy to murder police" charges laid against them. One of those judges, Justice Joanna Kubik, has been credibly said to be a twenty-six-time donor to the Liberal Party of Canada.[29] In fact, 77 percent of the judges in Canada are members of or donors to that very same Liberal Party.[30]

The Coutts Four were kept in "remand," a sort of legal purgatory in which you are a prisoner but get none of the rights afforded convicted felons. They were kept in this state for two years and often denied necessary medical care.[31] Defense counsel had to seek a narrow publication ban on certain unproven allegations by undercover officers that the media were repeating at high volume, knowing full well that this would prejudice any jury pool against them. The ban only prevented discussion of those allegations, not any other part of the case, but the media hid behind the ban for over two years, never asking why four men with no criminal records and no history of violence were denied bail and treated as political prisoners in a supposedly free and democratic country that affords certain rights and protections to the accused. The media had become agents of the Maple Gulag, and you should never forget that.

In February 2024, a week before the second anniversary of their arrests, Jerry Morin and Chris Lysak were released from remand, with all of the original charges against them dropped. Lysak pled guilty to a simple mishandling charge, which under normal circumstances would have involved only a fine, not two years in prison. Jerry Morin was kept in the gang unit of the Calgary Remand Centre and was denied any visit from his wife, Jaclyne Martin, for nineteen months. Jerry spent a great deal of time in solitary as well. Suffering major psychological trauma from his ordeal, Jerry signed off on a plea deal that he, his lawyers, and everyone involved knew was false in order to get himself out of there. The "conspiracy to murder police officers" charge was falling apart, and the Crown prosecutor in the case, Steven Johnston, knew he had nothing on Morin, Lysak, or Chris Carbert. So Johnston set his sights on Tony Olienick, the only "trucker" in the group and the most vocal critic of the Trudeau government.

Chris Carbert was brought along for the ride with Tony, for how can you prove a conspiracy charge with only one person? Johnston had nothing on Carbert, but because Chris's travel trailer was the site of the initial arrests and search, he was kept in custody and put on trial with Tony. Their trial didn't start until June 2024, twenty-eight months after they had been arrested. It lasted until August. The jury found them not guilty of the main charge of "conspiracy to murder police officers," but they were found guilty of mischief and possession of a weapon for a dangerous purpose, and Tony Olienick was found guilty of possession of an explosive device.

What that "dangerous purpose" was has been a mystery to many observers, given that they were found not guilty of the conspiracy charge, but a valuable reminder came out of this episode. In an interrogation conducted by the RCMP after he was arrested, Tony made the mistake of speaking without a lawyer present. He admitted that if the police were to move in on the protesters and start shooting at them he would defend himself and his fellow protesters. In Canada you have no right to self-defense, and any object you might employ in that self-defense, be it a hockey stick or a box of Tim Horton's donuts, becomes a "weapon for a dangerous purpose."

The media made a huge deal out of the explosive device charge against Tony.[32] All they had to do was to lie by omission. Until the very day that this piece of the puzzle was discussed at the trial, the media failed to inform people that the explosive in question was a ten-year-old industrial explosive found buried in storage on Tony's property, nearly 200 kilometers (125 miles) from Coutts and the protest. Tony's dump truck was often used to haul gravel and other aggregates from the quarrying operation he and his late father George ran. At trial, a government expert testified that the thing was rusted and essentially unusable, and a former associate of Tony's testified that this device was used for breaking loose stuck drill bits on industrial drills used for breaking up rocks and stone. The device was over a decade old, but because Tony didn't have a permit for it, they got him on a technicality, and the Canadian media was only too happy to make it look like he had "pipe bombs" to throw at the cops.

The biggest scandal in this ordeal involved how Crown Prosecutor Steven Johnston acted during the execution of search warrants at the Coutts protest site. During pretrial motions in July 2023, it was accidentally revealed that Johnston and fellow prosecutor Matthew Dalidowicz had been targeted in a motion to override solicitor-client privilege. Olienick's former counsel, Tonii Roulston, claimed to have evidence that Johnston and Dalidowicz gave unlawful direction to the RCMP, changing the nature of the RCMP's investigation on February 9,

2022. Unfortunately, the evidence was sealed in a closed-door session with only the Crown and lawyers for the accused present.[33]

The warrants Johnston had obtained for the RCMP to conduct searches of property near the protest site are alleged to have been obtained deceptively. The warrants had stipulated that the searches would be limited to looking for papers, computers, and other items related to organizing the protest, but Johnston allegedly told the cops to "grab everything, tear the place apart" at the raid. He also allegedly said that he would make the breaking of the bounds of the warrant legal after the fact. If that had been known in 2023, the Coutts Four might never have gone to trial, and probably would have been released immediately.

What possessed Johnston to pursue this peaceful protest with such zeal? We may never know, as over 27,000 government documents related to the Freedom Convoy were kept "confidential," over 16,000 have been declared "Secret," and another 372 have been labeled "Top Secret."[34]

Top secret? What are the authorities trying to hide?

Who railroaded the Coutts Four, a group of innocent men who did nothing but exercise their rights to peaceful assembly and expression? Were they fall guys so Justin Trudeau could show the Biden Administration that the Canadian government was doing something about those pesky truckers who were a pain in the sides of American automotive executives? According to documents revealed in a Freedom of Information Act request made by a small American gun-enthusiast blog, the Biden Administration workshopped ways to cooperate with Meta (Facebook) and Twitter to censor communications by those supporting the Convoy.[35] We *know* there is something to see here.

We will never know the full story unless and until the relevant documents are unclassified, but we do know this: hundreds of innocent Canadians have been and continue to be punished, people who are guilty of nothing but standing up for their fellow citizens against a government that was dissolving society under the cover of COVID.

Although many did not know it at the time, Trudeau's vengeful campaign against the citizens he made prisoners and against the truckers from whom he demanded compliance was made even more sinister by the fact that Trudeau was *at the very same time exempting from vaccine mandates migrant workers who came to Canada during the pandemic.* That's right: non-Canadians were exempt from Trudeau's punishing mandates.[36] According to MP Carla Qualtrough, Minister of Employment, Workforce Development and Disability Inclusion (gotta love the titles of these people who make life difficult for the working man), "Early on, temporary foreign workers were exempt from some restrictions into Canada and flexibilities were implemented to enable timely access to foreign workers." Those flexibilities included waiving the COVID vaccination requirement.[37]

During the Convoy, trucker Csaba Vizi, a Romanian immigrant to Canada who had escaped the authoritarian control of the Eastern Bloc, was beaten in the streets of Ottawa and had his back broken by the cops.[38] Absurdly, he was charged with mischief and had to endure three years of lawfare before he was found not guilty. Why was he wrong to protest the same mandate that was waived for thousands of foreign agricultural workers? A local government official named Marco Van Huigenbos, who volunteered to serve as a liaison between protesters at Coutts and the RCMP, was convicted of mischief and sentenced to four months in jail. I suppose he would have remained free if he had been liaising with Jamaican farmhands. Chris Barber, after being convicted of mischief, was persecuted further by the government of Ontario Premier Doug Ford, brother of the late and great mayor of the city of Toronto, Rob Ford. The Crown has sought to seize Barber's Kenworth, Big Red, and have it destroyed. Big Red is the center of Barber's business and became a powerful symbol of the Freedom Convoy— and therefore a powerful symbol to the Convoy's enemies. Court proceedings for this naked attempt at government thievery wrapped up just before this book went to print. Sanity prevailed, thank God; the Crown's attempt to confiscate Big Red were denied, and Chris Barber can keep on trucking.

Following his crushing of the Freedom Convoy, Justin Trudeau took a page from the Biden Administration to further punish the nation's truckers with massive increases in the Temporary Foreign Worker program, study permits, and something called the International Mobility Program. As a result, labor poured into the Canadian economy from overseas, and the Indo-Canadian trucking community in particular expanded its presence in the Canadian trucking market at the expense of those born and raised in Canada, men and women who cannot compete against indentured and low-paid drivers.

Under the Trudeau government, there were enormous increases in the issuance of work visas to foreign nationals in 2022, 2023, and 2024.[39] The increase in these work visas in 2023 and 2024 alone accounted for an additional 1.2 million workers, over and above those arriving via family reunification or other paths to permanent migration or residency. Just as we saw in the United States, the result of this influx has been a nosedive in wages, closure of indigenous companies, and layoffs of their drivers. As a Saskatoon-based friend of mine who works for a major freight agency put it to me, in his four decades of trucking he has never seen a market like this. Compounding these challenges is the tariff war between Canada and the United States, which has caused 70 percent of Canadian trucking companies to experience substantial losses.[40] "Our members' customers are facing a precipitous drop in demand for their goods which could leave trucks parked on the sidelines indefinitely," said the Canadian Trucking Alliance (CTA) recently. "More bad news could be the breaking point for many in the industry."[41]

Ironically, the CTA's leader, Stephen Laskowski, was a donor to Justin Trudeau and a willing participant in the smearing of the Freedom Convoy by Canadian media.[42] In the same way that members of the American Trucking Associations are feeling the pain from policies they begged for from the Biden Administration, Laskowski's members are also in deep shit. Trudeau may have crushed the Freedom Convoy, which was composed mainly of independents and smaller operators who would never be members of a lobby group like the CTA. But Trudeau's vindictive punishment of the Freedom Convoy and the deliberate flooding of Canada's labor market by recent arrivals have also punished large corporate trucking firms and the drivers who work for them. Perhaps Laskowski, like Trudeau, should have listened to the concerns of the Convoy and the millions of Canadians they stood for instead of smearing and trying to destroy them.

Conclusion

The End of the Road?

In the depths of the COVID regime, when many people were compelled to stay home and watch the world through screens, a previously obscure term suddenly became hot online vernacular: "supply chains." With seemingly everyone at home ordering everything they needed or wanted online, and the world of normal retail and supply mostly shut down, questions about how the world's system of production and distribution worked were suddenly front of mind. Until that point, as my wise fellow trucker Justin Martin opined, "The greatest trick The Supply Chain ever pulled was convincing people it doesn't exist."

Truckers, the most critical link in North America's supply chain, have nevertheless remained an afterthought.

It is because of their position as an afterthought that those who have abused the North American trucker for so long have been able to get away with it. But the cracks in the project of replacing and/or vindictively regulating us are beginning to show. The public can no longer afford to ignore what has become of the profession that kept their grocery stores, lumber yards, Amazon delivery vans, and gas stations full. The carnage on our roads, and the visibility of that carnage on social media, are making people notice and ask questions.

A comment in the form of a question I have heard from many people of late goes something like this: "Are they putting so many bad drivers on the road on purpose, to hasten the solution offered by autonomous-truck developers?" It sounds conspiratorial but is a fair enough question, given what people hear in the media from autonomous-vehicle boosters and tech fetishists. RoboTrucks' main selling feature is the perception that they are safer. So why not prime the public to accept the solution by creating more of the problem? There's an old saying about not attributing to malice that which can be more accurately explained by incompetence, but it seems to me what has happened to trucking, and truck drivers, can be attributed to both; the autonomous-vehicle-system companies are merely taking advantage of a situation whose causes go back many decades.

Is it conspiratorial to ask why the Biden and Trudeau administrations flooded the trucking industry with incompetent insourced labor? Were they really duped by the likes of the American Trucking Associations and the Canadian Trucking Alliance? Perhaps something deeper was going on behind the policy changes that encouraged the mass replacement of North American truckers.

In late 2017, a small group of truckers took to Washington, DC, to protest the ELD mandate, driving their rigs around the city in a slow-roll action that temporarily paralyzed traffic in parts of the nation's capital.[1] Similar protests took place in other cities, including Fresno, California.[2] Two years later, the loosely organized group "Black Smoke Matters" held more anti-ELD-mandate protests around the country.[3] Also in 2019, a cavalcade of Canadian truckers took the same route the Freedom Convoy would later take, adopting the "Yellow Vests" symbolism from *les gilets jaune* in France as they protested the government getting in the way of oil development—and thus many truckers' jobs—in Alberta.

The following year, in a foreshadowing of the Freedom Convoy, truckers' anti-lockdown protests took place in Oregon, New Hampshire, and back in DC, right in front of the White House.

Perhaps advisers to Biden and Trudeau, seeing these simmering protests, recalled the 1970s, when truckers' protests brought certain highways in the United States to a standstill and resulted in meetings with the feds, who ultimately offered concessions to some of the truckers' demands.[4] Under COVID, the regime was not interested in listening to anyone in a democratic fashion, except maybe those mostly peaceful protesters during the Summer of Love in 2020, when thirty people were killed and rioters destroyed billions of dollars in private and public property.

What's one sure way to prevent another effective mass-protest action from the nation's truckers? Replace them, by hook or by crook.

Is it all doom and gloom? Will the highways continue to take on the aspect of a scene from *Mad Max* or a slower-moving version of the *Fast and Furious* films? Will truckers continue to be treated like criminals under a regulatory regime imposed on them to cover up for the fact that the professionals among us have been pushed out of the industry? Is our own unique culture facing erasure?

There are glimmers of hope on some of these fronts.

On the regulatory side, it appears that the Trump Administration is listening to America's truckers, with Transportation Secretary Sean Duffy engaging on social media with truckers, advocacy organizations, and those parts of the trucking media ecosystem which aren't ignoring or attempting to downplay the chaos. On September 26, 2025, Duffy made a momentous announcement in a presser held shortly after yet another dash-cam video went viral showing an innocent motorist killed by an insourced trucker of dubious training and licensure. In addition to making some serious changes to the enforcement of federal requirements for CDLs and bringing recalcitrant states to heel for handing out CDLs willy-nilly to unvetted migrants, Duffy vindicated the project of making America's roads safer and returning the job and archetype of the trucker to its rightful and respected place: "In each of these tragedies, the drivers were non-domiciled! . . . That's why under President Trump's leadership, we have launched a nationwide audit of non-domiciled CDLs to get to the bottom of what we think is causing this crisis. We've heard from truckers, and safety advocates, and news reports, that something was seriously wrong. It was alleged that the open-border policies of the last administration have led to an exploitation of our nation's trucking licensing system. So today, I'm here to tell you that, after our audit, that those reports—they're all true!"[5]

I am not usually in the habit of thanking or acknowledging politicians for anything except being a pain in everyone's ass, but I will extend thanks and gratitude to Secretary Duffy for taking the War on Truckers seriously and engaging in corrective action. The changes he has made to the rampant abuse of "non-domiciled" and "limited term" CDLs will turn off one of the taps of labor arbitrage being used against truckers by some of America's largest corporations. My friends on the left—assuming there are any who are still pro-worker—should celebrate these moves. Why should Third World labor be brought here under conditions often amounting to indentured servitude just so your Amazon packages can be delivered for a few pennies cheaper—and at the cost of your fellow Americans being rendered unemployed?

What of the surveillance we are subjected to? It seems like driver-facing cameras will become a standard feature of a truck's cab, regardless of the safety and driving record of the guy or gal behind the wheel. But they're not the law of the land—*yet*—and I don't foresee that they will become so under this administration. Our friends at the Teamsters in Québec fought back against the imposition of these cameras by the very large food distribution company Sysco and beat them in court.[6] Will the Teamsters and other labor organizations fight back against the creep of the surveillance state into truckers' cabs and other workplaces in general? Though we are told that we can "vote with our feet" and don't have to take a job that requires driver-facing cameras, sooner or later the bastards will make it so there is no escape. I would advise my fellow drivers to have some self-respect and not offer their services to any company that requires them; maybe if enough of us do that, the industry will take safety more seriously instead of pretending that filming incidents does anything to prevent them.

As for electronic logging devices, well, there are still exceptions for those who work locally in less than a 150-mile radius from home, haul livestock, or have old enough equipment. Lean into the exceptions where you can—I know I will. ELDs are another example of surveillance technology being used as a cover for failing to maintain necessary barriers to entry into the industry or offering legitimate training programs. It's good to see Alberta pursue recognition of trucking as a skilled occupation, but most governments and their advisers in the ATA have fought tooth and nail to prevent "truck driver" from being considered such; it would cost them more money to pay competent operators, and they can't have that. I would advise my fellow drivers to join up with guys like Kim Wylie and Trent Lalonde in Saskatchewan, who are moving mountains in order to change this paradigm. In the U.S., the guys who organized the first ELD protest in Washington continue to hold an annual truckers' visibility event on the National Mall called 10-4 DC. Some truckers view asking the government to change things as a fool's errand, but at the end of the day the government makes the rules and manages the nation's highways. Why not join the likes of 10-4 DC in educating the bureaucrats and politicians about what's really going on in our industry? Five decades of the American Trucking Associations running the table on Washington is part of what got us here, and it's time to break the ATA's monopoly on being "our" voice in Washington.

Ten days before writing this conclusion I visited a small truck show in Norwich, New York. The eighth annual Tom "Uncle Bear" Safford Sr. Memorial Truck Show is held by the late Mr. Safford's son, Adam, and usually features a hundred or so rigs at the Chenango County fairgrounds. Proceeds from the show go toward cancer research. The show also helps preserve the vestiges of American trucking culture. Most of the trucks on display at Adam's show are working trucks; they all look great and are kept in tip-top shape, but they're not show ponies—these are the tools of American working men and women. Shows like Adam's are not all that uncommon, but they might take a bit of digging to find out about, given how much smaller they are than the Mid-America Trucking Show in Louisville. Representatives of the American Truck Historical Society can often be found at smaller regional shows, and they are doing their best to maintain the legacy of an industry that built and continues to maintain the economy that undergirds our society. If you are a budding trucker who wants to get into the business the old-fashioned way, with legitimate training and tutelage from people who know what they are doing, you ought to go to one of these shows and talk to people there; I'm sure you'll find something. Avoid the recruiters for big companies at all costs unless you want to be treated like meat in the seat and get washed out of the business *tout suite*. Most of the really big carriers are biding their time until they can replace you with a robot.

One of my friends, a young guy named Ryan who wants to become an owner-operator very badly, has some thoughts about this stage of the trucking industry and his place in it as a competent operator:

The people who insist that aesthetics don't matter, that trucking is strictly business, and a truck is just a tool to get work done as cheaply as possible, are missing or ignoring the fact that in virtually any other trade we could all be making more money in fewer hours without spending weeks away from home. Clearly there is something about trucking—incomprehensible to the spreadsheet brain of your average accountant—that draws us to it, but we don't agree on what exactly that means or what we're willing to compromise to be here.

As for me, I've had enough of being a half-assed cyborg in today's highly surveilled, mostly automated fiberglass and plastic aero trucks. I'm glad that many fuel-saving features are available for those who want them, but I'm an American—I shift gears, I piss standing up, and I resent not having a choice.

When I wake up early in the morning I put on steel-toed boots and a pearl-snap shirt and I set out to do my job with dignity, respect, and, when possible, good cheer. I do the right thing even when I'm not being watched by the cops, a safety manager, or the safety manager's AI assistant. I treat my work with a level of seriousness appropriate for an environment where a lack of skill, or more likely one lapse in judgement or attention, can easily kill half a dozen innocent people—as news reports show with increasing frequency despite our electronic babysitters.

Is there still a place for me in the trucking industry? After thirteen years of professional driving all I can say is that I honestly don't know. I'm about to take a huge step in my career and an enormous financial risk to find out— by buying an older, less automated truck and putting it to work full-time. We've all heard the cliché "Trucking isn't a job, it's a lifestyle." That's true. That's why the freedom to live in accordance with one's own values is so critically important. What I've come to realize is that if I can't do this job my way, there's no point in doing it at all.

Amen to that, brother.

What about the future? It seems like the question is not *if* robots will take over various sectors of the trucking industry but *when*. Though they have many hurdles yet to jump, RoboTrucks are not far over the horizon. And their Dr. Frankenstein creators are coming for your salary, dear driver, sooner or later. What to do? I would certainly advise the more competent and dedicated truckers to get specialized: the robots will come first for the low-hanging fruit of pin-to-pin middle-mile freight that doesn't require people or any particular considerations in transit. Markets that require human overseers will remain for some time yet, and some of them have been resisting the first stage of our replacement with insourced labor.

Policymakers in government should invest in retraining for those drivers who will eventually be displaced by autonomous technology. The government has spent hundreds of millions of dollars over the last four decades on training schools to put people into trucks; once we are pulled out of them, then what? What do you do when hundreds of thousands of truckers become unemployed? Seems only fair that you help them get retrained, or maybe force the beneficiaries of decades of taxpayer largesse—the megacarriers represented by the ATA—to come up with a plan for the drivers they want to replace. Maybe that's part of the reason some big carriers are moving to the "power only" subcontractor model— to once again wash their hands of any accountability for the people they abuse.

We all ought to be giving deep consideration to the consequences of the End of the Road. Its last miles should not be such a dangerous place for North American motorists, nor should it be so degrading for those of us expected to keep driving those miles before the switch is flipped on RoboTrucks. Truckers are better than that, and we deserve to be treated as such.

Keep on truckin'—while you still can.

Acknowledgments

To my long-suffering wife Jenna, thank you for your patience with me over the year it took for this book to be completed. For all our various disagreements, she has supported my writing of this tome while carrying the can for our household, and especially for our daughters, Vivian and Georgia. They are the love of my life, and all my efforts are for them. My mother- and father-in-law, Cindy Kramer and John Hallas, come in for a great deal of gratitude for helping us out in many ways.

This book would not have happened without my publisher at Creed & Culture, Jeremy Beer. To him and his business partner, Byron Smith, thanks for the opportunity! My editor, Bill Kauffman, has been one of the better "bosses" I've ever had—more or less hands off and encouraging when necessary. I've dealt with a few editors along the way in my shorter-form writings, and Bill really stands out; also, I think he probably worked harder on this project than I did.

Huge thanks to a tiny online forum called glibertarians.com, which hosted my first feature-length essay way back in 2017. A couple of years later it was read by the wonderful Oliver Bateman. Oliver invited me on his podcast, encouraged me to keep writing and start my own interview show and a Substack, and hooked me up with a few gigs. Oliver really Does The Work.

Another writer and editor to whom I owe unending gratitude is Batya Ungar-Sargon. Batya saw me tweeting like hell in defense of the Freedom Convoy and offered me a place in the pages of *Newsweek*. Batya has taken some slings and arrows in her own career, and no doubt some of them were for pulling a weirdo trucker out of obscurity to help defend those who had been fingered as Enemies of the State. Batya is the only mainstream journalist I know who expressed any concern or curiosity about the Coutts Four, and for that she deserves eternal credit and praise. Likewise, I want to thank Tucker Carlson for inviting me on his show to discuss the fates of Jerry Morin, Chris Lysak, Chris Carbert, and Tony Olienick. Amazing how two Americans cared more about the unjust treatment of these guys than nearly anyone in any position of power in Canada.

I have many to thank in the world of media who have offered me space to write and encouraged the defense of my fellow truckers: Oren Cass, Drew Holden, and Helen Andrews at American Compass; Julius Krein at *American Affairs Journal*; Geoff Shullenberger, Matthew Schmitz, and Ashley Frawley at *Compact*; Mark Granza of *IM—1776*; Matt Himes, Matthew Peterson, and Jill Savage at Blaze Media; Florence Read at UnHerd; Elena Lange at *Café Américain*; Laura Williams at the American Institute for Economic Research; Jude Russo at *The American Conservative*; Toby Young at the Mid-America Trucking Show; and the pseudonymous "Tyler Durden" of ZeroHedge. Many other American writers, podcasters, trucking-industry pros, and outside-the-box thinkers also deserve gratitude for helping me over the years: Matthew B. Crawford, Ross Kennedy, Rachel Premack, Justin "SuperTrucker" Martin (thanks for the memes and the research assistance!), Timothy Dooner, Clarissa Hawes, Rob Carpenter, J. P. Hampstead, Craig Fuller, Bog Beef and Maarek of the *Good Ol Boyz* podcast, James Pogue and Ashley Fitzgerald of the *Doomer Optimism* podcast, Grant Martsolf and Brandon Daily of the *Savage Collective*, Farahn Morgan, Joseph Keegin, Paul McNiel, Dr./Colonel Chris Ellis, Seneca Scott, and Andy and Keturah Hickman, as well as Ashley "Flatbed Red"—I appreciate all your encouragement and fellowship.

"Long Haul" Paul Marhoefer has become a great friend to me and contributed to this book. I've seen Paul perform live many times now, and it is always a magical experience. Tommy Salmons of the *Year Zero* podcast is a fellow trucker who has my back; you will never meet a finer Louisiana Swamp Creature. Other folks in the online trucking world who have helped me out, encouraged me, fought with me, or otherwise been great inspirations are Kevin "Let's Truck" Rutherford, Mike Williams of the *On the Road Aussie Trucking Podcast*, Tamie Stuttle and Desiree Wood of REAL Women in Trucking, Hunter and Pedro of *The Logistics Lounge* podcast, Bruce Outridge of the *Lead Pedal Podcast*, Matt Leffler, Charles Gracey, Ike Stephens, and Alex "Mutha Trucker" Mai, as well as Reed Loustalot, Evan, Hunter, and the rest of The TPC Crew. Thanks also to so many regulars on FreightX: Hillary and Jamie "Hell Bent" Hagen, Mike Lombard, Lee and Lisa Schmitt, Chris and Miranda Thomas, Trish Severson, Lora Andela, Taylor Barker, Isaac "Spud" McCarty, and Ryan "Squirt McGirt" Schefsky.

Special shout-outs to Shannon Everett, Harvey Beech, and Cliff Bates at American Truckers United, who have done yeoman work in exposing so much of the rot discussed in this book. Danielle Chaffin, daughter and granddaughter of some of the best old-school Tennessee truckers, has done incredible research into the corruption infesting the industry. All of you are the Best of the Best, really.

Many a podcaster and dissident journalist in Canada has had me on or otherwise encouraged me to do what I do and say what I say. Alexander Brown and Alex "Zoltan" Tirkanits of *Juno News* have been extremely receptive to my thoughts about the Canadian trucking industry. Trish Wood has had me on her wonderful podcast and been a great guide and confidante; what a shame that the CBC has no one like her anymore. Roxanne Halverson of the *Intrepid Viking* Substack questioned everything that went on with the Coutts Four. Donna Laframboise, another grand dame of Canadian journalism, did what very few media people do anymore, which is talk to working-class people, including many of those who in substantive ways helped the Freedom Convoy. Donna's work recalls the public-interest journalism of guys like Studs Terkel. Others at home in Canada who have spoken with me on the record or encouraged my work include Barry Bussey, Esq., of First Freedoms Foundation (Canada), Mocha Bezirgan, David Krayden, Ray McGinnis, Shaun Newman, Will Dove of *Iron Wire*, Black Horse of the *Red Ensign Podcast*, Dimes of *Blood $atellite*, "Giant" Gio Pannechetti, Kruptos, Fortissax, John Carter of *Postcards from Barsoom*, Jason James of Brave New Normal, Buck McYoung, Richard "R.B. Ham" Winteringham of *Beyond the Pale*, Jonathan "Right Blend" Villeneuve, Chris Dacey, Jodi Bruhn, Viva Frei, and last but not least, my favorite fellow expat,

Meghan Murphy. I also want to praise the friends and family who joined me in Ottawa that fateful weekend in January 2022: Andrew and Melanie Hamill and their girls Aya and Phoenix, Brett Hawes, Jeremy Reid, J. J. and Delia Kunnas, and my cousin Clayton L'Heureux and his wife Amber.

Tamara Lich and Chris Barber of the Freedom Convoy have made themselves available for numerous calls—no small task given their position as the most high-profile politically persecuted people in the Western world. If it weren't for them and everyone else in the Freedom Convoy, Canada would have continued down the dark path of the COVID regime.

I want to thank a very small and dedicated group of women who worked tirelessly to help the Coutts Four, essentially taking on another full-time job as quasi-paralegals, doing an incredible amount of legwork for the lawyers who defended the Four. Nikki Thom, Danielle Slettede, Margaret Mackay, and Jaclyne Martin are angels and the best that Canada has to offer.

James Year, Edward Escobar, Scott Douglass, and Will Cook helped me learn more about autonomous truck and vehicle technology. Through our many roundtables, phone calls, and exchanges of intel, a picture formed of what we need to be looking out for with the "clankers." James Year has been absolutely tireless on this front: his master's degree project from Syracuse University examined the impact of this technology on the truckers it seeks to replace. You can check it out at StealingFire.tech. Truckers Benjamin McCulley, Paulette Nobles, and Mitchell Riesgraf have also offered great insights into our looming replacement by robots.

Throughout the book I have referenced the work of academics who have spent much of their lives in deep study of the industry. Many thanks to Michael Belzer, Karen Levy, Steve Viscelli, Stephen Burks, Christopher Clarke, David Correll, and their colleagues and research teams. My fellow truckers would do themselves a favor by reading these authors' research and many books.

And now, not quite last and certainly not least, I thank the truckers to whom I owe so much for teaching me the right way to get down the road.

First off, to my father, Leonard Magill—thanks for everything, Dad. Wouldn't be here without you. (Literally!) Thanks also to my Uncle Chris, a great inspiration and role model, who presented me with unique opportunities in life. He's not trucking anymore, but he is escorting wide loads for the Paddocks at the ripe old age of eighty-two. This book is also dedicated, in part, to the memories of my grandfather, James Ewart Magill, and my late Uncle Bruce. Uncle Bruce taught me so much, and our careers had parallels: traveling far away from home, getting into forestry, hitchhiking, and living in fairly remote areas. I miss you, sir.

This book is formally dedicated to the memory of Marty Paddock, who passed away on November 28, 2025, after a fight with an aggressive cancer. In addition to being one of the best truckers and company owners in the business, Marty was a steadfast supporter, critic, and fan of my writing. He also generously offered commentary that was used in this book. His family, and the trucking community writ large, have suffered a great loss with his passing.

I owe the entire Paddock family no small debt of gratitude for teaching me most of what got me rolling as a young man and for being extremely tolerant of my wandering ways, always giving me my job back whenever I came home. Scott, Marty, and Mac Paddock were and are humble titans of the trucking industry, and you will find no better representatives of it. I was too young to meet their father, who started it all, the late and great Earl Paddock, who passed away when I was barely a teenager; their little brother Duncan, who bought me a lot of pizza as a young kid working in their yard, was also taken from us far too soon. The cast of characters who passed through their doors is too long to possibly list, but I do owe some shout-outs to a number of guys who work or have worked there: Wig, Skippy, Rod, Brandon, Ed Watkins, Jay Pendlebury, Bill "Little Cookies" Napper, the Van Herk Clan, the Baillies, Scotty and Colleen Tophen, Larry, Donny and Jerry in the shop, Mark "Boo-Boo" Cromwell, Jim "Hot Wheels" MacGregor, Bill Bentley, Winston "Five Dogs" Nelson, "Diesel" Danny Lucken, and Gene "Shammy" Champagne, as well as the late Hugh Beck, Donald Bakker, The Colonel, Hank VanderScheer, and Mark "Mouse" Williams, among many others. Someone ought to write a book about that joint.

Other truckers who have been great influences on my life, humble and unsung heroes and servants of their fellow man, include Jim Lengyel, the late Clifford R. Smith, Alden Paul, Trent Lalonde, Jamie Gravel, Gavin Smith and Nigel Frost of New Zealand, Norm Bilston, "Oil Can" Greg, Scotty Rowland, Spider and all the other drivers at Bonnie Rock Transport in Perth, "Steady Eddie" Plotnikoff, Dave Halliday at AFD, Guy Meister and Harold Jonker of the Freedom Convoy, Vince Sturge, and Aaron and Rick Jackson and their late father, Victor, as well as their stepdad, Jim Cronin, and the late Barry Etherington.

I'm also full of gratitude to my family, who have encouraged me along the way: my sister Rebecca, the most important rock I've had in my life; Ben, Logan, and cousin Samantha; and my Aunties Reeni and Kate, who have been bugging me to write since I was a teenager.

Thanks to those who chipped in to my modest GiveSendGo fundraiser or otherwise threw a few bucks toward this project: Lee and Lisa Schmitt, American Compass, Charles Haywood, Uncle Chris, Old Man with Candy, Chris Thomas, Batya, Sam, Detroit Supremacist, Brandon Daily, Rachel Premack, Rod McChesney, and anyone else who gave what they could. Thanks for helping me feed these kids!

To everyone who agreed to talk to me for the book, come on my podcast, or otherwise enriched my life along the way: thank you!

Two final acknowledgments, of a kind. First, the trucking industry has received a great deal of exposure recently, and it appears that the United States Department of Transportation is actually moving rather quickly to correct some of the problems discussed herein. As such, significant new developments may have taken place between the time of writing and final publication.

Second, I want to acknowledge that this book was written by me, a human, using only the Brave web browser and the Pages app that comes with a MacBook laptop. No artificial intellgience or large language models were used in the writing of this book whatsoever. But by now, you may have guessed that.

Notes

Introduction

1. Transport Canada, "Mandatory COVID-19 Vaccination Requirements for Federally Regulated Transportation Employees and Travellers," last updated October 30, 2021, https://www.canada.ca/en/transport-canada/news/2021/10/mandatory-covid-19-vaccination-requirements-for-federally-regulated-transportation-employees-and-travellers.html.
2. Andrew Lawton, "Mendicino's Office Wanted to Keep 'Crazies' in Freedom Convoy," *True North*, October 31, 2022, https://tnc.news/2022/10/31/mendicinos-office-convoy/.
3. Steve Viscelli, "Truck Stop: How One of America's Steadiest Jobs Turned into One of Its Most Grueling," *The Atlantic*, May 10, 2016, https://www.theatlantic.com/business/archive/2016/05/truck-stop/481926/.

1: A Family Tradition

1. Written by Mack in 1959, "I've Been Everywhere" was revised by Hank Snow in 1962 and immortalized by Johnny Cash.
2. See Kirkpatrick Sale, *Rebels Against the Future: The Luddites and Their War on the Industrial Revolution: Lessons for the Computer Age* (Addison-Wesley, 1995).
3. TransCanadaHighway.com, "History of the Trans-Canada Highway Construction," https://transcanadahighway.com/history/history-of-trans-canada-highway-construction/.

2: The Journeymen

1. Naomi J. Dunn, Susan A. Soccolich, and Jeffrey S. Hickman, "Commercial Motor Vehicle Driver Risk Based on Age and Driving Experience," National Surface Transportation Center for Excellence, Virginia Tech, April 17, 2020, https://vtechworks.lib.vt.edu/items/a73eaf6a-03fa-4f7f-b34c-deb67a33a4aa. The study's authors wrote: "Generally speaking, the first year of driving a CMV [Commercial Motor Vehicle] is riskier in terms of crash rates, crash involvement, and moving violations, regardless of age. Thus, motor carriers may want to focus on driver training, including engaging older, experienced drivers in driver mentoring programs to share their knowledge with inexperienced CMV drivers."

2. Student Borrower Protection Center, *Shadow Student Debt*, July 2020, https://protectborrowers.org/wp-content/uploads/2020/12/Shadow-Student-Debt.pdf.

3. Tanya Eiserer, "Trucking's Hidden Dangers: How an Unauthorized Driver Led to Fatal Fort Worth Pileup," television investigative report, WFAA, February 11, 2021, YouTube, 6 min., 48 sec., https://www.youtube.com/watch?v=xebV-Er-CMU&t=1s.

4. Tanya Eiserer and Mark Smith, "Trucking's Hidden Dangers: How an Unauthorized Driver Led to Fatal Fort Worth Crash in 130-Vehicle Pileup," WFAA, February 11, 2025, https://www.wfaa.com/article/news/local/investigates/fort-worth-texas-deadly-pileup-2021-crash-interstate-35-trucking-law/287-6235b5fa-0721-421b-bbf3-ac036ec87c64.

5. Super B-trains, more common in Canada than in the U.S., will make several appearances later in this book.

6 . For Australia, see Australian Government, Department of Infrastructure, Transport, Regional Development, Communications, Sport and the Arts, "Road Trauma Involving Heavy Vehicles—Annual Summaries," January 18, 2023, https://www.bitre.gov.au/publications/ongoing/road-trauma-involving-heavy-vehicles. For the United States, see United States Department of Transportation, Federal Motor Carrier Safety Administration, "Large Truck and Bus Crash Facts 2021," last updated November 4, 2024, https://www.fmcsa.dot.gov/safety/data-and-statistics/large-truck-and-bus-crash-facts-2021.

7 . World Bank Group, "Urban Population (% of total population) – Australia," https://data.worldbank.org/indicator/SP.URB.TOTL.IN.ZS?locations=AU.

8 . See John Gallagher, "Major Trucking Companies Seek Exemption for Driver Trainers," *FreightWaves*, July 27, 2023, https://www.freightwaves.com/news/major-trucking-companies-seek-exemption-for-driver-trainers. The money quote is as follows: "MTI, on behalf of the three companies, has asked the Safety Administration for an exemption from regulations requiring that a behind-the-wheel (BTW) training instructor have at least two years' experience driving a commercial motor vehicle or two years' experience as a BTW instructor. "MTI has had CDL training since 1991 and has always required our 'OTR' [over the road] trainers to have one year minimum

experience in order to train our students," wrote MTI Training Director William Griffin in the company's exemption application. "We have an extensive 'safety evaluation' process and only those that pass our evaluation process will be allowed to train. We have been extremely successful with this policy."

9. John Gallagher, "FMCSA Halts Study on Sexual Assault in Trucking," *FreightWaves*, August 29, 2025, https://www.freightwaves.com/news/fmcsa-halts-study-on-sexual-assault-in-trucking.

10. "Canadian Province Announces $54 Million Investment for Trucking Industry," Land Line Media, April 4, 2025, https://landline.media/canadian-province-announces-54-million-investment-for-trucking-industry, April 4, 2025

3: The War Begins

1. Layoffs and Bankruptcies section, *FreightWaves*, https://www.freightwaves.com/news/category/news/business/layoffs-and-bankruptcies.

2. "Long Haul" Paul Marhoefer, host, *Over the Road*, podcast, episode 3, "A Brief History of Trucking in America," March 19, 2020, https://static1.squarespace.com/static/5d39b277b437ad00019c4c8f/t/5e6ac130c489752bc2a5248a/1584054593532/Ep3_Transcript_A+Brief+History+of+Trucking+in+America.pdf; an alternative access point for the same text is https://www.overtheroad.fm/episodes/a-brief-history-of-trucking-in-america.

3. https://www.barrons.com/articles/federal-reserve-inflation-1970s-stagflation-crisis.

4. https://www.presidency.ucsb.edu/documents/motor-carrier-act-1980-statement-signing.

5. Michael H. Belzer, *Sweatshops on Wheels: Winners and Losers in Trucking Deregulation* (Oxford University Press, 2000).

6. Belzer, *Sweatshops on Wheels*, 64.

7. Rachel Premack, "Why Trucking Embraces Alarming Turnover Rates," *FreightWaves*, November 22, 2023, https://www.freightwaves.com/news/why-trucking-embraces-alarming-turnover-rates. Unlike most companies in the deregulated market, the Paddocks pay their drivers handsomely and have a turnover rate in the single digits. Many large carriers burn through 94 percent of their driver workforce every year.

4: Welfare on Wheels

1. "ATA Releases Updated Driver Shortage Report and Forecast," press release, American Trucking Associations, July 23, 2019, https://www.trucking.org/news-insights/ata-releases-updated-driver-shortage-report-and-forecast.

2. J. F. Casey, "An Assessment of the Truck Driver Shortage," *Transportation Executive Update* 1, no. 1 (1987): 20–23, https://trid.trb.org/View/353903.

3. Knight-Ridder, "Trucking Firms Face Driver Shortage," *Spokesman-Review* (Spokane), November 15, 1987.

4. Don Kirkman, reporting for Scripps Howard, "Truckers Are Going to Be in Demand," *Free Lance-Star* (Fredericksburg, VA), December 10, 1987.

5. Denise Gellene, "Driver Shortage Spurs Company Incentive Plans," *Los Angeles Times*, February 25, 1990.

6. Steve Viscelli, *The Big Rig: Trucking and The Decline of the American Dream* (University of California Press, 2016), 40.

7. For more on the WIOA, see the subheading "Workforce Innovation & Opportunity act (WIOA)" in "10 Ways to Pay for CDL Training: Programs, Grants, Paid Training," Smart Trucking, https://www.smart-trucking.com/pay-for-cdl-training/#h-workforce-innovation-opportunity-act-wioa; for more on Pell Grants, see the subheading "Pell Grants for CDL Training" in the same article," https://www.smart-trucking.com/pay-for-cdl-training/#h-pell-grants-for-cdl-training; regarding the 2023 grants from the Biden Administration, see Federal Motor Carrier Safety Administration, "Biden-Harris Administration Announces Grants to Improve the Commercial Driver's Licensing Process and Get More Safe Truck Drivers on the Road," September 14, 2023, https://www.fmcsa.dot.gov/newsroom/biden-harris-administration-announces-grants-improve-commercial-drivers-licensing-process.

8. Viscelli, *Big Rig*, 41.

9. Greg Rosalsky, "Is There Really a Truck Driver Shortage?," Planet Money, NPR, May 25, 2021, https://www.npr.org/sections/money/2021/05/25/999784202/is-there-really-a-truck-driver-shortage.

10. Stephen V. Burks and Kristen Monaco, "Is the U.S. Labor Market for Truck Drivers Broken?," *Monthly Labor Review* (U.S. Bureau of Labor Statistics), March 2019, https://doi.org/10.21916/mlr.2019.5.

11. Steve Viscelli and Eric Balcom, *Ensuring the Supply of Agricultural Truck Drivers: What the State of California Can Do* (UC Berkeley Labor Center, 2023), 2, https://laborcenter.berkeley.edu/wp-content/uploads/2023/09/Ensuring-the-Supply-of-Agricultural-Truck-Drivers.pdf.

12. Viscelli and Balcom, *Ensuring the Supply*, 2.

13. Mark Schremmer, "Buttigieg: 300,000 Truckers Leave Industry Every Year," Land Line Media, April 28, 2022, https://landline.media/buttigieg-300000-truckers-leave-industry-every-year.

14. Conversation with the author.

15. Viscelli and Balcom, *Ensuring the Supply*, 5.

16. Stephen V. Burks, Arne Kildegaard, Jason Miller, and Kristen Monaco, *When Is High Turnover Cheaper? A Simple Model of Cost Tradeoffs in a Long Distance Truckload Motor Carrier, with Empirical Evidence and Policy Implications* (IZA Institute of Labor Economics, September 2023), 31, https://docs.iza.org/dp16477.pdf.

17. Rachel Premack, "Washington Lawmakers Still Believe There's a Truck Driver Shortage," *FreightWaves*, November 8, 2022, https://www.freightwaves.com/news/washington-lawmakers-still-believe-theres-a-truck-driver-shortage.

18. Global Insight and American Trucking Associations, *The U.S. Truck Driver Shortage: Analysis and Forecasts*, 2005, https://books.google.com/books/about/The_U_S_Truck_Driver_Shortage.html?id=VTwdAQAAMAAJ.

19. Bob Costello and Alan Karickhoff, *Truck Driver Shortage Analysis 2019* (American Trucking Associations, 2019), https://www.trucking.org/sites/default/files/2020-01/ATAs%20Driver%20Shortage%20Report%202019%20with%20cover.pdf.

20. "Nunn Leads Bipartisan Bill to Address Truck Driver Shortage," press release, Congressman Zach Nunn, March 27, 2025, https://nunn.house.gov/2025/03/27/nunn-leads-bipartisan-bill-to-address-truck-driver-shortage/.

21. "Nunn Leads Bipartisan Bill."

22. "Zach Nunn: Top Industries 2023–2024," OpenSecrets, https://www.opensecrets.org/members-of-congress/zach-nunn/industries?cid=N00048870&cycle=2024.

23. Nicolás Rivero, "The Infrastructure Bill Will Put Teenage Truckers on US Roads," Quartz, last updated July 20, 2022, https://qz.com/2089831/the-infrastructure-bill-will-put-teenage-truckers-on-us-roads.

24. James Jaillet, "Trucker Pay Has Plummeted in the Last 30 Years, Analyst Says," *Overdrive*, updated March 7, 2016, https://www.overdriveonline.com/business/article/14889914/trucker-pay-has-plummeted-in-the-last-30-years-analyst-says.

25. "10-4! Employment and Wages of Truck Drivers in 2015," *TED: The Economics Daily* (U.S. Bureau of Labor Statistics), https://www.bls.gov/opub/ted/2016/10-4-employment-and-wages-of-truck-drivers-in-2015.htm. Click on the link "View Chart Data."

26. Pamella De Leon, "Truck Driver Pay Falls Behind Other Careers, Widening a $3,500 Wage Gap," *Commercial Carrier Journal*, updated April 22, 2025, https://www.ccjdigital.com/business/article/15743117/truck-driver-pay-falls-behind-other-careers-widening-a-3500-wage-gap.

27. "ATA Statement on GOT Truckers Act," press release, American Trucking Associations, November 9, 2023, https://www.trucking.org/news-insights/ata-statement-got-truckers-act.

28. "American Trucking Assns," OpenSecrets, https://www.opensecrets.org/orgs/american-trucking-assns/summary?id=D000000177.

29. *The Churn: A Brief Look at the Roots of High Driver Turnover in U.S. Trucking* (OpenSecrets, 2025), https://www.ooida.com/white-paper-request/?result=The%20Churn%20-%20A%20Brief%20Look%20at%20the%20Roots%20of%20High%20Driver%20Turnover%20in%20U.S.%20Trucking&file=22981.

5: The Trucker as Indentured Servant

1. Girish Kumar Anshul, "Protests Across Canada as 70,000 International Students Face Deportation," *India Today*, August 27, 2024, https://www.indiatoday.in/world/canada-news/story/international-foreign-students-face-deportation-canada-

federal-immigration-policy-changes-cut-immigration-justin-trudeau-2588601-2024-08-27.

2. Benjamin Lorr, *The Secret Life of Groceries: The Dark Miracle of the American Supermarket* (Avery, 2020).

3. Lorr, *Secret Life of Groceries*, 89.

4. Lorr, *Secret Life of Groceries*, 75–112.

5. Viscelli, *Big Rig*, 44.

6. Viscelli, *Big Rig*, 46.

7. Viscelli, *Big Rig*, 47.

8. Viscelli, *Big Rig*, 48.

9. Lorr, *Secret Life of Groceries*, 94.

10. Viscelli, *Big Rig*, 110.

11. Viscelli, *Big Rig*, 109.

12. Viscelli, *Big Rig*, 140–51.

13. Brett Murphy, "Rigged: Forced into Debt. Worked Past Exhaustion. Left with Nothing," *USA Today*, June 16, 2017, https://www.usatoday.com/pages/interactives/news/rigged-forced-into-debt-worked-past-exhaustion-left-with-nothing/.

14. Murphy, "Rigged."

15. Murphy, "Rigged."

16. I'm not exaggerating. Consider this report from Investment Monitor: "AP Moller-Maersk increased its earnings before interest and tax almost five-fold to $4.1bn in the second quarter of 2021, compared with the same quarter in 2020, while Cosco Shipping's profits of $6.77bn (42.9bn yuan) for the first six months of 2021 dwarf the $299.98m profit made in the first six months of 2020." See Martin Kaspar, "The Record Profits of Shipping Companies Will Contribute to Their Demise," *Investment Monitor*, https://www.investmentmonitor.ai/logistics/shipping-profits-supply-chain-demise/.

17. Federal Motor Carrier Safety Administration, "Crash Statistics" (data as of 9/26/25), https://ai.fmcsa.dot.gov/CrashStatistics/Visualization; Government of Canada, "Canadian Motor Vehicle Traffic Collision Statistics: 2023," https://tc.canada.ca/en/road-transportation/statistics-data/canadian-motor-vehicle-traffic-collision-statistics/2023/canadian-motor-vehicle-traffic-collision-statistics-2023.

18. On Super B-trains, see chapter 2, including n. 5.

19. At least not yet. Reform is afoot in the province of Alberta.

20. Canadian Museum of Immigration at Pier 21, "Canadian Multiculturalism Policy, 1971," https://pier21.ca/research/immigration-history/canadian-multiculturalism-policy-1971.

21. "Temporary Foreign Worker Program Misuse Sanctioned by Harper Government, Union Says," CBC, updated August 17, 2014, https://www.cbc.ca/news/canada/calgary/temporary-foreign-worker-program-misuse-sanctioned-by-harper-government-union-says-1.2737422.

22. "How Punjabis Came to Dominate Trucking Industry in Canada," *The Canadian Bazaar*, May 1, 2022, https://www.thecanadianbazaar.com/how-punjabis-came-to-dominate-trucking-industry-in-canada/.

23. Ontario Trucking Association, "Mag: Immigrants More than Half of Truck Drivers in Major Cities," September 27, 2018, https://ontruck.org/mag-immigrants-more-than-half-of-truck-drivers-in-major-cities.

24. Kathy Tomlinson, "How an Immigration Scheme Steers Newcomers into Canadian Trucking Jobs—and Puts Lives at Risk," *The Globe and Mail*, October 5, 2019, https://web.archive.org/web/20191008005205/https://www.theglobeandmail.com/canada/article-foreign-truck-drivers-canada-immigration-investigation/.

25. Tomlinson, "How an Immigration Scheme Steers Newcomers."

26. Tomlinson, "How an Immigration Scheme Steers Newcomers."

27. Annabel Makhwaya, "Kenya Secures American Jobs Deal for Truck Drivers Through Nebraska Partnership," Kenya Insights, September 8, 2025, https://kenyainsights.com/kenya-secures-american-jobs-deal-for-truck-drivers-through-nebraska-partnership/.

28. Kennedy Rotich, "Kenyan PS Njogu Seeks Employment Partnerships for Kenyan Truck Drivers with Werner Enterprises in Nebraska, US," Kenyan Diaspora Media, June 2, 2024, https://www.thekenyandiaspora.com/stories/747/Kenyan-PS-Njogu-seeks-employment-partnerships-for-Kenyan-truck-drivers-with-Werner-Enterprises-in-Nebraska-US.

29. Gord "Anti-Social Media Defluencer" Magill (@GordMagill), "Driver Shortage Scam News Continues," September 9, 2025, https://x.com/GordMagill/status/1965510193082761273.

30. John Kingston, "Werner Faces Social Media Storm over Kenyan Driver Rumors," *FreightWaves*, September 10, 2025, https://www.freightwaves.com/news/werner-faces-social-media-storm-over-kenyan-driver-rumors; Tyson Fisher, "Road Rumors: Did Nebraska, Werner Open the Door to Kenyan Truck Drivers?," Land Line Media, September 12, 2025, https://landline.media/road-rumors-did-nebraska-werner-open-the-door-to-kenyan-truck-drivers/; Jake Lawson, "Governor Pillen Insists Nebraska Is Not Recruiting Kenyan Truck Drivers After Evnen Trade Mission," KOLN (Lincoln, NE), September 11, 2025, https://www.1011now.com/2025/09/11/gov-pillen-insists-nebraska-is-not-recruiting-kenyan-truck-drivers-after-evnen-trade-mission/.

31. American Truckers (@atutruckers), Nebraska Governor's Office's response to American Truckers' FOIA request, September 11, 2025, https://x.com/atutruckers/status/1966271362135187561.

6: Panopticons of the Interstate, or The Hitchhikers You Don't Want

1. Lyndel L. Erwin, "The Motor Carrier Exemption under the Fair Labor Standards Act," Worklaw Network, July 31, 2019, https://www.worklaw.com/blog/the-motor-carrier-exemption-under-the-fair-labor-standards-act.

2. As usual, the government ignored us. The "Trucker Listening Sessions" put on by the Federal Motor Carrier Safety Administration while it was considering this rule drew furious criticism of ELDs from truckers themselves, but the mandate was imposed anyway.

3. U.S. Department of Transportation, Federal Highway Administration, "MAP-21: Moving Ahead for Progress in the 21st Century," last modified November 7, 2018, https://www.fhwa.dot.gov/map21/; Truck Safety Coalition, "P.A.T.T.," https://trucksafety.org/about-tsc/patt/; Todd Dills, "OOIDA Hits FMCSA with Lawsuit to Block ELD Mandate, Calls Rule Arbitrary and Unconstitutional," *Overdrive*, updated April 6, 2016, https://www.overdriveonline.com/electronic-logging-devices/article/14890055/ooida-hits-fmcsa-with-lawsuit-to-block-eld-mandate-calls-rule-arbitrary-and-unconstitutional.

4. Long Haul Paul Marhoefer, host, *Over the Road* podcast, episode 1, "The Biggest Tailgate in Trucking," https://www.overdriveonline.com/overdrive-radio/podcast/14897423/over-the-road-podcast-episode-1-the-eld-mandate-and-more.

5. H.R. 6159, 115th Congress (2018), https://www.congress.gov/115/bills/hr6159/BILLS-115hr6159ih.xml.

6. "Editorial: FMCSA's Listening, Will You Talk?," Transport Topics, March 28, 2018, https://www.ttnews.com/articles/editorial-fmcsas-listening-will-you-talk.

7. Michael Belzer, "Sweatshops on Wheels with Trucker and Academic Dr. Michael Belzer," interview by Gord Magill, *Autonomous Truck(er)s*, Substack, September 11, 2023, https://autonomoustruckers.substack.com/p/sweatshops-on-wheels-with-trucker.

8. David H. C. Correll, "Written Testimony of David HC Correll, PhD: Written Testimony for House Committee on Transportation and Infrastructure," 117th Cong., November 17, 2021, https://www.congress.gov/117/meeting/house/114233/witnesses/HHRG-117-PW00-Wstate-CorrellD-20211117.pdf.

9. Brent Davis, "150 Loblaw Drivers Losing Jobs at Cambridge Distribution Centre," *Waterloo Region Record*, January 5, 2021, https://www.therecord.com/business/150-loblaw-drivers-losing-jobs-at-cambridge-distribution-centre/article_6a4cd233-0805-52d9-b64a-b97a96e800fe.html.

10. Detention time was drivers' number four concern in 2024. See American Transportation Research Institute, *Critical Issues in the Trucking Industry – 2024*, October 2024, https://truckingresearch.org/wp-content/uploads/2024/10/ATRI-Top-Industry-Issues-2024.pdf.

11. Matt Cole, "ELDs and Highway Safety: Crashes, Injuries and Fatalities Rise Post-Mandate," *Overdrive*, updated October 28, 2022, https://www.overdriveonline.com/csas-data-trail/article/15301876/crashes-injuries-and-fatalities-up-posteld-mandate.

12. James Jaillet, "Study: Under ELDs, Crash Rates Flat but Unsafe Driving Violations Are Up," *Overdrive*, February 4, 2019, https://www.overdriveonline.com/electronic-

logging-devices/article/14895792/study-under-elds-crash-rates-flat-but-unsafe-driving-violations-are-up.

13. Karen Levy, *Data Driven: Truckers, Technology, and the New Workplace Surveillance* (Princeton University Press, 2022), 55.

14. Levy, *Data Driven*, 48.

15. Original Trucking Barbie 2.0, YouTube, https://www.youtube.com/watch?v=J-gbPHAsHw (video no longer available).

16. Alex Leslie and Dan Murray, *Issues and Opportunities with Driver-Facing Cameras* (American Transportation Research Institute, 2023), https://truckingresearch.org/2023/04/issues-and-opportunities-with-driver-facing-cameras/.

17. Mike Williams, interview by Gord Magill, "Comparing Notes on Issues in Trucking Between North America and Australia with Mike Williams of *On the Road Aussie Trucking Podcast*," *Autonomous Truck(er)s*, Substack, May 28, 2025, https://autonomoustruckers.substack.com/p/comparing-notes-on-issues-in-trucking.

18. Matthew B. Crawford, *Shop Class as Soulcraft: An Inquiry into the Value of Work* (Penguin, 2009), 7.

19. Matthew B. Crawford, "Seeing like Google: Mapmaking as an Instrument of Empire," *Archedelia*, Substack, May 18, 2023, https://mcrawford.substack.com/p/seeing-like-google.

20. "I-40 Trucker Arrested After Ignoring Barricades," *Newport (TN) Plain Talk*, January 22, 2025, https://www.newportplaintalk.com/news/article_33a8ee24-d766-11ef-b52a-3785b1bee2b7.html.

21. Michelle Chenowith, "Semi Recovered Following January Bridge Collapse on Dale Bend Road," River Valley Now (Russellville, AR), updated August 14, 2019, https://www.rivervalleynow.com/local_news/semi-recovered-following-january-bridge-collapse-on-dale-bend-road/article_9de1f7d2-bea7-11e9-b648-c345910fa2a8.html.

22. "California CDL Fraud Scheme Ends with 20 Convictions," *Overdrive*, November 22, 2022, https://www.overdriveonline.com/life/article/15303513/california-cdl-fraud-scheme-ends-with-20-convictions.

23. https://www.gps.gov/support/user/mapfix/truck-traffic/. On aging GPS satellites, see https://payloadspace.com/rise-and-stall-of-gps-the-average-age-of-gps-satellites-hits-13-years/.

24. Clarissa Hawes, "Foreign Truckers Allege US Job Offers Turned into Human-Trafficking Scheme," *FreightWaves*, March 25, 2021, https://www.freightwaves.com/news/foreign-truckers-allege-us-job-offers-turned-into-human-trafficking-scheme.

25. Danielle Chaffin and Justin Martin, interview by Gord Magill, "How to Take Out the Trash with Danielle Chaffin and Justin 'Supertrucker' Martin," *Autonomous Truck(er)s*, Substack, June 28, 2025, https://autonomoustruckers.substack.com/p/how-to-take-out-the-trash-with-danielle.

26. Danielle Chaffin, "Electronic Logging Devices: Perception vs Reality," *Maybe Danielle*, Substack, July 17, 2025, https://maybedanielleee.substack.com/p/electronic-logging-devices-perception.

27. Breck Dumas, "Cargo Theft in US and Canada Soars to Record in 2024," Fox Business, January 24, 2025, https://www.foxbusiness.com/economy/cargo-theft-us-canada-soars-record-2024.

28. Alex Lockie, "ELD Tampering: CVSA Drafts New Inspections Bulletin to Combat 'Dangerous Trend,'" *Overdrive*, updated July 27, 2025, https://www.overdriveonline.com/regulations/article/15751118/new-outofservice-rules-coming-for-eld-tampering-logbook-fraud.

7: Interstate United Nations?

1. 49 C.F.R. 391.11(b)(2), available through Code of Federal Regulations: A Point in Time eCFR System, provided by the National Archives, last updated September 29, 2025, https://www.ecfr.gov/current/title-49/subtitle-B/chapter-III/subchapter-B/part-391.

2. An Oregon DOT link that used to host this has been scrubbed.

3. American Truckers United, "The Broken Road: America's Highway Safety Epidemic," https://americantruckers.com/crash-data/.

4. Federal Motor Carrier Safety Administration, "Crash Statistics," MCMIS snapshot date September 26, 2025, FARS snapshot date December 31, 2023, https://ai.fmcsa.dot.gov/CrashStatistics/CrashQueryTool?tab=Summary&type=&report_id=1&crash_type_id=4&datasource_id=1&time_period_id=2&report_date=0&vehicle_type=1&state=NAT&domicile=ALL&measure_id=1&operation_id=null; Lynn Hulsey, "Fatalities in Large Truck Crashes Are Up 48% Since 2009," *Dayton Daily News*, June 1, 2021, https://www.daytondailynews.com/local/fatalities-in-large-truck-crashes-are-up-48-since-2009/OVRFW4RABBAC3DG4HG6M3NMG2Y/#:~:text=Injuries%20in%20crashes%20involving%20large,in%202019%2C%20the%20data%20show.

5. This is not the same Harjinder Singh who collapsed the bridge in Arkansas.

6. U.S. Department of Transportation, "Trump's Transportation Secretary Announces Investigation into Deadly Florida Truck Crash, Shares Preliminary Findings," August 19, 2025, https://www.transportation.gov/briefing-room/trumps-transportation-secretary-announces-investigation-deadly-florida-truck-crash.

7. Gord Magill, "Welcome to the Jungle, Part Two," *Autonomous Truck(ers*, Substack, March 27, 2025, https://autonomoustruckers.substack.com/p/welcome-to-the-jungle-part-two.

8. Beasley Allen Law Firm, "Beasley Allen Files Lawsuit Against Trucking Companies Responsible for Fiery I-65 Crash That Killed 10," press release, August 9, 2021,

https://www.beasleyallen.com/article/beasley-allen-files-lawsuit-for-i-65-crash-that-killed-10.

9. Rob Carpenter, "The Pruitt Alabama Crash: A Deep Dive into Institutional Failure; Part 1," *The Tea*, Substack, September 24, 2025, https://www.talkingwreckless.com/p/the-pruitt-alabama-crash-a-deep-dive; Carpenter, "The Pruitt Crash, Part Two: Lives Depend How [sic] You Manage Your Tech," *The Tea*, Substack, September 24, 2025, https://www.talkingwreckless.com/p/the-pruitt-crash-part-two-lives-depend.

10. Federal Motor Carrier Safety Administration, "Trump's Transportation Secretary Sean P. Duffy: Truck Drivers Who Want to Share Our Roads Must Share Our Language," April 28, 2025, https://www.fmcsa.dot.gov/newsroom/trumps-transportation-secretary-sean-p-duffy-truck-drivers-who-want-share-our-roads-must.

11. Amir Vera and Raja Razek, "Colorado Governor Reduces Sentence of Truck Driver Who Was Given 110 Years in Fatal Crash," CNN, updated December 30, https://www.cnn.com/2021/12/30/us/colorado-rogel-aguilera-mederos-sentence-commuted/index.html.

12. Alex Lockie, "Non-English Speaking Carriers More Dangerous than Drug, Speeding Violators:? Study," *Overdrive*, updated August 10, 2025, https://www.overdriveonline.com/regulations/article/15752375/elp-violators-more-dangerous-than-drug-speeding-violators-study. Note that MC Advantage is owned by *Overdrive*'s parent company, Fusable.

13. Ash-har Quraishi, Amy Corral, Charlie Brooks, et al., "Amazon Trucking Contractors Have Higher Rates of Safety Violations, CBS News Investigation Finds," CBS News, December 2, 2024, https://www.cbsnews.com/news/amazon-trucking-contractors-have-higher-rates-of-safety-violations/.

14. Christopher Weaver, "Amazon Routinely Hired Dangerous Trucking Companies, with Deadly Consequences," *Wall Street Journal*, September 22, 2022, https://web.archive.org/web/20221013113742/https://www.wsj.com/articles/amazon-trucks-crash-safety-11663793491; Quraishi, Corral, Brooks, et al., "Amazon Trucking Contractors."

15. J.B. Hunt, "Keep Moving with Power Only," https://www.jbhunt.com/carriers/power-only; Swift Logistics, "Swift Logistics: Providing Quality Freight Capacity at an Unmatched Scale," https://www.swifttrans.com/services/swift-logistics; Werner Enterprises, "Everything You Want to Know About Power Only Loads (Updated: November 2024)," November 6, 2024, https://www.werner.com/blog/carriers/everything-you-want-to-know-about-power-only-loads/.

16. Executive Office of the President of the United States, "Fact Sheet: The Biden-Harris Administration Trucking Action Plan to Strengthen America's Trucking Workforce," December 16, 2021, https://bidenwhitehouse.archives.gov/briefing-room/statements-releases/2021/12/16/fact-sheet-the-biden-%E2%81%A0harris-administration-trucking-action-plan-to-strengthen-americas-trucking-workforce/.

17. Executive Office of the President of the United States, "Fact Sheet."

18. Executive Office of the President of the United States, "Fact Sheet."

19. Walt Bogdanich and Michael Forsythe, "McKinsey Advised Purdue to Pay Rebates To Distributors for OxyContin Overdoses," *New York Times*, November 28, 2020.

20. Alex Lockie, "Biden, 'Driver Shortage' Myth Caused CDL-Vetting 'Crisis': Punjabi Trucking Association CEO," *Overdrive*, updated June 25, 2025, https://www.overdriveonline.com/regulations/article/15748790/biden-trucking-plan-and-crisis-of-unvetted-drivers-raman-dhillon.

21. Lockie, "Biden, 'Driver Shortage' Myth."

22. Lockie, "Biden, 'Driver Shortage' Myth."

23. Gord Magill, "The Replacement of American Truckers," *Autonomous Truck(er)s*, Substack, March 1, 2025, https://open.substack.com/pub/autonomoustruckers/p/the-replacement-of-american-truckers; "verticals" is industry vernacular for lanes/segments/freight-service types.

24. Executive Office of the President of the United States, "Fact Sheet: The Biden Administration's Unprecedented Actions to Expand and Improve Trucking Jobs," April 4, 2022, https://roar-assets-auto.rbl.ms/files/76551/Biden%20update%201.pdf.

25. For more on CDL scams, see Rob Carpenter's work: Rob Carpenter, "The Fraud Factory: Corrupt CDL Programs That Put Killers Behind the Wheel; Part 1," *The Tea*, Substack, September 30, 2025, https://www.talkingwreckless.com/p/the-fraud-factory-corrupt-cdl-programs; Carpenter, "Day 28 Part 2: Complete CDL Fraud Case Repository (2001–2025)," *The Tea*, Substack, September 30, 2025, https://www.talkingwreckless.com/p/day-28-part-2-complete-cdl-fraud.

26. American Truckers (@atutruckers), "Why did South Carolina Dump 77,580 truck drivers into the system in 2021?," March 4, 2025, https://x.com/atutruckers/status/1896956428163908056.

27. U.S. Department of Transportation, "Biden-Harris Administration Announces Grants to Improve the Commercial Driver's Licensing Process and Get More Safe Truck Drivers on the Road," press release, September 14, 2023, https://roar-assets-auto.rbl.ms/files/76552/Biden%20update%202.pdf.

28. Federal Motor Carrier Safety Administration, "Biden-Harris Administration Provides Millions to Boost Trucking Workforce Programs," press release, August 26, 2024, https://roar-assets-auto.rbl.ms/files/76553/Biden%20update%203.pdf.

29. Danielle Chaffin, "What the Heck Is a Chameleon Carrier?," *Maybe Danielle*, Substack, July 26, 2025, https://www.highwayveritas.com/p/what-the-heck-is-a-chameleon-carrier.

30. "Eastern European Trucking Companies Are in Trouble: Driver Crisis," by Trucking Made Successful, YouTube, 8 min., 45 sec., https://www.youtube.com/watch?v=ogrASv7Pbt8.

31. Hawes, "Foreign Truckers Allege."

32. Clarissa Hawes, "Video Shows 'Ghost Co-Driver' Added to Trucker's ELD to Skirt HOS Rules," *FreightWaves*, March 30, 2023, https://www.freightwaves.com/news/video-shows-ghost-co-driver-added-to-truckers-eld-to-skirt-hos-rules.

33. "Inside Serbia: The Hidden Hub of U.S. Freight Outsourcing," featuring Paul-Bernard Jaroslawski and Aleks Bates, posted by Freight Caviar, YouTube, 38 min., 37 sec., https://www.youtube.com/watch?v=z6eHOX5cnEw&t=5s. The Super Ego billboard appears at about 1:25; the quoted statement is made at about 20:45.

34. "SuperEgo [sic] Class Action Lawsuit," https://superegoclassaction.com/. The suit was filed by the firm of Hughes Socol Piers Resnick & Dym, Ltd.

35. "SuperEgo Class Action Lawsuit."

36. https://balkantruckers.us/. The text is in Serbian.

37. Gord Magill, "Highway to Hell: Mass Influx of Foreign-Born Truckers Cause Carnage on American Roads," Blaze Media, March 10, 2025, https://www.theblaze.com/align/highway-to-hell-mass-influx-of-foreign-born-truckers-cause-carnage-on-american-roads.

38. American Trucking Associations, "No, Millions of Foreign Truck Drivers Aren't Flooding into the U.S.," blog post, March 12, 2025, https://www.trucking.org/news-insights/no-millions-foreign-truck-drivers-arent-flooding-us.

39. American Trucking Associations, "ATA Thanks Trump Administration for Responding to Industry Concerns," press release, April 28, 2025, https://www.trucking.org/news-insights/ ata-thanks-trump-administration-responding-industry-concerns.

40. Alex Lockie, "Enforcing Trump's English Language Mandate 'Not Part of California Law': CHP," *Overdrive*, updated August 3, 2025, https://www.overdriveonline.com/regulations/article/15751741/california-highway-patrol-not-enforcing-trumps-elp-mandate-for-truck-drivers.

41. U.S. Department of Transportation, "President Trump's Transportation Secretary Sean P. Duffy Announces Nationwide Audit of States Issuing Non-Domiciled Commercial Driver's Licenses," June 27, 2025, https://www.transportation.gov/briefing-room/president-trumps-transportation-secretary-sean-p-duffy-announces-nationwide-audit.

8: Truckzilla—Invasion of the RoboTrucks

1. Aurora Innovation, Inc., "Aurora Begins Commercial Driverless Trucking in Texas, Ushering in a New Era of Freight," press release, May 1, 2025, https://ir.aurora.tech/news-events/press-releases/detail/119/aurora-begins-commercial-driverless-trucking-in-texas-ushering-in-a-new-era-of-freight.

2. Aurora Innovation, Inc., "Aurora Begins Driverless Operations at Night and Opens Phoenix Terminal," press release, July 30, 2025, https://ir.aurora.tech/news-events/

press-releases/detail/122/aurora-begins-driverless-operations-at-night-and-opens-phoenix-terminal.

3. Kara Swisher, host, *On with Kara Swisher*, podcast, "The Man Making Self-Driving Trucks," recorded May 6, 2023, published June 5, 2023, https://podcasts.apple.com/si/podcast/the-man-making-self-driving-trucks/id1643307527?i=1000615690752.

4. Rahul Kalvapalle, "The Road Ahead: Raquel Urtasun's Startup to 'Unleash Full Power of AI' on Self-Driving Cars," https://www.utoronto.ca/news/road-ahead-raquel-urtasun-s-startup-unleash-full-power-ai-self-driving-cars. See also Waabi, "Introducing the Waabi Driver," https://waabi.ai/introducing-the-waabi-driver/.

5. Waabi, "Partnering with Uber Freight to Build an Industry-First Solution for AI-Powered Autonomous Truck Deployment at Scale," https://waabi.ai/waabi-uber-freight/.

6. Aurora Innovation, Inc., "Cautionary Statement Regarding Forward-Looking Statements," 2024, https://d1io3yog0oux5.cloudfront.net/_5a5495cc325297e7773d6f2bcb5d750f/aurora/db/856/7972/pdf/Investor+Presentation-+July+2024.pdf.

7. On drone operators, see Pratap Chatterjee, "A Chilling New Post-Traumatic Stress Disorder: Why Drone Pilots Are Quitting in Record Numbers," Salon, March 6, 2015, https://www.salon.com/2015/03/06/a_chilling_new_post_traumatic_stress_disorder_why_drone_pilots_are_quitting_in_record_numbers_partner/.

8. Autonomous Mobility Ensuring Regulation, Innovation, Commerce, and Advancement Driving Reliability in Vehicle Efficiency and Safety Act, 119th Congress (2025), https://fong.house.gov/sites/evo-subsites/fong.house.gov/files/evo-media-document/fong_010_xml.pdf.

9. Congressman Vincent Fong, "Congressman Fong Introduces Landmark Legislation to Streamline AV Trucking and Strengthen National Supply Chain," press release, July 24, 2025, https://fong.house.gov/media/press-releases/congressman-fong-introduces-landmark-legislation-streamline-av-trucking-and.

10. Fong, "Congressman Fong Introduces Landmark Legislation."

11. Stephen Moore, "China Is Winning the Trucking Arms Race," *Washington Examiner*, July 2, 2025, https://web.archive.org/web/20250702115332/https://www.washingtonexaminer.com/restoring-america/faith-freedom-self-reliance/3460260/china-is-winning-the-trucking-arms-race/.

12. Shruti Sinha, "Autonomous Vehicle Security Market to Reach USD 4.8 billion by 2032," Telematics Wire, April 22, 2025, https://telematicswire.net/autonomous-vehicle-security-market-to-reach-usd-4-8-billion-by-2032/.

13. Steve Vassallo, "Missionary Misfits: Meet a Former Fighter Pilot, Current Autonomous Vehicles Road Warrior," *Forbes*, updated October 19, 2020, https://www.forbes.com/sites/stevevassallo/2020/10/17/missionary-misfits-meet-a-former-fighter-pilot-current-autonomous-vehicles-road-warrior/.

14. M. L. Cummings and Ben Bauchwitz, "Identifying Research Gaps Through

Self-Driving Car Data Analysis," journal article accepted for publication by *IEEE Transactions on Intelligent Vehicles*, https://ieeexplore.ieee.org/stamp/stamp.jsp?tp= &arnumber=10778107. For the final, published version, see *IEEE Transactions on Intelligent Vehicles*, December 4, 2024, https://www.doi.org/10.1109/TIV.2024. 3506936.

15. Amber DaSilva, "Human Drivers Avoid Crashes 99.999819% of the Time, Self-Driving Cars Need to Be Even Safer," Jalopnik, February 28, 2023, https://www. jalopnik.com/self-driving-car-vs-human-99-percent-safe-crash-data-1850170268/.

16. Levy, *Data Driven*, 125–26.

17. Gord Magill, "Teaching the Robots Through Worker Surveillance—On Hirschbach and Aurora and Their Guinea Pig Drivers," *Autonomous Truck(er)s*, Substack, June 1, 2025, https://autonomoustruckers.substack.com/p/teaching-the-robots-through-worker.

18. David Wichner, "Feds Probe Crash of TuSimple Self-Driving Truck in Tucson," Tucson.com, August 1, 2022, https://tucson.com/news/local/business/article_ e37b6d6c-11e4-11ed-84d4-93d14a32fc7a.html.

19. John Worthen, "What's Next for TuSimple after Last Month's Multi-Million Dollar Lawsuit Settlement?," The Trucker, September 11, 2024, https://www.thetrucker. com/trucking-news/business/whats-next-for-tusimple-lawsuit-after-last-months-multi-million-dollar-lawsuit-settlement.

20. Lindland v. TuSimple, Inc., 21-CV-417 JLS (MDD) (S.D. Cal. Mar 08, 2022), available through vLex.com, https://case-law.vlex.com/vid/lindland-v-tusimple-inc-933177582.

21. Rebecca Bellan, "TuSimple Addresses Autonomous Truck Crash During Q2 Earnings Call," TechCrunch, August 2, 2022, https://techcrunch.com/2022/08/02/ tusimple-addresses-autonomous-truck-crash-during-q1-earnings/.

22. Kate O'Keeffe and Heather Somerville, "Self-Driving Truck Accident Draws Attention to Safety at TuSimple," *Wall Street Journal*, August 1, 2022, https://www. wsj.com/business/autos/self-driving-truck-accident-draws-attention-to-safety-at-tusimple-11659346202.

23. Matthew B. Crawford, *Why We Drive: Toward a Philosophy of the Open Road* (HarperCollins, 2020), 39.

24. Crawford, *Why We Drive*, 42.

25. Aurora Innovation, Inc., "Cautionary Statement." https://d1io3yog0oux5.cloudfront. net/_5a5495cc325297e7773d6f2bcb5d750f/aurora/db/856/7972/pdf/Investor+ Presentation-+July+2024.pdf.

26. Levy, *Data Driven*, 124.

27. JD Vance, "JD Vance on His Faith and Trump's Most Controversial Policies," interview by Ross Douthat, *Interesting Times with Ross Douthat*, podcast, May 21, 2025, https://podcasts.apple.com/us/podcast/jd-vance-on-his-faith-and-trumps-most-

controversial/id1438024613?i=1000709244230. All subsequent quotations from Douthat and Vance in this chapter are taken from this podcast episode.

28. Richard Bishop, "Gatik and Loblaw Partner to Bring First Ever Driverless Deliveries to Canada," *Forbes*, November 23, 2020, https://www.forbes.com/sites/richardbishop1/2020/11/23/gatik-and-loblaw-partner-to-bring-first-ever-driverless-deliveries-to-canada/.

29. Gatik, "Gatik and Isuzu Team Up to Mass-Produce SAE Level 4 (L4) Production-Ready Autonomous Trucks Powered by NVIDIA," March 20, 2025, https://gatik.ai/news/blog/gatik-isuzu-mass-production-powered-by-nvidia/.

30. JD Vance (@JDVance), "I think this guy is smart, but comparing globalization to tech advancement strikes me as very wrong," X, August 3, 2025, https://x.com/jdvance/status/19521183399406133372.

31. Andrew Yang, interview by Joe Rogan, host, *The Joe Rogan Experience*, podcast, episode 1245, February 12, 2019, https://open.spotify.com/episode/5t6lRzTYcVmivceC9HXQQB?si=64519c71c0be4d22&nd=1&dlsi=736d5da6f17946bc.

32. Tucker Carlson, "Ben Shapiro and Tucker Carlson Debate the Impact of Driverless Cars," interview by Ben Shapiro, posted by IDW Clips, YouTube, 10 min., 56 sec., https://www.youtube.com/watch?v=o5zPKxpPHFk.

33. Bleecker Street Research, "Aurora Innovation (AUR): Highway Robbery," May 14, 2025, https://www.bleeckerstreetresearch.com/research/aurora-innovation-aur.

34. Aurora Innovation, Inc., "Research: Autonomous Trucks Can Reduce Emissions and Fight Climate Change," April 30, 2024, https://ir.aurora.tech/news-events/press-releases/detail/94/research-autonomous-trucks-can-reduce-emissions-and-fight-climate-change.

35. Isaac Asimov, "The Evitable Conflict," in *I, Robot* (Bantam, 2004/1950).

36. Myra Blanco, Jon Atwood, Holland Vasquez, and Tammy E. Trimble, *Human Factors Evaluation of Level 2 and Level 3 Automated Driving Concepts*, Report No. DOT HS 812 182 (National Highway Traffic Safety Administration, 2015), https://www.researchgate.net/publication/281640555_Human_Factors_Evaluation_of_Level_2_and_Level_3_Automated_Driving_Concepts.

37. Sale, *Rebels Against the Future*, 68.

9: The Truck Stops of Babel

1. Jubitz, "Our History," https://jubitz.com/our-history/.

2. Helen Regan, "Half of India Couldn't Access a Toilet 5 Years Ago. Modi Built 110M Latrines – but Will People Use Them?," https://edition.cnn.com/2019/10/05/asia/india-modi-open-defecation-free-intl-hnk-scli/index.html.

3. Wolfgang Wendland via The Disrespected Trucker (@DisrespectedThe), "Welcome to America!," X, June 14, 2025, https://x.com/DisrespectedThe/status/1934058711145705827.

4. Jaweed Kaleem, "How a Rural Oklahoma Truck Stop Became a Destination for Sikh Punjabis Crossing America," *Los Angeles Times*, June 27, 2019, https://www.latimes.com/nation/la-na-col1-sayre-oklahoma-sikhs-20190627-story.html.

5. American Transportation Research Institute, *Critical Issues in the Trucking Industry – 2019*, October 2019, https://truckingresearch.org/wp-content/uploads/2019/10/ATRI-Top-Industry-Issues-2019-FINAL.pdf.

6. Evan Shelley, "Parking Anxiety with Evan Shelley, CEO of Truck Parking Club," interview by Gord Magill, *Autonomous Truck(er)s*, Substack, March 25, 2025, https://autonomoustruckers.substack.com/p/parking-anxiety-with-evan-shelley.

7. Michael Rainer and Chasaty Rainer, "Booker's Dude Ranch—Recreating Old School Truck Stop Hospitality," interview by Gord Magill, *Autonomous Truck(er)s*, Substack, August 26, 2025, https://autonomoustruckers.substack.com/p/bookers-dude-ranch-recreating-old. All the following quotations from the Rainers are taken from this Substack interview.

10: Punishment by Castration

1. OOIDA Foundation, "EPA's Myopic Cost Benefit Analysis," white paper, November 3, 2014, https://www.ooida.com/white-paper-request/?result=EPA%27s%20Myopic%20Cost%20Benefit%20Analysis&file=2227.

2. OOIDA Foundation, "EPA's Myopic Cost Benefit Analysis," 3–4.

3. Scott Neuman and Chris Arnold, "After Years of Trying, the U.S. Government May Finally Mandate Safer Table Saws," NPR, April 2, 2024, https://www.npr.org/2024/04/02/1241148577/table-saw-injuries-safety-sawstop-cpsc.

4. "Final Sentences Handed Down in Michigan Emissions 'Delete' Case," *Overdrive*, February 28, 2024, https://www.overdriveonline.com/regulations/article/15665196/final-sentences-handed-down-in-michigan-emissions-delete-case.

5. Brad Anderson, "North Carolina Shop Fined $10M for Selling Diesel Emissions Defeat Devices," Carscoops, September 16, 2024, https://www.carscoops.com/2024/09/north-carolina-shop-fined-10-million-for-selling-diesel-emissions-defeat-devices/.

6. "Emissions Deletes Net Small Fleet $101K Worth in Fines, Probation," *Overdrive*, March 5, 2025, https://www.overdriveonline.com/regulations/article/15739146/emissions-deletes-net-small-fleet-owner-101k-worth-in-fines-probation.

7. Clair McFarland, "Trump Pardons Cheyenne Diesel Delete Mechanic Troy Lake," *Cowboy State Daily*, November 7, 2025.

8. "40 CFR § 1037.635 – Glider Kits and Glider Vehicles," Legal Information Institute, https://www.law.cornell.edu/cfr/text/40/1037.635.

9. Jeremy Wolfe, "How Trump Is Changing Emissions Standards This Year," FleetOwner, January 22, 2025, https://www.fleetowner.com/emissions-efficiency/article/55262337/how-trump-is-changing-emissions-standards-fleets-operating-costs.

10. Wolfe, "How Trump Is Changing."

11. Jim Park, "Are Manual Transmissions Being Regulated out of Existence?," Trucknews.com, December 11, 2024, https://www.trucknews.com/equipment/are-manual-transmissions-being-regulated-out-of-existence/1003192008/.

12. Rob Carpenter, "Trucking's Race to the Bottom and Driver Non-Appreciation Week," *The Tea*, Substack, September 8, 2025, https://www.talkingwreckless.com/p/truckings-race-to-the-bottom-and.

13. Kenworth, "Kenworth Announces Sunset of the Iconic W900, T800, and C500 Models," March 19, 2025, https://www.kenworth.com/about-us/news/kenworth-announces-sunset-of-the-iconic-w900-t800-and-c500-models/. PACCAR is the company that owns Kenworth, Peterbilt, and a number of other truck manufacturers.

14. Henry Hazlitt, *Economics in One Lesson* (Ludwig von Mises Institute, 2008; first published 1946), 5.

11: Who Speaks for Truckers?

1. François Laporte, "Statement by François Laporte, President of Teamsters Canada," Teamsters Canada, https://teamsters.ca/blog/2022/02/07/the-real-enemy-for-truckers-is-covid-19/.

2. https://x.com/BiancaDonolo/status/1489337512866713601.

3. Thaddeus Russell, *Out of the Jungle: Jimmy Hoffa and the Remaking of the American Working Class* (Knopf, 2001), 150.

4. Russell, *Out of the Jungle*, 170.

5. Sean O'Brien, "'I'll Win with or Without You,' Teamsters Union President Reveals Kamala Harris's Famous Last Words," interview by Tucker Carlson, *Tucker Carlson Show*, first aired January 2025, 1 hr., 9 min., 31 sec., https://tuckercarlson.com/tucker-show-sean-obrien.

6. Weaver, "Amazon Routinely Hired Dangerous Trucking Companies."

7. Quraishi, Corral, Brooks, et al., "Amazon Trucking Contractors Have Higher Rates of Safety Violations."

8. Tyler Durden, "Biden Handed Out CDLs Like Candy," ZeroHedge, April 4, 2025, https://www.zerohedge.com/political/biden-handed-out-cdls-candy-now-us-highways-are-public-national-security-nightmare.

9. Charles Creitz, "Teamsters' Boss O'Brien Lauds Trump Tariffs, Says Attention Should Be on 'Massive' CEO Compensation," Fox News, July 23, 2025, https://www.foxnews.com/politics/teamsters-boss-obrien-lauds-trump-tariffs-says-attention-should-massive-ceo-compensation.

10. Sean Saldana, "The Complicated Legacy of César Chávez," Kut News, October 17, 2022, https://www.kut.org/texasstandard/2022-10-17/cesar-chavez-complicated-legacy-united-farm-workers-immigration.

11. Owner-Operator Independent Drivers Association, "Who We Are," https://www.ooida.com/who-we-are/.

12. American Trucking Associations, "Chris Spear, President and CEO," https://www.trucking.org/bio/chris-spear.

13. American Trucking Associations, "Chris Spear."

14. Commercial Vehicle Safety Alliance—Automated Commercial Motor Vehicle Working Group and the Federal Motor Carrier Safety Administration, *Final Report*, October 2019, https://www.cvsa.org/wp-content/uploads/CVSA-FMCSA-ADS-Report.pdf.

15. Robin Hutcheson, "FMCSA's Hutcheson: Nothing Is Final Until It's Final," interview by Scott Thompson and Mark Schremmer, hosts, *Land Line Now*, podcast, October 21, 2022, https://landline.media/podcasts/fmcsas-hutcheson-nothing-is-final-until-its-final/.

12: Necessary Parasites

1. Paul-Bernard Jaroslawski, "The Ten Largest Freight Brokerages by Revenue," Freight Caviar, May 31, 2023, https://www.freightcaviar.com/the-ten-largest-freight-brokerages-by-revenue/.

2. Federal Motor Carrier Safety Administration, registration statistics page, https://ai.fmcsa.dot.gov/registrationstatistics/customreports.aspx#OpAuthData.

3. Transportation Intermediaries Association, "about us" page, https://www.tianet.org/.

4. Cameron B. Ritter, *Confessions of a Freight Broker* (self-published on Amazon, 2024).

5. Ritter, *Confessions of a Freight Broker*, 44.

6. Long Haul Paul [Marhoefer], "Broker 'Confessions' Novel Aims at Seedy Underbelly of Digital Freight Culture," *Overdrive*, updated December 2, 2024, https://www.overdriveonline.com/overdrive-extra/article/15709245/confessions-of-a-freight-broker-sends-up-seedy-middlemen.

7. "49 CFR § 371.3 – Records to Be Kept by Brokers," Legal Information Institute, https://www.law.cornell.edu/cfr/text/49/371.3.

8. Adam Wingfield, "Too Many Trucks, Not Enough Freight—Why Rates Aren't Rising Yet," *FreightWaves*, February 25, 2025, https://www.freightwaves.com/news/too-many-trucks-not-enough-freight-why-rates-arent-rising-yet.

9. Courtney Reagan and Scott Zamost, "Cargo Thieves Are Attacking the U.S. Supply Chain at Alarming Rates," CNBC, May 9, 2025, https://www.cnbc.com/2025/05/09/cargo-thieves-attack-supply-chain.html.

10. U.S. Transportation Security Administration, "TWIC," https://www.tsa.gov/twic.

11. Islamic Circle of North America, untitled article on "usury," https://icna.org/the-burden-of-interest-why-islam-prohibits-usury/.

12. https://howmuch.net/articles/outgoing-remittances-from-usa.

13. Jagdeep Singh Insurance Agency, Inc., website home page, https://www.jsinghagency.com/; US Trucking Directory, https://www.ustruckingdirectory.com/punjabi-truck-insurance-california.php. https://www.thebainsfirm.com/punjabi-truck-drivers.

14. Matthew Sellers, "Court Dismisses Negligence Lawsuit Against State Farm over

Fatal USPS Truck Crash," InsuranceBusiness, March 14, 2025, https://www.insurancebusinessmag.com/us/news/legal-insights/court-dismisses-negligence-lawsuit-against-state-farm-over-fatal-usps-truck-crash-528601.aspx.

15. Tyson Fisher, "Texas Supreme Court to Hear Werner's Baffling Nuclear-Verdict Case," Land Line Media, September 5, 2024, https://landline.media/texas-supreme-court-to-hear-werners-baffling-nuclear-verdict-case/.

16. Krystyna Shchedrina, "Trucking Companies Hit with $165M in Nuclear Verdicts in the U.S. in 2023," November 29, 2024, https://www.trucknews.com/transportation/trucking-companies-hit-with-165m-in-nuclear-verdicts-in-the-u-s-in-2023/1003191698/.

13: The Truckers Strike Back

1. Dave Naylor, "Trudeau Calls the Unvaccinated Racist and Misogynistic Extremists," *Western Standard*, December 29, 2021, https://www.westernstandard.news/news/trudeau-calls-the-unvaccinated-racist-and-misogynistic-extremists/article_a3bacece-2e14-5b8c-bf37-eddd672205f3.html.

2. Government of Canada, "Question Period Note: Temporary Foreign Worker (TFW) Program (Including Travel Issues)," March 17, 2022, https://search.open.canada.ca/qpnotes/record/esdc-edsc%2CEWDDI-JUN2022-019.

3. Michael P. Senger, "Trudeau Had No Scientific Basis for Ban on Unvaccinated Travelers in Canada, Court Docs Reveal," *The New Normal*, Substack, August 2, 2022, https://www.michaelpsenger.com/p/trudeau-had-no-scientific-basis-for. Senger cites Rupa Subramanya, "Court Documents Reveal Canada's Travel Ban Had No Scientific Basis," *The Free Press*, Substack, August 2, 2022, https://www.thefp.com/p/court-documents-reveal-canadas-travel.

4. Derek Fildebrandt, "How Trudeau Bought the Media," *Western Standard*, October 10, 2020, https://www.westernstandard.news/features/how-trudeau-bought-the-media/article_58fdf7e6-39b9-5e78-a174-4a132b58a767.html.

5. Jonathan Bradley, "Which Media Were Included in Trudeau's $10 Million Top-Up Fund," https://www.canadaland.com/media-in-trudeaus-10-million-top-up-fund/.

6. Geoff Russ, "Half of Private Canadian Journalism Could Now Be Government Supported," The Hub, November 30, 2023, https://thehub.ca/2023/11/30/half-of-private-canadian-journalism-could-now-be-government-supported/.

7. Mark Gollom, "Carney Pledges $150M to 'Underfunded' CBC," CBC News, April 4, 2025, https://www.cbc.ca/news/politics/mark-carney-cbc-funding-1.7501902.

8. Matt Cole, "Owner-Ops, Groups: COVID Hours Waiver Should Open Door for More HOS Flexibility," Overdrive, updated October 7, 2022, https://www.overdriveonline.com/regulations/article/15300833/covid-hours-waiver-should-open-door-for-hos-flexibility.

9. Anderson Economic Group, "UPDATED 'Freedom Convoy' Disruptions: Direct

Loss Tally Surpasses One Quarter Billion Dollars," February 14, 2022, https://www. andersoneconomicgroup.com/freedom-convoy-disruptions-a-single-week-of-direct-lost-wages-estimated-at-over-51m-for-michigans-auto-industry/.

10. Nick Taylor-Vaisey, "Washington Pressed Ottawa to Shut Down 'Freedom Convoy' Blockades," Politico, November 24, 2022, https://www.politico.com/news/2022/11/24/washington-ottawa-freedom-convoy-00070817.

11. Executive Office of the President of the United States, "Readout of President Biden's Call with Prime Minister Justin Trudeau of Canada," press release, February 11, 2022, https://bidenwhitehouse.archives.gov/briefing-room/statements-releases/2022/02/11/readout-of-president-bidens-call-with-prime-minister-justin-trudeau-of-canada/.

12. David Fraser, "Texts Reveal Feds' Communications Strategy Before 'Freedom Convoy' Arrival," Canada's National Observer, November 1, 2022, https://www.nationalobserver.com/2022/11/01/news/texts-insight-feds-communications-strategy-freedom-convoy-arrival.

13. Marieke Walsh and Janice Dickson, "Ottawa Eyed Using Emergencies Act Early in Protest, RCMP Texts Suggest," *Globe and Mail*, October 27, 2022, https://www.theglobeandmail.com/politics/article-emergencies-act-inquiry-rcmp-opp-lucki/.

14. Much of the information in this chapter has come to me via personal interviews with the people involved. Some also comes from court documents. My *Autonomous Truck(er)s* Substack, accessible at https://autonomoustruckers.substack.com, includes more details about and discussion of this entire ugly episode.

15. "Defence Calls Coutts Murder-Conspiracy Trial 'Un-Canadian,' Accuses RCMP of Lying," CBC News, July 11, 2024, https://www.cbc.ca/news/canada/calgary/defence-calls-coutts-murder-conspiracy-trial-un-canadian-accuses-rcmp-of-lying-1.7261403.

16. "RCMP Arrest 11 Coutts Protesters on Weapons-Related Charges," *Lethbridge News*, February 14, 2022, https://lethbridgenewsnow.com/2022/02/14/rcmp-arrest-11-coutts-protesters-on-weapons-related-charges/.

17. "4 Alberta Border Protesters Charged with Conspiring to Murder RCMP Officers," CBC News, February 15, 2022, https://www.cbc.ca/news/canada/calgary/coutts-protest-charges-laid-court-appearance-bail-1.6352482.

18. Gord Magill, "Canadian Feds to Seize Iconic 'Big Red' as Freedom Convoy Persecution Rolls On," *The Blaze*, April 26, 2025, https://www.theblaze.com/align/canadian-feds-to-sieze-iconic-big-red-as-freedom-convoy-persecution-rolls-on.

19. Donna Laframboise, *Thank You, Truckers! Canada's Heroes and Those Who Helped Them* (Independently published, 2025).

20. Cosmin Dzsurdzsa, "CBC Anchor Invents Conspiracy About Russia Orchestrating Freedom Convoy," *True North*, January 29, 2022, https://tnc.news/2022/01/29/cbc-anchor-invents-conspiracy-about-russia-orchestrating-freedom-convoy/.

21. Abbas Rana and Peter Mazereeuw, "Bucking the National Trend, Liberals' Riding Associations Out-Fundraised Conservatives by $2-Million in 2022," *The Hill Times*, March 25, 2024, https://www.hilltimes.com/story/2024/03/25/bucking-national-

trends-liberal-riding-associations-out-raise-conservatives-by-2-million-in-2022/
415534/.

22. Sara Frizzell and Shaamini Yogaretnam, "Convoy Protest Organizers Tamara Lich, Chris Barber, Pat King Arrested in Ottawa," CBC News, February 17, 2022, https://www.cbc.ca/news/canada/ottawa/tamara-lich-chris-barber-arrested-ottawa-1.6355960.

23. David Fraser, "Convoy Leaders' Trial Will Settle Criminal Question—But Debates Will Rage On," CBC News, September 4, 2023, https://www.cbc.ca/news/canada/ottawa/convoy-leaders-trial-will-settle-criminal-question-but-debates-will-rage-on-1.6956416.

24. Jen Hodgson, "Lich, Barber to Receive Verdict Thursday in Canada's Longest Mischief Trial," *Western Standard*, https://www.westernstandard.news/news/lich-barber-to-receive-verdict-thursday-in-canadas-longest-mischief-trial/63672.

25. Sheila Gunn Reid, "Liberals Torch $21M Fighting Convoy Lawsuits—and That's Just the Civil Side," *Rebel News*, September 19, 2025, https://www.rebelnews.com/liberals_torch_21m_fighting_convoy_lawsuits_and_thats_just_the_civil_side.

26. Jen Hodgson, "UPDATED: Freedom Convoy Leaders Lich, Barber Found Guilty of Mischief, Not Guilty of Intimidation, Obstruction," *Western Standard*, April 3, 2025, https://www.westernstandard.news/news/breaking-judge-dismisses-crowns-conspiracy-theory-charge-in-lich-barber-trial/63691.

27. Ian Bailey, "Convoy Organizers Lich, Barber Receive 18-Month Conditional Sentences," *Globe and Mail*, October 7, 2025, https://www.theglobeandmail.com/canada/article-tamara-lich-chris-barber-sentence-trucker-convoy/.

28. Donald Best, "Denying Bail to the Coutts Four Is a Political Decision and Act," July 8, 2023, https://donaldbest.ca/denying-bail-to-the-coutts-four-is-a-political-decision-and-act/.

29. 42nd Parliament, 1st Session, edited Hansard number 189, June 7, 2017, https://www.ourcommons.ca/DocumentViewer/en/42-1/house/sitting-189/hansard. Scroll down to the statement by Ms. Marilyn Gladu. See also https://autonomoustruckers.substack.com/p/on-the-coutts-verdict-part-two.

30. Kate Schneider and Christopher Nardi, "Trudeau's Law Society: Exclusive Data Analysis Reveals Liberals Appoint Judges Who Are Party Donors," *National Post*, August 11, 2023, https://nationalpost.com/feature/exclusive-data-analysis-reveals-liberals-appoint-judges-who-are-party-donors.

31. Nikki Thom, "Persecution of Coutts Political Prisoners via Denial of Medial Treatment," *Autonomous Truck(er)s*, Substack, April 15, 2024, https://autonomoustruckers.substack.com/p/persecution-of-coutts-political-prisoners.

32. See, for example, Bill Graveland, "RCMP Found Pipe Bombs of Accused, Coutts Murder-Conspiracy Trial Told," *National Post*, June 28, 2024, https://nationalpost.com/news/canada/coutts-murder-conspiracy-trial-10; and "Jurors Ask About Pipe Bomb While Discussing Verdict in Coutts Murder-Conspiracy Trial," *Lethbridge*

News, August 2, 2024; https://lethbridgenewsnow.com/2024/08/02/jurors-ask-about-pipe-bomb-while-discussing-verdict-in-coutts-murder-conspiracy-trial/.

33. Gord Magill, "On the Continued Persecution of Canadian Political Prisoners Tony Olienick and Chris Carbert," *Autonomous Truck(er)s*, Substack, May 21, 2025, https://autonomoustruckers.substack.com/p/on-the-continued-persecution-of-canadian.

34. "Report Says 87% of Freedom Convoy Documents Were Never Released," *Toronto Sun*, May 21, 2024, https://torontosun.com/news/national/report-says-87-of-freedom-convoy-documents-were-never-released.

35. John Crump, "FOIA Shows Disinformation Governance Board Was Trying to Censor the Freedom Convoy," *AmmoLand* (blog), August 6, 2024, https://www.ammoland.com/2024/08/foia-shows-disinformation-governance-board-was-trying-to-censor-the-freedom-convoy/#ixzz8iABXdTYr.

36. Government of Canada, "Question Period Note: Temporary Foreign Worker (TFW) Program (Including Travel Issues)," March 17, 2022, https://search.open.canada.ca/qpnotes/record/esdc-edsc%2CEWDDI-JUN2022-019.

37. Government of Canada, "Question Period Note."

38. Yael Halon, "Canadian Trucker Beaten by Police Says He Won't Be Intimidated," Fox News, February 21, 2022, https://www.foxnews.com/media/canadian-truck-driver-beaten-by-police.

39. Immigration, Refugees and Citizenship Canada, "Canadian Immigration Statistics," https://immigrationstatistics.ca/.

40. Canadian Trucking Alliance, "70% of Carriers See Freight Drop; Further Tariffs Could Be 'Breaking Point': CTA Survey," April 15, 2025, https://cantruck.ca/70-of-carriers-see-freight-drop-further-tariffs-could-be-breaking-point-cta-survey/.

41. Canadian Trucking Alliance, "70% of Carriers See Freight Drop."

42. "Canadian Trucking Alliance President Donated to Liberals in 2018," *The Post Millennial*, January 26, 2022, https://thepostmillennial.com/canadian-trucking-alliance-president-donated-to-liberals-in-2018; Canadian Trucking Alliance, "Canadian Trucking Alliance Statement to Those Engaged in Road/Border Protests," January 22, 2022, https://cantruck.ca/canadian-trucking-alliance-statement-to-those-engaged-in-road-border-protests/.

Conclusion: The End of the Road?

1. Steve Martinez and David Cullen, "Truckers Take to the Streets to Protest ELD Rule," Heavy Duty Trucking, October 6, 2017, https://www.truckinginfo.com/142514/truckers-take-to-the-streets-to-protest-elds.

2. Lewis Griswold, "A New Big Rig Logbook Is Supposed to Make Roadways Safer, but Some Truckers Hate It," *Fresno Bee*, October 6, 2017, https://www.fresnobee.com/news/local/article177323516.html.

3. "Truck Drivers Hold 'Slow Roll' Protests Nationwide," Eyewitness News, WABC-TV (New York City), April 15, 2019, https://abc7ny.com/post/truck-drivers-hold-slow-roll-protests-nationwide/5245311/.

4. Joseph A. Williams, "When Truckers Shut Down America to Protest Oil Prices—and Became Folk Heroes," *History*, last updated May 28, 2025, https://www.history.com/articles/oil-crisis-1973-truck-strike.

5. Rob Carpenter, "FMCSA Issues Emergency Rule Restricting Non-domiciled CDLs," *FreightWaves*, September 26, 2025, https://www.freightwaves.com/news/fmcsa-issues-emergency-rule-restricting-non-domiciled-cdls; "Secretary Duffy Delivers Major Announcement on Safety and Trucking," announcement by U.S. Transportation Secretary Sean P. Duffy and Federal Motor Carrier Safety Administration Chief Counsel Jesse Elison, September 26, 2025, posted by the U.S. Department of Transportation, YouTube, 32 min., 35 sec., https://www.youtube.com/watch?v=I_SdVkHnGsg.

6. "Are Driver-Facing Cameras Legal?," CDLLife, June 23, 2020, https://cdllife.com/2020/are-driver-facing-cameras-legal/.

CREED AND CULTURE